Contents Table

Section 6: Advanced Customization and Integration

Section 7: Change Management and User Training

Section 8: Monitoring and Performance Optimization

Section 9: Scaling and Expanding ServiceNow Capabilities

Section 10: Case Studies and Real-World Implementations

Section 11: Compliance and Security Considerations

Section 12: Continuous Improvement and Future Prospects

Appendices

- Appendix A: Glossary of ServiceNow HR Terms
- Appendix B: Useful Resources and Tools for HR Professionals
- Appendix C: Training and Certification Programs for ServiceNow HR
- Appendix D: FAQs on Implementing ServiceNow for HR
- Appendix E: Further Reading and Industry Insights

~ Conclusion

Welcome & What You'll Learn

Welcome to "Implementing ServiceNow for HR: Transforming Human Resources with Digital Workflows." This book has been crafted to guide HR professionals, IT leaders, project managers, and digital transformation enthusiasts through the process of leveraging ServiceNow to enhance HR operations. Our aim is to demystify the complex process of implementing ServiceNow's HR capabilities, streamline workflows, and create a digital environment where HR teams can thrive.

Why ServiceNow for HR?

Human Resources (HR) departments worldwide are evolving from traditional, manual processes to a more dynamic and automated approach. ServiceNow stands out as a leading platform that empowers HR teams to deliver exceptional service through its comprehensive suite of digital tools and workflows. By adopting ServiceNow, HR teams can move beyond paper-based tasks and fragmented systems to achieve improved efficiency, better data management, and a more engaging employee experience.

What You Can Expect from This Book

In this guide, we will take you through every critical aspect of implementing ServiceNow for HR, from understanding its fundamentals to scaling it for global operations. You will gain insights into how to align your HR technology with organizational goals, effectively plan and configure the platform, and manage the change required for successful user adoption. The chapters are structured to provide a clear and actionable roadmap, enabling you to harness the power of ServiceNow to its fullest.

Key Areas Covered

Here's an overview of what you'll learn throughout this book:

1. **Introduction to ServiceNow and HR Digital Transformation**: Explore the role of ServiceNow in modern HR operations, the evolution of HR technology, and the significant benefits of digital workflows.
2. **Planning and Preparation for Implementation**: Understand the steps for assessing organizational needs, defining project scopes, assembling the right team, budgeting, and preparing data for migration.
3. **ServiceNow Platform Essentials**: Familiarize yourself with the architecture, user roles, navigation, dashboards, and data security protocols necessary for HR-focused implementations.
4. **Configuring ServiceNow for HR Processes**: Delve into setting up portals, designing workflows, automating case management, and integrating with existing HR systems for seamless operation.
5. **HR Service Delivery Modules in Depth**: Learn how to manage employee documentation, onboarding/offboarding, HR ticketing, and benefits administration through ServiceNow's capabilities.
6. **Advanced Customization and Integration**: Discover how to customize workflows with Flow Designer, utilize advanced scripting, integrate with third-party applications, and incorporate AI.
7. **Change Management and User Training**: Uncover strategies for managing change, training HR teams, and designing user guides to ensure adoption and engagement.
8. **Monitoring and Performance Optimization**: Gain skills in tracking performance metrics, conducting audits, fine-tuning processes, and troubleshooting.
9. **Scaling and Expanding Capabilities**: Learn best practices for global operations, multi-language support, analytics, and enhancing self-service portals.
10. **Case Studies and Real-World Implementations**: Read about successful implementations, lessons learned, and specific use cases tailored for various industries.
11. **Compliance and Security Considerations**: Understand how to ensure data protection compliance, implement security protocols, and audit HR workflows.

12. **Continuous Improvement and Future Prospects**: Discover strategies for ongoing workflow enhancements, future upgrades, and leveraging new features.

Who This Book is For

This comprehensive guide is designed for:

- **HR Leaders and Professionals** seeking to understand how to implement digital solutions for HR.
- **IT and ServiceNow Administrators** involved in configuring and managing the platform for HR needs.
- **Project Managers** overseeing the implementation and integration of ServiceNow within HR departments.
- **Business Analysts and Consultants** looking to advise organizations on digital transformation for HR.

How to Use This Book

The structure of this book allows you to start from the basics and progress to more advanced topics. If you're entirely new to ServiceNow or its application in HR, we recommend beginning from the first chapter and working your way through sequentially. However, if you're more experienced and seeking insights on specific topics, feel free to jump to the relevant chapters that suit your needs.

By the end of this book, you will have an in-depth understanding of how to leverage ServiceNow for HR, from initial planning through advanced customization and scaling for future growth. We hope this book serves as a practical resource for your HR digital transformation journey.

Welcome aboard, and let's begin!

Section 1:
Introduction to ServiceNow and HR Digital Transformation

Understanding the Role of ServiceNow in Modern HR

The landscape of Human Resources (HR) has transformed significantly in recent years, driven by rapid advancements in technology and the increasing expectations of the modern workforce. At the forefront of this digital evolution is ServiceNow, a comprehensive platform designed to enhance and automate various business functions, including HR. In this chapter, we delve into the essential role that ServiceNow plays in reshaping HR operations, improving employee experiences, and driving efficiency.

The Need for Technological Evolution in HR

Historically, HR processes were predominantly manual, heavily reliant on paperwork, and often fragmented across different systems. This approach led to inefficiencies, delays, and a disjointed employee experience. In an era where organizations strive for speed, accuracy, and employee satisfaction, the traditional model no longer suffices.

The demand for a cohesive, digital-first solution has never been greater. HR departments now need tools that integrate seamlessly, automate routine tasks, and provide actionable insights. ServiceNow has emerged as a game changer, offering a platform that aligns with these needs and supports HR's transformation from a reactive, process-oriented function to a proactive, service-oriented partner within the business.

What ServiceNow Brings to HR

ServiceNow's platform is designed to manage complex HR operations through a single, integrated interface. Its capabilities extend beyond basic automation, addressing the holistic needs of HR, including case management, employee onboarding and offboarding, knowledge management, and service delivery.

Key Roles of ServiceNow in HR

1. **Centralized HR Service Management**: ServiceNow consolidates HR services into one streamlined portal, enabling HR teams to manage and deliver services efficiently. This centralized approach helps eliminate silos and fosters better collaboration within HR and between departments.
2. **Automation of Routine Tasks**: One of the most notable contributions of ServiceNow to HR is its automation capabilities. Tasks such as employee onboarding, status updates, and document management can be automated to free up HR staff for more strategic activities.
3. **Enhanced Employee Experience**: ServiceNow's user-friendly interface and self-service options empower employees to access information, submit requests, and track the status of their inquiries with ease. This self-service model reduces the volume of repetitive questions HR teams handle and improves response times.
4. **Improved Compliance and Data Management**: Managing employee data securely is a top priority for HR. ServiceNow's platform offers robust data protection features that help ensure compliance with regulatory standards. Its built-in reporting tools also facilitate audits and compliance checks.

5. **Scalability and Customization**: HR needs evolve as organizations grow. ServiceNow supports this growth by allowing extensive customization to meet unique business needs and scaling up to accommodate increased demand. This flexibility makes it an invaluable asset for companies of all sizes, from small businesses to global enterprises.

How ServiceNow Transforms Key HR Functions

Employee Onboarding and Offboarding

A seamless onboarding experience sets the stage for employee satisfaction and long-term retention. ServiceNow simplifies the onboarding process by automating the creation of accounts, scheduling training, and tracking completion of necessary tasks. Similarly, during offboarding, ServiceNow ensures that access is revoked, documentation is completed, and exit procedures are followed consistently.

Case and Knowledge Management

HR teams often deal with a high volume of inquiries and cases. ServiceNow's case management system helps categorize, prioritize, and resolve cases efficiently. Paired with knowledge management features, HR can create a repository of information that employees can access for common issues, reducing the workload on HR personnel and fostering a self-service culture.

Workflow Automation

The platform's workflow capabilities enable HR to design processes that automate approvals, route tasks, and ensure that no steps are missed. This is particularly useful for managing leave requests, benefits administration, and compliance-related tasks.

The Strategic Advantage of ServiceNow in HR

Implementing ServiceNow is not just about improving existing processes; it is about redefining HR's role within an organization. With the administrative workload reduced, HR professionals can pivot their focus towards strategic initiatives such as talent development, employee engagement, and fostering a culture of continuous improvement.

Moreover, by integrating ServiceNow with existing HR software and systems, organizations can create a unified ecosystem that supports data-driven decision-making. This interconnectedness enhances the overall efficiency of HR operations and aligns them with broader business objectives.

Conclusion

Understanding the role of ServiceNow in modern HR is the first step in recognizing its potential impact on your organization. As you progress through this book, you will learn not only how to implement ServiceNow effectively but also how to maximize its benefits to create an HR department that is both proactive and responsive. In the following chapters, we will explore the evolution of HR technology, delve deeper into ServiceNow's features, and begin laying the groundwork for a successful implementation.

The Evolution of HR Technology Solutions

The journey of Human Resources (HR) technology has been marked by significant advancements, moving from manual processes to the modern, digital-first solutions that drive efficiency and enhance the employee experience today. Understanding this evolution is crucial for appreciating the transformative role that platforms like ServiceNow play in the contemporary HR landscape. In this chapter, we explore the key phases of HR technology's development and the pivotal innovations that have shaped it.

The Early Days: Paper-Based Systems

Before the advent of computer technology, HR departments managed their operations through labor-intensive, paper-based systems. Employee records were stored in physical files, and HR tasks, such as payroll and benefits administration, were handled manually. This era was characterized by:

- **High administrative burden**: HR professionals spent substantial time on repetitive tasks such as filing, document retrieval, and data entry.
- **Limited accessibility and data integrity**: Paper records were prone to misplacement, damage, or unauthorized access, impacting the reliability of HR data.
- **Time-consuming processes**: Processing payrolls, tracking leave balances, and handling employee benefits required significant manual effort, leading to inefficiencies.

The Advent of HR Software: 1980s–1990s

The introduction of personal computers and early software solutions in the 1980s and 1990s marked the initial wave of digitization in HR. This era saw the emergence of basic HR Management Systems (HRMS) that provided tools for:

- **Data digitization**: Early HRMS platforms allowed for electronic storage and retrieval of employee data, making record-keeping more efficient.
- **Payroll processing**: Software solutions simplified payroll tasks, automating calculations and payment processing.
- **Improved reporting**: HR professionals gained the ability to generate simple reports to track employee attendance and payroll summaries.

However, these systems were limited in scope, offering only siloed functionalities that did not integrate well with other business processes. They primarily focused on transactional tasks, leaving strategic HR initiatives underdeveloped.

The Rise of Integrated HR Systems: 2000s

The early 2000s witnessed a significant leap in HR technology with the development of more sophisticated and integrated Human Resource Information Systems (HRIS). These systems combined various HR functionalities into a unified platform, supporting functions such as:

- **Employee lifecycle management**: From recruitment and onboarding to performance management and offboarding, HRIS provided comprehensive tools for managing the employee journey.
- **Data analytics**: The integration of analytics allowed HR teams to track key performance metrics and make data-driven decisions.
- **Workflow automation**: Basic workflow automation reduced the manual burden on HR teams, streamlining repetitive processes such as leave approvals and employee evaluations.

The adoption of integrated HRIS led to better collaboration among HR professionals and other departments. Nevertheless, these systems often required substantial investment in IT infrastructure and were less adaptable to the evolving needs of dynamic workforces.

The Cloud Revolution: Late 2000s–2010s

With the advancement of cloud technology, the late 2000s and 2010s marked the shift towards cloud-based HR platforms, which offered several transformative benefits:

- **Accessibility and mobility**: HR professionals could access systems from any device, enhancing productivity and responsiveness.
- **Scalability**: Cloud platforms allowed businesses to scale their HR operations up or down without significant infrastructure changes.
- **Reduced costs**: Organizations benefited from lower capital expenditure as cloud-based solutions shifted costs to subscription-based models.

The emergence of Software-as-a-Service (SaaS) platforms like Workday, SAP SuccessFactors, and others revolutionized HR technology by enabling more flexibility, faster updates, and integration capabilities with other enterprise software.

The Era of Strategic HR: Late 2010s–Present

In recent years, HR has evolved from being an administrative function to playing a strategic role within organizations. Modern HR technology solutions now focus on enhancing the employee experience and aligning HR processes with business goals. Key developments in this phase include:

- **Artificial Intelligence (AI) and machine learning**: These technologies power predictive analytics for talent management, automate complex tasks, and improve decision-making.
- **Employee self-service portals**: Empowering employees to manage their own information, request time off, and access HR resources enhances their experience and reduces the burden on HR teams.
- **Integration with broader business functions**: Modern HR platforms connect seamlessly with finance, IT, and other departments, fostering cross-functional collaboration.

ServiceNow emerged during this era as a leader in workflow automation and service management, filling the gap between HR operations and enterprise-wide digital transformation. By integrating with existing HR systems and offering robust customization capabilities, ServiceNow has enabled organizations to build efficient, scalable, and secure HR ecosystems.

The ServiceNow Advantage

As organizations seek comprehensive solutions that can adapt to their unique needs, ServiceNow has positioned itself as a key player in modern HR transformation. Its platform allows HR teams to:

- **Centralize operations**: ServiceNow unifies HR processes on a single platform, facilitating better coordination and visibility.
- **Enhance automation**: With advanced workflow tools and AI-driven capabilities, HR professionals can automate complex tasks and free up time for strategic initiatives.
- **Support a digital-first culture**: ServiceNow's user-centric design and self-service features promote employee engagement and align with the needs of today's tech-savvy workforce.

Conclusion

The evolution of HR technology solutions reflects the broader journey of HR itself—from a support function bogged down by manual tasks to a strategic partner enabled by digital tools. ServiceNow exemplifies the culmination of decades of technological advancements, offering HR teams a powerful platform for transforming their operations and fostering a more dynamic and effective workplace.

Benefits of Implementing ServiceNow for HR Processes

The decision to implement ServiceNow within an HR department represents a significant step towards operational excellence and digital transformation. By leveraging the capabilities of ServiceNow, HR teams can automate processes, enhance employee satisfaction, and streamline service delivery. This chapter delves into the key benefits of implementing ServiceNow for HR processes and how it can fundamentally reshape an organization's HR function.

1. Enhanced Efficiency Through Automation

One of the most immediate and impactful benefits of ServiceNow is the automation of repetitive and time-consuming tasks. HR professionals often face a myriad of routine activities such as managing employee requests, updating records, and processing leave applications. ServiceNow's workflow automation capabilities allow HR teams to:

- **Reduce manual workload**: Automated workflows handle common HR processes, freeing up HR staff to focus on more strategic initiatives.
- **Accelerate processing times**: By automating approvals and notifications, ServiceNow significantly cuts down response and processing times.
- **Minimize errors**: Automation reduces the chances of human error in data entry and process execution, ensuring more reliable outcomes.

2. Improved Employee Experience

ServiceNow empowers employees by providing a user-friendly, self-service platform where they can access HR services without delay. This feature is crucial for organizations aiming to create a positive and engaging work environment. Benefits include:

- **24/7 accessibility**: Employees can submit requests, check the status of their cases, and access HR information at their convenience, enhancing their overall experience.
- **Simplified communication**: The platform enables streamlined communication between HR teams and employees, reducing wait times and improving transparency.
- **Personalized services**: ServiceNow's ability to create customized HR portals allows employees to find relevant information and services tailored to their needs, fostering satisfaction and reducing frustration.

3. Centralized HR Operations

Managing disparate HR tools and processes can be complex and lead to inefficiencies. ServiceNow provides a centralized platform that consolidates HR functions into a single, cohesive interface. This centralization leads to:

- **Improved coordination**: HR teams can manage various processes, from onboarding to case management, all within the same system, facilitating better teamwork and alignment.
- **Streamlined data management**: With data stored in a unified platform, HR departments can eliminate data silos, reduce duplication, and ensure a single source of truth.
- **Comprehensive reporting**: ServiceNow's reporting and analytics capabilities allow HR leaders to gather insights from a central repository, aiding in strategic decision-making.

4. Enhanced Compliance and Data Security

HR departments are responsible for handling sensitive employee data and ensuring compliance with local, national, and international regulations. ServiceNow offers robust data protection measures that support compliance needs:

- **Secure data handling**: The platform includes advanced security protocols to protect HR data from unauthorized access and breaches.
- **Automated compliance checks**: ServiceNow can help maintain compliance by automating tasks related to data retention policies, employee record management, and auditing procedures.
- **Built-in audit trails**: HR teams can benefit from ServiceNow's audit logs, which provide a clear record of actions taken within the system, simplifying compliance reporting and investigations.

5. Scalability for Growing Organizations

As companies grow and evolve, their HR needs change as well. ServiceNow is designed to scale with an organization's growth, supporting more complex and larger-scale HR operations:

- **Adaptability**: ServiceNow's platform is highly configurable, allowing organizations to adapt their HR workflows and services to accommodate growth and new business requirements.
- **Global support**: The platform can be customized to support multi-language and multi-currency needs, making it an ideal choice for multinational organizations.
- **Integration capabilities**: ServiceNow integrates seamlessly with existing HR systems and third-party applications, ensuring that organizations can extend its capabilities as needed.

6. Data-Driven Insights for Strategic HR

Modern HR departments require access to data-driven insights to improve decision-making and drive strategy. ServiceNow's analytics and reporting features provide HR professionals with:

- **Real-time data**: Access to up-to-date information helps HR leaders make informed decisions quickly.
- **Performance tracking**: HR teams can monitor the efficiency of their processes and identify areas for improvement using built-in performance metrics.
- **Predictive analytics**: By leveraging ServiceNow's AI-powered analytics tools, HR can forecast trends, anticipate workforce needs, and proactively address potential challenges.

7. Enhanced Collaboration and Integration

HR processes often overlap with other business functions, such as IT, finance, and operations. ServiceNow facilitates cross-departmental collaboration by integrating with various business systems:

- **Unified service delivery**: HR, IT, and other departments can collaborate on projects and processes seamlessly through ServiceNow's shared platform.
- **Integrated workflows**: Processes that require input or action from multiple departments can be automated end-to-end, improving coordination and reducing bottlenecks.
- **Custom integrations**: ServiceNow's flexibility allows for integrations with a wide range of third-party applications, enhancing the platform's functionality and ensuring a holistic approach to HR service management.

Conclusion

The benefits of implementing ServiceNow for HR processes extend far beyond simple task automation. By adopting ServiceNow, organizations can transform their HR departments into strategic assets that contribute to overall business success. From enhancing efficiency and employee experience to supporting compliance and scalability, ServiceNow equips HR teams with the tools they need to thrive in an increasingly digital workplace.

An Overview of ServiceNow's HR Service Delivery Module

ServiceNow's HR Service Delivery (HRSD) module is at the forefront of transforming how HR services are managed and delivered in modern organizations. It is designed to simplify and enhance HR processes, aligning them with broader organizational goals and improving the overall employee experience. This chapter provides an in-depth overview of the HRSD module, highlighting its key components and the value it adds to HR operations.

What is the HR Service Delivery Module?

The HR Service Delivery module within ServiceNow is a suite of applications and tools that streamline HR processes by automating service requests, improving case management, and providing comprehensive self-service options for employees. It supports the end-to-end management of HR services and is designed to enhance productivity, accuracy, and employee engagement.

The module offers a centralized platform where HR teams can manage tasks more effectively, collaborate across functions, and ensure that HR processes are executed efficiently. By integrating HRSD with other business systems, organizations can create a seamless workflow that bridges the gap between HR and other departments.

Core Components of the HRSD Module

1. Case and Knowledge Management

ServiceNow's case and knowledge management features enable HR teams to handle employee inquiries and issues systematically. Key aspects include:

- **Case Management**: Facilitates the tracking, assignment, and resolution of employee cases, ensuring that HR teams manage inquiries efficiently and transparently.
- **Knowledge Management**: Provides a centralized repository of information that employees and HR staff can access to find answers to common questions, reducing repetitive inquiries and empowering self-service.

2. Employee Service Center

The Employee Service Center is a user-friendly portal that acts as a one-stop shop for employees seeking HR support. It offers:

- **Self-Service Capabilities**: Employees can submit requests, track their progress, and find resources independently, improving satisfaction and reducing HR's workload.
- **Personalized Experiences**: Tailored content ensures that employees see relevant information based on their roles and previous interactions.

3. Lifecycle Event Management

Managing employee lifecycle events such as onboarding, transfers, and offboarding can be complex. ServiceNow's HRSD module simplifies these processes through:

- **Automated Workflows**: Automates the tasks and notifications associated with each lifecycle event, ensuring a smooth transition for employees and compliance with internal policies.
- **Task Coordination**: Coordinates tasks across departments like IT and facilities, ensuring all aspects of onboarding or offboarding are handled without oversight.

4. HR Case Management

The HR Case Management application provides HR teams with a structured approach to managing cases from initiation to resolution. This includes:

- **Automated Case Assignment**: Routes cases to the appropriate HR personnel based on predefined rules, ensuring prompt and accurate responses.
- **Progress Tracking**: HR staff can monitor the status of cases in real time, providing visibility and ensuring timely follow-ups.

5. HR Knowledge Base

An integral part of effective HR service delivery is the knowledge base that supports employees and HR teams. The knowledge base:

- **Centralizes Information**: Stores documents, policies, FAQs, and guidelines that employees can easily access.
- **Reduces Case Volume**: By providing clear and accessible information, HR teams can reduce the number of inquiries that require personal intervention.

Key Benefits of Using the HRSD Module

1. Improved HR Productivity

The automation of routine tasks and streamlined case management enable HR teams to allocate more time to strategic initiatives. With structured workflows and automated notifications, HR staff can focus on high-impact activities that add value to the organization.

2. Enhanced Employee Engagement

Employees benefit from faster service delivery, transparent processes, and easy access to information. The self-service portal provides a seamless experience that aligns with modern expectations for workplace technology, fostering trust and satisfaction.

3. Consistency and Compliance

ServiceNow's HRSD module helps maintain consistency in HR processes by enforcing standard procedures and ensuring that policies are followed. Built-in compliance features and audit trails also aid in meeting regulatory requirements and preparing for audits.

4. Scalability for Growing Organizations

Whether an organization is expanding locally or globally, the HRSD module is designed to scale efficiently. It supports multi-language and multi-currency needs, making it suitable for organizations with diverse workforces across different regions.

How the HRSD Module Integrates with Other ServiceNow Applications

A significant advantage of using ServiceNow's HRSD module is its seamless integration with other ServiceNow applications and external systems. This integration facilitates:

- **Cross-Departmental Collaboration**: HR teams can work closely with IT, finance, and facilities management to handle requests that involve multiple departments.
- **Enhanced Reporting and Analytics**: Integrating with ServiceNow's analytics tools provides HR leaders with deeper insights into service metrics, helping to optimize performance and identify areas for improvement.
- **Unified Platform Experience**: Employees benefit from a consistent interface when accessing various services, reducing confusion and enhancing the user experience.

Real-World Applications of HRSD

Organizations that have implemented ServiceNow's HRSD module have reported significant improvements in their operations. For example:

- **Reduced Case Handling Time**: By automating routine tasks and efficiently routing cases, HR teams can resolve inquiries faster.
- **Higher Employee Satisfaction Scores**: The use of self-service portals and clear communication channels contributes to an improved perception of HR services.
- **Lower Administrative Overheads**: Automation and streamlined processes lead to a decrease in manual workload, reducing the need for extensive HR administrative support.

Conclusion

The HR Service Delivery module in ServiceNow is a transformative tool that modernizes HR processes, making them more efficient, consistent, and employee-focused. As you continue through this book, you will learn more about how to configure, implement, and optimize the HRSD module to meet your organization's specific needs and enhance your HR service delivery.

Key Features of ServiceNow for HR Workflow Automation

In today's dynamic business environment, the ability to automate HR workflows is essential for maximizing efficiency and delivering a superior employee experience. ServiceNow's platform is equipped with a suite of features specifically designed to optimize HR processes, making them more streamlined, accurate, and responsive. This chapter provides an in-depth look at the key features of ServiceNow that enable HR workflow automation and transform traditional HR practices.

1. HR Service Management (HRSM)

HR Service Management (HRSM) serves as the foundation for automating and organizing HR workflows within ServiceNow. This feature facilitates a centralized approach to handling various HR tasks, including case management and employee inquiries. Key benefits include:

- **Automated Case Assignment**: HRSM uses predefined rules to route employee cases to the appropriate HR personnel, ensuring that inquiries are handled quickly and efficiently.
- **End-to-End Case Tracking**: HR professionals can track the progress of cases from initiation to resolution, providing transparency and accountability in HR services.
- **Self-Service Options**: The platform allows employees to submit requests and access support resources through an intuitive interface, reducing the workload on HR teams.

2. Workflow Designer and Automation Tools

One of ServiceNow's standout features for HR workflow automation is its Workflow Designer. This tool enables HR teams to build custom workflows that fit the specific needs of their organization. Features include:

- **Drag-and-Drop Interface**: The no-code/low-code environment allows HR professionals to create complex workflows without deep technical expertise.
- **Automated Task Management**: Tasks are automatically assigned, monitored, and completed according to the defined process flow, ensuring that all necessary steps are followed consistently.
- **Conditional Logic**: Workflows can incorporate conditional logic to handle different scenarios, making processes adaptable to various needs.

3. Employee Service Center

The Employee Service Center is a central hub where employees can access all HR services and resources. This feature significantly enhances HR workflow automation by:

- **Enabling Self-Service**: Employees can find answers to common questions, submit service requests, and track their progress independently, which reduces repetitive interactions for HR teams.
- **Streamlining Access to Information**: The center integrates with the organization's knowledge base, allowing employees to find solutions faster.
- **Mobile Compatibility**: Employees can access the service center through mobile devices, ensuring support is available anytime and anywhere.

4. Integration with Existing Systems

ServiceNow's ability to integrate with other HR and enterprise systems is a significant advantage for workflow automation. By connecting with platforms such as payroll systems, applicant tracking systems (ATS), and other HR software, ServiceNow can:

- **Automate Data Transfers**: Reduce the need for manual data entry by automatically syncing information between systems.
- **Enhance Process Continuity**: Integrated workflows ensure that related tasks, such as onboarding and offboarding, are seamlessly executed across multiple systems.
- **Improve Reporting and Analytics**: Data from various sources can be combined to provide comprehensive insights into HR operations and performance.

5. Lifecycle Event Management

Managing employee lifecycle events, such as onboarding, promotions, and offboarding, can be complex and time-consuming. ServiceNow's Lifecycle Event Management feature automates these processes by:

- **Coordinating Cross-Departmental Tasks**: Ensures that tasks involving multiple departments (e.g., IT, facilities) are completed on schedule.
- **Automating Notifications and Approvals**: Keeps all stakeholders informed and engaged through automated notifications and approval workflows.
- **Standardizing Processes**: Provides templates for common lifecycle events, allowing HR teams to maintain consistency across different cases.

6. Robotic Process Automation (RPA)

ServiceNow incorporates Robotic Process Automation (RPA) to enhance its workflow automation capabilities. RPA bots can perform repetitive, rule-based tasks that would otherwise require human intervention, such as:

- **Data Entry and Transfer**: Bots can input data into various systems, eliminating manual entry and minimizing errors.
- **Routine Reporting**: Automated generation of reports and dashboards helps HR teams track metrics without dedicating time to data collection and analysis.
- **Email Management**: RPA can automatically send emails or notifications based on specific triggers, ensuring timely communication without manual effort.

7. Advanced Reporting and Analytics

The ability to monitor, analyze, and optimize HR workflows is crucial for continuous improvement. ServiceNow provides comprehensive reporting and analytics tools that help HR teams:

- **Track Key Performance Indicators (KPIs)**: Real-time insights into workflow performance allow HR teams to identify bottlenecks and areas for improvement.
- **Generate Custom Reports**: ServiceNow's reporting engine enables the creation of tailored reports that align with an organization's specific needs.
- **Predict Trends**: Leveraging predictive analytics, HR leaders can forecast trends and prepare proactive strategies to manage workload and resource allocation.

8. Integration of Artificial Intelligence (AI) and Machine Learning (ML)

ServiceNow's use of AI and ML in HR workflows can further automate and enhance processes. These technologies contribute by:

- **Automating Decision-Making**: AI-driven tools can recommend actions based on historical data and current conditions, streamlining processes such as candidate screening and performance evaluations.
- **Personalizing Employee Interactions**: Machine learning algorithms can tailor the employee experience by suggesting relevant articles or services based on previous interactions.
- **Continuous Learning**: The platform's machine learning capabilities adapt over time, making workflows more efficient as they gather more data and refine their functions.

Conclusion

ServiceNow's suite of features for HR workflow automation goes beyond basic task automation, offering a holistic approach to enhancing HR operations. By integrating powerful tools such as workflow designers, lifecycle event management, RPA, and AI, ServiceNow provides HR teams with the means to deliver more efficient, accurate, and engaging services. This foundation enables organizations to transform their HR departments into strategic partners that contribute to business success.

Setting the Stage: Why Digital Workflows Matter in HR

In the modern workplace, the pressure on HR departments to deliver fast, accurate, and efficient services is higher than ever. Employees expect seamless interactions, while organizations seek streamlined processes that reduce costs and increase productivity. Digital workflows have emerged as the solution to meet these demands, offering an approach that transforms HR into a more agile, responsive, and strategic function. This chapter explains why digital workflows matter in HR and sets the stage for how ServiceNow can be leveraged to maximize their benefits.

The Evolution of HR Processes

Traditionally, HR processes were characterized by manual workflows and paperwork. Whether it was handling onboarding, responding to employee inquiries, or managing payroll, HR teams spent significant time and effort completing routine tasks. These manual processes came with several challenges:

- **Inefficiency**: Manual handling of tasks slowed down response times, reduced productivity, and often introduced errors.
- **Lack of Standardization**: Processes varied between HR personnel, leading to inconsistencies in service delivery.
- **Limited Visibility**: Tracking the progress of HR requests and maintaining oversight was difficult without a centralized system.

As businesses became more complex and employee expectations evolved, the need for more efficient, automated, and transparent HR processes became clear.

The Benefits of Digital Workflows in HR

Implementing digital workflows transforms the way HR operates, bringing numerous benefits to both the HR team and the broader organization. Here's why digital workflows are essential for HR:

1. Increased Efficiency and Productivity

Automating routine tasks allows HR teams to focus on high-value activities that contribute to strategic goals. With digital workflows:

- **Process automation** reduces the time required to complete repetitive tasks such as leave requests, benefits enrollment, and document approvals.
- **Task routing** ensures that requests are automatically assigned to the right person or department, speeding up response times and enhancing productivity.

2. Enhanced Employee Experience

A positive employee experience is directly tied to how smoothly HR services are delivered. Digital workflows support this by:

- **Providing self-service options**: Employees can submit requests, access policies, and track the progress of their inquiries through user-friendly portals.
- **Ensuring faster response times**: Automated notifications and case tracking keep employees informed and reduce waiting periods.
- **Simplifying interactions**: With digital workflows, employees don't have to navigate multiple channels or deal with lengthy approval processes, making their interactions with HR more streamlined.

3. Standardized Processes

Consistency in HR processes is crucial for fairness and compliance. Digital workflows help:

- **Enforce standard procedures**: Predefined workflows guide HR staff through processes step-by-step, ensuring that each task is handled consistently.
- **Maintain compliance**: Automated checks and balances embedded in workflows help ensure adherence to internal policies and external regulations.
- **Reduce errors**: Automated workflows minimize manual data entry, which is prone to mistakes.

4. Improved Data Management and Accessibility

Digital workflows centralize HR data and make it easily accessible. This leads to:

- **Better record-keeping**: All employee interactions and requests are logged and stored within a single system, making information retrieval straightforward.
- **Data-driven decision-making**: HR leaders can leverage analytics from workflow data to identify trends, make informed decisions, and optimize processes.
- **Enhanced security**: Digital workflows often come with built-in data protection measures, ensuring sensitive information is handled securely.

5. Adaptability and Scalability

As organizations grow, their HR needs evolve. Digital workflows provide the flexibility and scalability needed to support this growth:

- **Easy modifications**: Workflows can be updated or expanded to reflect new processes or organizational changes without significant downtime.
- **Scalable solutions**: Digital workflows can be adapted to accommodate an increasing number of employees, locations, or services as the company grows.

Why ServiceNow Stands Out

ServiceNow is a leading platform for implementing digital workflows in HR due to its comprehensive features and adaptability. ServiceNow's HR Service Delivery module provides the necessary tools to automate, track, and manage HR processes efficiently. The platform stands out because:

- **It integrates seamlessly with existing systems**, ensuring continuity across different HR functions.
- **It supports end-to-end workflow automation**, covering the entire employee lifecycle from recruitment to offboarding.
- **It includes analytics and reporting capabilities**, enabling HR teams to measure performance and optimize workflows continuously.

Real-World Impact of Digital Workflows in HR

Organizations that have transitioned from manual processes to digital workflows have seen significant improvements:

- **Increased responsiveness**: HR departments can handle more requests with the same number of staff, leading to faster response times.
- **Enhanced employee satisfaction**: Employees appreciate being kept in the loop and having access to self-service options.
- **Operational cost savings**: Automation reduces the need for extensive manual labor, cutting down operational expenses.

For example, an HR department that previously took days to approve leave requests could reduce processing times to mere hours by implementing an automated digital workflow. Such efficiencies translate to a more productive HR team and a better employee experience.

Conclusion

Digital workflows are not just a trend; they are a fundamental shift in how HR services are delivered. By automating processes, standardizing tasks, and enhancing data management, digital workflows empower HR teams to operate more efficiently and strategically. ServiceNow provides the tools and flexibility needed to implement these workflows effectively, making it an indispensable partner in modern HR digital transformation.

Section 2:
Planning and Preparation for Implementation

Assessing Organizational Needs and Readiness

Embarking on the journey to implement ServiceNow for HR requires thorough preparation and a clear understanding of your organization's current state and objectives. The first step in this process is to assess your organizational needs and readiness. This chapter outlines the key areas to evaluate and provides a structured approach to ensure your organization is prepared for a successful implementation.

The Importance of Assessing Organizational Readiness

A successful implementation of ServiceNow depends on more than just choosing the right software. It involves understanding how well your organization can adapt to new processes, systems, and workflows. Properly assessing readiness helps to:

- **Identify gaps** in current processes that the new system should address.
- **Ensure alignment** between HR objectives and broader business goals.
- **Facilitate smoother adoption** by preparing stakeholders for change.
- **Mitigate risks** associated with system integration and data migration.

Steps to Assess Organizational Needs and Readiness

1. Conduct a Comprehensive Process Audit

Start by evaluating your current HR processes to identify inefficiencies and areas for improvement. Key questions to consider include:

- **What processes are currently manual or semi-automated?**
- **Where are the most significant delays or bottlenecks?**
- **Which HR tasks are repetitive and could benefit from automation?**

Documenting existing workflows helps to map out how ServiceNow can be integrated to fill these gaps and enhance overall efficiency.

2. Engage Key Stakeholders

Stakeholder engagement is critical to understanding the broader implications of implementing ServiceNow. Include:

- **HR leaders and teams** who will use the platform daily.
- **IT specialists** who will manage integration and support.
- **Executive sponsors** to ensure alignment with strategic business goals.

Gather feedback on current pain points and desired features in a new system. This will not only inform your implementation strategy but also foster early buy-in from stakeholders, which is vital for smooth adoption.

3. Assess Technical Infrastructure

Before implementing ServiceNow, it's essential to review your organization's current technical infrastructure. This step ensures that your systems can support ServiceNow's requirements:

- **Evaluate existing HR software and tools**: Identify which systems ServiceNow will need to integrate with (e.g., payroll systems, ATS).
- **Check system compatibility**: Ensure that your infrastructure (servers, networks, etc.) can handle ServiceNow's platform capabilities.
- **Determine data storage and security protocols**: ServiceNow requires robust data handling and security measures. Ensure that your IT team is prepared for compliance with these standards.

4. Analyze Workforce Readiness

Understanding how ready your workforce is for digital transformation is crucial. This involves:

- **Assessing skill levels**: Determine if the HR team has the technical skills to work with ServiceNow or if training will be needed.
- **Measuring openness to change**: Gauge the willingness of employees to adopt new workflows and technologies.
- **Identifying training needs**: Develop a training plan tailored to different user roles to ensure everyone can use the system effectively once it is deployed.

5. Define Clear Objectives and Success Metrics

To ensure that the implementation aligns with your business goals, clearly define what success looks like. Objectives might include:

- **Reducing process times** by a certain percentage.
- **Improving employee satisfaction scores** related to HR services.
- **Enhancing data accuracy** through automated workflows.

Once objectives are defined, establish key performance indicators (KPIs) to measure the success of the implementation, such as response times, case resolution rates, and user adoption levels.

Addressing Potential Barriers to Readiness

Identifying potential challenges early on can help mitigate risks and pave the way for a smoother implementation. Common barriers include:

- **Resistance to change**: Some HR team members may be hesitant to adopt new systems. Address this by clearly communicating the benefits and providing hands-on training.
- **Budget constraints**: Ensure the budget allocated for implementation covers not just the software costs, but also training, data migration, and integration expenses.
- **Data migration complexity**: Moving data from legacy systems to ServiceNow can be complicated. Engage IT teams early to plan for secure, accurate data transfer.

Tools and Methods for Assessing Readiness

Leverage the following tools and methods to conduct a thorough readiness assessment:

- **Surveys and feedback forms**: Collect insights from HR and other departments to identify current challenges and desired outcomes.
- **Workshops and meetings**: Hold discussions with stakeholders to gather qualitative data and build consensus.
- **Readiness assessment checklists**: Use structured checklists to evaluate technical, procedural, and workforce readiness comprehensively.
- **Pilot programs**: Run a pilot with a small subset of the HR team to identify any adjustments needed before full-scale implementation.

Creating an Implementation Roadmap

After assessing your organization's readiness and gathering all necessary data, develop an implementation roadmap that outlines:

- **Phased approach**: Plan for incremental rollouts starting with high-impact areas.
- **Timeline and milestones**: Set realistic deadlines for each phase of the project.
- **Resource allocation**: Assign roles and responsibilities to project team members to ensure clarity.

Conclusion

Assessing your organization's needs and readiness for ServiceNow implementation is an essential step to ensure a successful deployment. By auditing current processes, engaging stakeholders, analyzing technical infrastructure, and addressing workforce readiness, you lay the groundwork for a seamless transition. This proactive approach minimizes risks and positions your HR department to fully leverage the capabilities of ServiceNow, transforming it into a more efficient and strategic asset.

Defining Project Scope and Objectives

Defining the project scope and setting clear objectives are critical steps in the successful implementation of ServiceNow for HR. These elements serve as the foundation of your project, ensuring alignment among stakeholders and guiding your team through each phase of the implementation. In this chapter, we will discuss the importance of defining project scope and objectives, outline the key components involved, and provide practical steps to create an effective project blueprint.

The Importance of Defining Project Scope

The project scope outlines the boundaries of what the ServiceNow implementation will cover. It is essential for:

- **Setting clear expectations**: Ensures all stakeholders understand what is included in the project and what is not.
- **Preventing scope creep**: Helps maintain focus by preventing unplanned expansions that could delay timelines and increase costs.
- **Allocating resources effectively**: Clarifies which resources are needed for different project phases and tasks.

Key Elements of Project Scope

When defining your project scope for ServiceNow implementation, consider the following components:

1. Objectives and Deliverables

Clearly state what the project aims to achieve. This includes:

- **Primary goals**: For example, automating specific HR processes, improving response times, or enhancing employee self-service capabilities.
- **Key deliverables**: The tangible outcomes of the project, such as an HR service portal, automated workflows for onboarding, and integrated case management systems.

2. Inclusions and Exclusions

Specify what is within the scope of the project and what falls outside it:

- **In-scope activities**: These could include data migration, configuring custom workflows, training HR staff, and integrating third-party systems.
- **Out-of-scope activities**: Such as updating non-HR related modules or implementing unrelated ServiceNow features.

3. Stakeholder Roles and Responsibilities

Identify who will be involved in the project and their responsibilities:

- **Project manager**: Oversees the entire project, ensuring timelines and goals are met.
- **HR team leads**: Provide input on HR processes and collaborate on workflow designs.
- **IT specialists**: Handle technical aspects like system integration and data migration.
- **Change management team**: Manages user adoption and training efforts.

4. Project Constraints and Assumptions

Document any constraints that could affect the project, such as budget limitations, availability of resources, or regulatory requirements. Also, outline key assumptions that influence your planning, such as access to current HR data or the readiness of existing systems for integration.

Setting Clear Objectives

Establishing well-defined objectives provides a roadmap for achieving the desired outcomes of the project. Objectives should be **SMART**—Specific, Measurable, Achievable, Relevant, and Time-bound.

Examples of SMART Objectives:

- **Reduce HR response times** for employee requests by 40% within six months of implementation.
- **Automate at least 80%** of routine HR tasks within three months of going live.
- **Achieve a 90% user adoption rate** among HR staff within the first quarter post-implementation through targeted training and support.

Aligning Objectives with Business Goals

Ensure that the objectives align with broader organizational goals, such as improving operational efficiency, enhancing employee satisfaction, or supporting digital transformation initiatives. This alignment will secure executive support and ensure that the implementation delivers value beyond the HR department.

Steps to Define Project Scope and Objectives

1. Collaborate with Stakeholders

Conduct workshops and meetings to gather input from key stakeholders. Discuss their expectations, identify pain points in current HR processes, and align on what the new system should accomplish.

2. Develop a Project Charter

Create a project charter that outlines the scope, objectives, key stakeholders, timeline, and resource allocation. The project charter serves as a guiding document throughout the implementation process and can be referenced to keep the project on track.

3. Break Down the Scope into Phases

Segment the project scope into manageable phases. For example:

- **Phase 1**: Configure and launch the HR service portal.
- **Phase 2**: Automate onboarding and offboarding workflows.
- **Phase 3**: Integrate existing HR systems for seamless data flow.

4. Establish Success Criteria

Determine how success will be measured for each objective. This might include quantitative metrics like reduced processing times and qualitative measures such as improved user feedback.

5. Document and Communicate the Plan

Once the scope and objectives are defined, document them in detail and communicate them to all project stakeholders. Regular updates and open channels for feedback will keep everyone informed and engaged.

Common Challenges and Solutions

Challenge: Scope Creep

Solution: Regularly review the project scope and objectives with stakeholders. Address any proposed changes formally and assess their impact on the timeline and budget before approval.

Challenge: Vague Objectives

Solution: Revisit objectives to ensure they meet the SMART criteria. Specificity and measurability are crucial for tracking progress and assessing outcomes.

Challenge: Conflicting Priorities Among Stakeholders

Solution: Prioritize objectives based on business impact and resource availability. Ensure executive sponsors mediate and align conflicting priorities.

Conclusion

Defining the project scope and setting clear objectives are foundational steps that set the tone for a successful ServiceNow implementation. These steps help maintain focus, prevent costly deviations, and ensure that the project delivers the intended value. With a well-defined scope and objectives, your organization will be positioned for a smoother implementation journey and more impactful results.

Building the Right Implementation Team

Assembling the right implementation team is a critical step in ensuring the successful deployment of ServiceNow for HR. The complexity of such projects requires a diverse group of individuals with different skill sets, roles, and responsibilities. In this chapter, we will outline how to build an effective implementation team, the key roles involved, and best practices for promoting collaboration and accountability throughout the project.

The Importance of a Strong Implementation Team

The success of a ServiceNow implementation hinges on the capabilities and coordination of the team driving the project. A well-rounded team ensures:

- **Efficient project management**: Tasks are completed on time, within budget, and aligned with project goals.
- **Comprehensive knowledge**: Team members contribute their expertise from various areas such as HR, IT, and change management.
- **User adoption**: Engaging key stakeholders early on helps promote user acceptance and smoother transition.

Key Roles in an Implementation Team

1. Project Manager

The project manager is responsible for overseeing the entire implementation process. Their responsibilities include:

- **Developing and managing the project timeline**.
- **Coordinating team efforts** and ensuring alignment with project goals.
- **Communicating progress** to stakeholders and senior management.
- **Mitigating risks** and resolving issues as they arise.

2. HR Process Experts

HR process experts bring in-depth knowledge of current HR processes and identify areas where ServiceNow can add the most value. Their role includes:

- **Mapping existing workflows** to ServiceNow functionalities.
- **Defining new processes** that leverage the capabilities of the platform.
- **Providing insights** to customize HR modules effectively.

3. IT Specialists

IT specialists handle the technical aspects of the implementation, such as system integration and data migration. Their responsibilities include:

- **Ensuring system compatibility** and seamless integration with existing HR and enterprise software.
- **Configuring and customizing** the platform as needed.
- **Addressing security and compliance requirements**.
- **Supporting data migration** and maintaining data integrity.

4. ServiceNow Implementation Partner

Collaborating with a ServiceNow-certified partner or consultant can significantly improve the chances of a successful implementation. They provide:

- **Expert guidance** on best practices for configuration and deployment.
- **Technical support** for complex customizations.
- **Training resources** to equip your team with the necessary skills for post-implementation management.

5. Change Management Lead

The change management lead ensures that the human aspect of the implementation is not overlooked. Their tasks include:

- **Creating change management plans** to support user adoption.
- **Developing training programs** for HR staff and end-users.
- **Communicating project updates** and benefits to the broader organization.
- **Collecting feedback** to refine processes and address concerns.

6. Business Analysts

Business analysts bridge the gap between technical teams and HR process experts. They are essential for:

- **Documenting business requirements** and translating them into technical specifications.
- **Validating that solutions align** with the organization's needs and objectives.
- **Supporting testing and quality assurance** to ensure that the system meets expectations.

7. Training and Support Team

The training and support team prepares HR staff and other users for the new system. Their responsibilities include:

- **Developing training materials** such as user guides and tutorials.
- **Conducting training sessions** and workshops.
- **Providing ongoing support** post-implementation to handle user queries and troubleshoot issues.

Best Practices for Building and Managing the Team

1. Select a Balanced Mix of Skills

Ensure that the team includes both technical experts and HR professionals to cover all aspects of the implementation. A balanced team can navigate both the technical configuration of ServiceNow and the nuances of HR processes.

2. Define Roles and Responsibilities Clearly

Establish clear responsibilities for each team member to avoid overlaps and confusion. Use a Responsibility Assignment Matrix (RAM) to outline who is responsible for each task and who should be consulted or informed.

3. Foster Open Communication

Regular team meetings and updates are essential for keeping the project on track. Use collaboration tools like Slack or Microsoft Teams to facilitate ongoing communication and document progress.

4. Ensure Stakeholder Involvement

Engage key stakeholders throughout the project to gain their feedback and buy-in. This involvement helps in refining the project scope and ensures that the final implementation aligns with business goals.

5. Implement a Feedback Loop

Create a system for collecting feedback from team members and stakeholders during each project phase. This helps in identifying potential issues early and allows for timely adjustments.

6. Prioritize Training and Knowledge Transfer

A successful implementation doesn't end at deployment. Ensure that the team provides comprehensive training for HR teams and establishes a knowledge transfer plan so that internal staff can manage the system post-launch.

Overcoming Common Challenges

Challenge: Skill Gaps

Solution: Partner with a ServiceNow-certified consultant or train existing team members through workshops and courses.

Challenge: Lack of Coordination

Solution: Use project management tools such as Jira or Trello to organize tasks, track progress, and assign responsibilities clearly.

Challenge: Resistance to Change

Solution: Include a change management lead who can focus on communication, training, and support to foster a culture of acceptance and enthusiasm for the new system.

Conclusion

Building the right implementation team is essential for a smooth and successful ServiceNow deployment. By assembling a diverse group of experts and defining their roles clearly, you lay the groundwork for an efficient implementation process. Remember, fostering collaboration, maintaining open communication, and prioritizing training will ensure that your team not only completes the project successfully but also sets the stage for long-term adoption and utilization.

Planning Budget and Resource Allocation

Effective budget planning and resource allocation are essential for a smooth and successful ServiceNow implementation. A well-thought-out budget and resource plan helps ensure that the project stays on track, avoids unforeseen financial challenges, and maximizes the impact of the implementation. This chapter will guide you through creating a comprehensive budget and allocating resources efficiently to support the deployment of ServiceNow for HR.

The Importance of Budget Planning

Proper budget planning enables organizations to:

- **Identify and control costs** associated with the implementation.
- **Ensure funding is available** for all phases of the project, from initial setup to post-implementation support.
- **Reduce financial risks** by anticipating potential cost overruns and establishing contingencies.
- **Secure executive buy-in** by presenting a clear and justified financial plan.

Key Budget Components to Consider

When planning the budget for ServiceNow implementation, include the following key components:

1. Licensing and Subscription Costs

ServiceNow operates on a subscription-based model. The costs will vary based on:

- **Modules required**: The HR Service Delivery module and any additional functionalities.
- **Number of users**: How many HR staff and employees will access the platform.
- **Contract length**: Multi-year agreements may offer cost benefits over shorter contracts.

2. Implementation and Integration Services

These costs cover professional services needed for:

- **Initial configuration** and setup.
- **Customizations and integrations** with existing HR systems and software.
- **Data migration** from legacy systems to ServiceNow. Engaging a ServiceNow-certified implementation partner can add to these expenses but often brings expertise that accelerates the project timeline and enhances outcomes.

3. Training and User Education

Training is critical for the successful adoption of ServiceNow. Budget for:

- **Workshops and training sessions** for HR staff and IT teams.
- **Development of training materials** such as guides, videos, and tutorials.
- **Ongoing support** to ensure users remain confident and proficient post-implementation.

4. Change Management and Communication

Implementing ServiceNow is a significant change that requires a dedicated plan for managing this transition. Allocate budget for:

- **Change management experts** who can drive user adoption strategies.
- **Communication campaigns** to keep stakeholders informed and engaged.
- **Feedback tools** to gather user input and address concerns early.

5. Infrastructure and Technical Requirements

Ensure that the organization's technical environment can support ServiceNow. Costs in this area may include:

- **Server upgrades or additional storage** if needed.
- **Network enhancements** to ensure optimal performance.
- **IT resources** for maintaining and supporting the system during and after implementation.

6. Contingency Fund

Unforeseen expenses can arise during any implementation. Setting aside 10-15% of the total budget as a contingency helps:

- **Mitigate risks** associated with unexpected technical challenges or extended timelines.
- **Cover additional training or support needs** that may become apparent after the system goes live.

Allocating Human Resources

Equally important to budgeting is the allocation of human resources to ensure the project progresses smoothly. Here's how to allocate resources effectively:

1. Project Management Team

A dedicated project manager is essential for overseeing timelines, deliverables, and stakeholder communication. Ensure this role is staffed with someone experienced in HR technology implementations or complex IT projects.

2. Subject Matter Experts (SMEs)

Engage HR process experts and team leads to provide input on workflows, best practices, and user needs. Their involvement is vital during the configuration and customization phases.

3. IT and Technical Team

Assign IT professionals who can handle system integration, data migration, and any infrastructure updates. They should work closely with the implementation partner to align the platform with existing technologies.

4. Change Management Lead

Appoint a change management lead to develop and execute the communication and training plan, ensuring user buy-in and a smooth transition to the new platform.

5. Training and Support Staff

Allocate team members responsible for creating training materials, conducting training sessions, and offering ongoing support to HR staff and other users.

Creating a Budget Plan

Step 1: Estimate Costs by Phase

Break down the budget into project phases:

- **Planning and preparation**
- **Implementation and configuration**

- **Training and change management**
- **Post-implementation support**

Step 2: Prioritize Spending

Identify which areas will deliver the most value and allocate resources accordingly. For example, if user adoption is a top priority, invest more in training and change management.

Step 3: Review and Validate

Collaborate with financial controllers or budget analysts to validate the budget plan and ensure it aligns with the organization's financial guidelines. This step helps prevent potential pushback during executive approval.

Step 4: Present a Comprehensive Business Case

Prepare a business case that outlines the anticipated ROI (return on investment) from implementing ServiceNow. Include metrics such as expected productivity gains, reduced HR workload, and improved employee satisfaction.

Tips for Effective Budget Management

- **Track expenses continuously**: Use project management software to monitor costs and resource allocation in real-time.
- **Adjust as needed**: Be prepared to reallocate resources if priorities shift during the project.
- **Communicate transparently**: Keep stakeholders informed of budget status, especially if adjustments or additional funding are required.

Conclusion

Planning budget and resource allocation is a crucial step that sets the stage for a successful ServiceNow implementation. By considering all key cost components, allocating human resources effectively, and developing a clear and detailed budget plan, your organization can pave the way for a smooth deployment. Proper budget management ensures that your project remains financially feasible and delivers the expected benefits.

Establishing Key Performance Indicators (KPIs)

Establishing Key Performance Indicators (KPIs) is a fundamental part of the planning and preparation phase for implementing ServiceNow in HR. KPIs help you measure the success of your project, track performance, and ensure that the new system meets its intended objectives. This chapter will guide you through the process of defining meaningful KPIs, aligning them with your project goals, and using them to drive continuous improvement.

Why KPIs Matter in ServiceNow Implementation

KPIs are vital for several reasons:

- **Measuring Success**: KPIs provide clear metrics to evaluate whether the implementation is achieving its goals, such as improved efficiency or enhanced user satisfaction.
- **Driving Accountability**: Setting KPIs holds the implementation team accountable and ensures that everyone is focused on delivering measurable results.
- **Informing Decisions**: KPIs offer actionable insights that can guide adjustments to processes and workflows, ensuring continuous optimization.
- **Building Stakeholder Confidence**: Demonstrating progress through KPIs helps maintain the confidence and support of stakeholders.

Types of KPIs for HR ServiceNow Implementation

KPIs can be broken down into several categories based on the aspect of the implementation they measure. Here are some of the most relevant KPI types for HR:

1. Operational Efficiency KPIs

These KPIs measure how well HR processes are being optimized. Examples include:

- **Average Time to Resolve Cases**: The time taken from when an HR case is opened until it is resolved.
- **Process Automation Rate**: The percentage of HR processes automated through ServiceNow compared to those still requiring manual intervention.
- **Task Completion Rate**: The percentage of tasks completed within a set timeframe.

2. User Adoption KPIs

User adoption KPIs gauge how effectively HR staff and employees are embracing the new system:

- **User Training Completion Rate**: The percentage of HR staff who have completed training on the new system.
- **Active User Ratio**: The proportion of HR users actively engaging with ServiceNow tools compared to the total number of trained users.
- **User Satisfaction Scores**: Survey results measuring user satisfaction with the new processes and system.

3. Performance and Productivity KPIs

These KPIs focus on improvements in the productivity of the HR team:

- **Reduction in Manual Workload**: The decrease in time HR staff spend on manual tasks after implementing ServiceNow.
- **Improved Response Time**: The time it takes for HR to respond to employee requests or inquiries.
- **Case Handling Efficiency**: The number of cases handled per HR representative within a specific period.

4. Employee Experience KPIs

These KPIs measure the impact of the implementation on the overall employee experience:

- **First Response Time**: The average time it takes for an employee's case or request to receive an initial response.
- **Self-Service Utilization Rate**: The percentage of employees using self-service tools provided by ServiceNow.
- **Feedback and NPS (Net Promoter Score)**: Surveys to determine how likely employees are to recommend HR services within the organization.

How to Define Effective KPIs

1. Align with Business Objectives

Ensure that KPIs are aligned with the broader goals of your HR department and the organization. For example, if a key objective is to enhance employee satisfaction, KPIs should include metrics related to response times and satisfaction surveys.

2. Make KPIs SMART

KPIs should be:

- **Specific**: Clearly defined and detailed.
- **Measurable**: Quantifiable to allow for precise tracking.
- **Achievable**: Realistic and within the reach of your resources.
- **Relevant**: Aligned with the overall goals of the implementation.
- **Time-bound**: Have a set timeframe for achieving the targets.

3. Involve Stakeholders in KPI Selection

Engage HR leaders, project managers, and IT specialists to contribute their input when selecting KPIs. This collaboration ensures that the metrics chosen reflect the priorities of all relevant parties.

4. Focus on Leading and Lagging Indicators

- **Leading indicators** provide predictive insights and help identify potential issues early, such as training completion rates.
- **Lagging indicators** show results after processes have occurred, such as improvements in response times or case resolution rates.

Tools for Tracking and Measuring KPIs

Use tools within ServiceNow to track and report on KPIs effectively:

- **ServiceNow Performance Analytics**: Offers dashboards and reports that can visualize KPI trends and progress over time.
- **Integrated Reporting Tools**: Leverage the reporting capabilities within ServiceNow to create custom KPI reports tailored to HR needs.
- **Feedback and Survey Modules**: Collect user feedback directly through ServiceNow to measure satisfaction and adoption rates.

Setting Baselines and Targets

Before launching the implementation, establish baseline metrics for each KPI to understand your starting point. This helps set realistic targets and allows for clear comparisons as the project progresses.

Example of Baseline and Target Setting:

- **Current average case resolution time**: 5 days.
- **Target after ServiceNow implementation**: 2 days within the first 6 months.

Continuous Monitoring and Adjustment

KPI tracking should not be a one-time task. Implement a system for continuous monitoring, allowing your team to:

- **Identify trends** and proactively address issues.
- **Make data-driven decisions** to optimize processes.
- **Adjust KPIs** as the project evolves or as business objectives shift.

Regularly review KPI performance during project meetings, and use the data to inform any changes needed in workflows or training.

Conclusion

Establishing and tracking KPIs is crucial for the successful implementation of ServiceNow for HR. By aligning KPIs with business goals, ensuring they are SMART, and continuously monitoring them, your organization can measure progress effectively, adapt when needed, and achieve a successful transformation.

Preparing Data for Migration

Data migration is a crucial part of implementing ServiceNow for HR. Ensuring that the transfer of data from legacy systems to the new platform is accurate and seamless can make the difference between a successful and challenging implementation. This chapter will guide you through the process of preparing data for migration, emphasizing best practices, potential challenges, and strategic steps to ensure a smooth transition.

The Importance of Data Preparation in ServiceNow Implementation

Preparing data for migration is essential because:

- **Data accuracy** directly impacts the functionality and reliability of the new system.
- **Seamless workflows** require comprehensive data mapping to integrate effectively with ServiceNow processes.
- **Compliance and security** mandates are more easily met when data is properly handled during migration.

Key Steps for Data Preparation

1. Conduct a Data Audit

Before initiating the data migration process, conduct a comprehensive audit of existing HR data. This includes:

- **Identifying data sources**: List all systems that currently store HR data, such as payroll software, employee databases, and document management systems.
- **Evaluating data quality**: Check for errors, inconsistencies, and outdated information that need correction or elimination.
- **Classifying data types**: Categorize data by its relevance and sensitivity to prioritize what needs migration.

2. Clean and Validate Data

Data cleaning ensures that the migrated data is accurate, complete, and consistent. To achieve this:

- **Remove duplicates and obsolete records**: Eliminate redundant data and information that is no longer relevant.
- **Standardize data formats**: Ensure consistent formatting for dates, names, and other data fields to align with ServiceNow's requirements.
- **Validate key data points**: Verify critical data fields such as employee IDs, contact details, and job roles for accuracy.

3. Map Data Fields

Data mapping involves matching fields from the legacy system to corresponding fields in ServiceNow. This step is crucial for maintaining data integrity:

- **Create a data mapping template**: Document how each field in the source system corresponds to the destination system.
- **Identify mandatory fields**: Ensure all required fields for ServiceNow functionality are populated in the data mapping template.
- **Review with stakeholders**: Have HR and IT teams validate the data mapping to avoid discrepancies during migration.

4. Plan for Data Segmentation

Not all data needs to be migrated at once. Segmenting data into manageable groups can help streamline the migration process:

- **Prioritize recent and relevant data**: Migrate the most current and frequently used data first to minimize disruptions to daily operations.
- **Archive historical data**: Consider archiving older data that is not immediately needed but may be required for future reference or compliance purposes.
- **Define data ownership**: Assign ownership to specific data segments so that responsible team members can oversee their accuracy and completeness.

Best Practices for Data Migration

1. Develop a Data Migration Plan

A structured plan ensures that each phase of the migration process is accounted for:

- **Set a timeline**: Define clear start and end dates for the data migration process.
- **Allocate resources**: Assign roles and responsibilities, including data migration specialists, HR team members, and IT support.
- **Create a risk management strategy**: Identify potential risks, such as data loss or compatibility issues, and develop contingency plans.

2. Perform Test Migrations

Testing the migration process before the final transfer helps identify any issues:

- **Run pilot tests**: Migrate a small data set to ServiceNow to check for errors and address them early.
- **Analyze test results**: Ensure that data integrity is maintained, and workflows are functioning as expected after the pilot migration.
- **Refine the process**: Use insights from test migrations to adjust the strategy and make improvements.

3. Ensure Compliance and Security

Data migration often involves handling sensitive employee information, so it's important to:

- **Adhere to data protection regulations**: Follow GDPR, CCPA, or other relevant data privacy laws to safeguard employee data.
- **Encrypt data**: Use encryption protocols during data transfer to prevent unauthorized access.
- **Limit access**: Only allow authorized personnel to handle data during the migration process to reduce the risk of breaches.

Common Challenges and How to Overcome Them

Challenge: Data Incompatibility

Solution: Work with IT specialists to identify data fields that may not align with ServiceNow's format and transform them into compatible formats during the mapping process.

Challenge: Data Loss

Solution: Perform regular backups before and during the migration process. Implement verification procedures post-migration to confirm data completeness.

Challenge: Extended Downtime

Solution: Schedule migrations during low-activity periods, such as after work hours or over weekends, to minimize disruptions.

Challenge: Resistance to Change

Solution: Communicate the benefits of ServiceNow and the improved data handling it offers to HR staff. Provide training to ensure familiarity with data processes on the new platform.

Post-Migration Validation

After completing the data migration, it's essential to validate that everything has transferred correctly:

- **Run data audits**: Conduct comprehensive checks to ensure all data is present and accurate in ServiceNow.
- **Verify workflow functionality**: Test workflows that depend on the migrated data to confirm seamless operation.
- **Gather feedback**: Collect input from HR users to identify any discrepancies or usability issues that may have surfaced post-migration.

Conclusion

Preparing data for migration is a complex but vital step in implementing ServiceNow for HR. By conducting thorough data audits, cleaning and validating data, and using strategic mapping and testing, your organization can ensure a smooth transition. Following best practices and addressing common challenges proactively will lay the groundwork for an effective and reliable ServiceNow deployment that enhances HR processes and workflows.

Section 3:
ServiceNow Platform Essentials

Introduction to ServiceNow Platform Architecture

Understanding the architecture of the ServiceNow platform is crucial for effectively leveraging its capabilities and ensuring smooth integration with existing HR systems. The platform's architecture underpins its performance, scalability, and flexibility, enabling organizations to manage HR processes efficiently and drive digital transformation. In this chapter, we will explore the core components and structure of ServiceNow's architecture, explaining how each element contributes to a cohesive and powerful HR service delivery solution.

Overview of ServiceNow Platform Architecture

The ServiceNow platform is built on a cloud-based, multi-instance architecture designed to deliver robust service management capabilities. Its architecture can be broken down into several core layers, each contributing unique functionalities:

1. Multi-Instance Cloud Architecture

Unlike many multi-tenant platforms, ServiceNow operates on a multi-instance architecture. Each customer has their own instance, allowing for:

- **Customized configurations**: Each organization can tailor the platform to meet its unique HR needs without affecting other users.
- **Enhanced security**: Data isolation ensures that each instance remains independent, providing greater data protection and compliance.
- **Optimized performance**: Independent instances mean that high demand or customization in one organization does not impact others.

2. ServiceNow Platform Layers

The platform's architecture is divided into several key layers that work together to provide a seamless user experience:

a. User Interface Layer

- **Purpose**: The user interface (UI) is what HR professionals and employees interact with when using ServiceNow. It is designed to be user-friendly, customizable, and responsive across devices.
- **Components**: Dashboards, service portals, and custom interfaces that allow users to access HR services, submit requests, and track case progress.

b. Application Layer

- **Purpose**: Houses the various applications and modules available within ServiceNow, such as the HR Service Delivery (HRSD) module.
- **Components**: Core applications include HR Case Management, Employee Service Center, and Lifecycle Event Management. Custom applications can also be built using the ServiceNow Application Creator.

c. Processing Layer

- **Purpose**: Facilitates the execution of workflows and business logic. This layer handles automated processes such as approvals, notifications, and data updates.
- **Components**: The processing layer uses scripting and workflow engines, including Flow Designer and Business Rules, to automate HR tasks and integrate with external systems.

d. Data Layer

- **Purpose**: Manages the storage, retrieval, and management of data within ServiceNow.
- **Components**: The data layer is composed of a relational database (built on MySQL) that stores information such as employee records, case histories, and service requests. ServiceNow's data model supports a variety of data types and relationships.

Core Platform Components

1. ServiceNow Database

At the heart of ServiceNow's architecture is its relational database. This database enables robust data management, supporting a wide range of data types and complex relationships. Key features include:

- **Data Security**: ServiceNow offers granular access control, ensuring data privacy and compliance with standards like GDPR.
- **CMDB (Configuration Management Database)**: Provides a single source of truth for all data related to IT and HR services, facilitating better decision-making and process optimization.

2. Integration Capabilities

ServiceNow's architecture is designed to integrate seamlessly with other enterprise systems, ensuring cohesive workflows and data synchronization. Key integration methods include:

- **APIs (Application Programming Interfaces)**: REST and SOAP APIs allow ServiceNow to connect with external HR systems, payroll software, and other business applications.
- **IntegrationHub**: A native tool that facilitates the creation and management of integrations, reducing the need for extensive coding and development.

3. Flow Designer and Workflow Engine

The workflow engine and Flow Designer are pivotal for automating processes in ServiceNow. They enable:

- **No-code/low-code workflow creation**: Users can build and manage workflows through an intuitive drag-and-drop interface.
- **Advanced scripting capabilities**: For more complex use cases, scripting allows for customized logic and automation.

4. Performance Analytics and Reporting

Performance analytics provides insights into HR operations, helping HR leaders monitor KPIs and make data-driven decisions. This component includes:

- **Real-time dashboards**: Visual representations of data that track key HR metrics, such as case resolution times and employee satisfaction rates.
- **Historical trend analysis**: Helps identify patterns and areas for improvement over time.

5. Security Framework

ServiceNow's architecture includes a comprehensive security framework that protects data and ensures compliance:

- **Role-based access control (RBAC)**: Users have access to information and functions based on their roles, enhancing security and data integrity.
- **Encryption and compliance features**: End-to-end encryption ensures data privacy, and ServiceNow is compliant with various regulatory standards.

Advantages of ServiceNow Architecture for HR

1. Scalability

ServiceNow's cloud-based architecture allows HR operations to scale as the organization grows. Whether expanding to new locations or adding more users, the platform supports seamless scaling without performance degradation.

2. Customization and Flexibility

With a multi-instance approach, organizations can tailor their instance to their specific needs. This means HR teams can:

- **Create custom workflows** to match internal HR processes.
- **Adapt interfaces** to ensure an intuitive user experience for employees.

3. Enhanced Performance and Reliability

Because each organization has its own instance, ServiceNow maintains high performance and reliability. Maintenance or customization in one instance does not affect others, ensuring consistent uptime and user satisfaction.

4. Robust Data Management

ServiceNow's data architecture supports extensive data handling capabilities, essential for managing employee information, service requests, and case data. The centralized data model ensures easy retrieval and reporting.

Conclusion

ServiceNow's platform architecture is a robust, scalable, and secure foundation that supports comprehensive HR service delivery. By understanding its key components, from the user interface to the processing and data layers, organizations can better leverage its capabilities to enhance HR processes.

Core Capabilities of ServiceNow for HR

ServiceNow is a comprehensive platform designed to streamline HR service delivery by digitizing and automating processes. Understanding the core capabilities of ServiceNow for HR is essential for fully leveraging its potential and achieving maximum efficiency in HR operations. This chapter will cover the main functionalities of ServiceNow that enhance HR workflows, improve employee experiences, and drive operational excellence.

Overview of Core Capabilities

ServiceNow's HR Service Delivery (HRSD) module is built to automate and improve the delivery of HR services across the employee lifecycle. Its core capabilities include:

1. HR Case Management

HR Case Management is a cornerstone feature that helps HR teams manage employee inquiries and requests efficiently:

- **Case creation and tracking**: Employees can submit HR requests through a centralized portal, and HR teams can track the progress of each case in real time.
- **Automated routing and prioritization**: The system automatically routes cases to the appropriate HR specialist and assigns priority based on pre-set criteria.
- **Collaboration tools**: HR professionals can collaborate with team members, share notes, and attach relevant documents to cases.

2. Employee Service Center

The Employee Service Center is a unified portal where employees can access HR services and resources:

- **Self-service capabilities**: Employees can find answers to common questions, submit service requests, and track their progress without needing to contact HR directly.
- **Knowledge base integration**: Provides employees with access to articles, FAQs, and guides to resolve queries independently.
- **Personalized experience**: The portal can be customized to show relevant content and services based on the employee's role, location, or department.

3. Lifecycle Event Management

Lifecycle Event Management simplifies complex HR processes related to key employee lifecycle events:

- **Onboarding and offboarding**: Automates checklists and task assignments to ensure a smooth transition for new hires or departing employees.
- **Employee transfers and promotions**: Coordinates the necessary steps for internal job changes, including updating systems and notifying relevant departments.
- **Automated workflows**: Reduces manual effort by triggering pre-defined workflows that handle document collection, task tracking, and communications.

4. HR Knowledge Management

Knowledge Management in ServiceNow helps HR teams create and manage a repository of articles and documentation:

- **Content creation and curation**: HR professionals can easily develop knowledge articles and keep them updated.

- **Access controls**: Manage who can view or contribute to the knowledge base, ensuring that sensitive information is protected.
- **Integration with case management**: Articles can be linked to HR cases to provide employees with quick access to relevant information.

5. Performance Analytics for HR

Performance Analytics is essential for monitoring the effectiveness of HR services and making data-driven decisions:

- **Custom dashboards and reports**: HR leaders can create tailored dashboards that display key performance metrics such as case resolution times and employee satisfaction.
- **Real-time insights**: Provides up-to-date data to monitor ongoing HR operations and identify areas for improvement.
- **Trend analysis**: Helps track changes over time, enabling HR teams to forecast future performance and prepare accordingly.

6. HR Integrations and APIs

ServiceNow supports integrations with various third-party HR and enterprise systems to ensure seamless data flow and process continuity:

- **Pre-built integrations**: Connects with popular HR systems such as Workday and SAP SuccessFactors.
- **APIs and IntegrationHub**: Enables custom integrations with other tools and platforms for advanced use cases and data synchronization.
- **Single sign-on (SSO)**: Enhances user convenience and security by allowing employees to log in with their existing enterprise credentials.

7. HR Workflow Automation

Workflow automation streamlines routine HR tasks and ensures consistent execution of processes:

- **Visual workflow builder**: Use the Flow Designer to create automated workflows without extensive coding knowledge.
- **Conditional logic and triggers**: Define rules that trigger specific actions based on conditions such as employee type or request urgency.
- **Approval processes**: Automate approval chains for requests like leave applications or benefits changes.

8. Mobile Capabilities

ServiceNow's mobile functionality allows HR services to be accessed from anywhere, supporting remote and hybrid work environments:

- **Mobile app access**: Employees and HR teams can manage cases, submit requests, and access information via their mobile devices.
- **Push notifications**: Keeps employees updated on the status of their requests and ensures timely communication.

Benefits of ServiceNow's Core Capabilities for HR

1. Improved Efficiency

Automating manual tasks and streamlining processes reduce HR's workload, allowing the team to focus on strategic initiatives. Features such as workflow automation and case management minimize repetitive administrative work, leading to higher productivity.

2. Enhanced Employee Experience

The Employee Service Center and self-service capabilities empower employees to find solutions and submit requests independently, reducing wait times and improving satisfaction. Personalization ensures that employees receive information relevant to their needs, enhancing their overall experience.

3. Greater Process Consistency

ServiceNow ensures that HR processes are standardized across the organization. Automated workflows ensure that every request follows the same approval path and task assignments, reducing errors and maintaining compliance.

4. Data-Driven Insights

With Performance Analytics, HR leaders gain access to comprehensive data that helps in decision-making and strategy formulation. The ability to track KPIs and measure outcomes leads to continuous improvement in HR service delivery.

5. Scalability and Flexibility

ServiceNow's architecture and integrations allow HR capabilities to scale with organizational growth. Whether an organization is expanding its workforce or adding new service lines, ServiceNow adapts to support increased demand without significant reconfiguration.

Use Case Example: Onboarding Workflow Automation

Consider an organization onboarding new employees. Before implementing ServiceNow, HR had to manually coordinate tasks such as collecting documents, arranging orientations, and setting up accounts. With ServiceNow:

- **A custom onboarding workflow** is set up that triggers once an offer is accepted.
- **Automated task assignments** are sent to relevant departments, such as IT for system access and facilities for workspace preparation.
- **New hires receive personalized onboarding plans** and access to self-service resources via the Employee Service Center.

This streamlined process not only saves HR time but also ensures a seamless experience for new employees, boosting their engagement and productivity from day one.

Conclusion

ServiceNow offers a suite of core capabilities that enhance HR service delivery by automating tasks, enabling data-driven decision-making, and improving employee experiences. Understanding and leveraging these capabilities is essential for HR departments aiming to modernize their workflows and maximize operational efficiency.

Understanding User Roles and Permissions

Managing user roles and permissions is a vital aspect of any HR system, and ServiceNow is no exception. By implementing structured user roles and permissions, organizations can safeguard sensitive data, maintain compliance, and ensure that HR operations run smoothly. This chapter will explore the fundamentals of ServiceNow's user roles and permissions, the benefits of proper role management, and best practices for assigning and maintaining user access.

The Importance of User Roles and Permissions

Defining and managing user roles and permissions are critical for:

- **Ensuring data security**: Protecting sensitive HR information from unauthorized access.
- **Maintaining compliance**: Adhering to data privacy regulations, such as GDPR and CCPA, which mandate strict access controls.
- **Enhancing workflow efficiency**: Assigning appropriate access to users ensures that they have the tools and information necessary for their roles, without being overwhelmed by irrelevant data or capabilities.

Overview of User Roles in ServiceNow

ServiceNow uses a role-based access control (RBAC) model. This approach means that access permissions are determined based on the user's role within the organization. Each role defines a set of permissions that dictate what the user can view, create, modify, or delete within the platform.

Key Role Types in ServiceNow

1. **Admin Role**
   - **Permissions**: Full access to all system features, data, and configuration settings.
   - **Use Case**: Assigned to IT administrators or HR system managers responsible for overseeing platform setup, configurations, and high-level management tasks.
2. **HR Administrator Role**
   - **Permissions**: Access to all HR-specific modules, data, and workflow settings. Can create and manage HR cases, set up new HR services, and modify HR-related configurations.
   - **Use Case**: HR department leaders who need comprehensive access to manage day-to-day HR operations.
3. **HR Specialist Role**
   - **Permissions**: Limited to specific HR tasks such as managing employee requests, processing HR cases, and viewing relevant HR data.
   - **Use Case**: Assigned to HR team members handling specific HR functions, such as case management or employee onboarding.
4. **Employee Role**
   - **Permissions**: Basic access to the Employee Service Center, where they can submit HR requests, view status updates, and access approved HR resources.
   - **Use Case**: Standard employees who interact with HR services for submitting requests, accessing self-service resources, or tracking their cases.
5. **IT Support Role**
   - **Permissions**: Access to the technical configuration and support areas relevant to maintaining the ServiceNow platform, including integrations, performance checks, and system health monitoring.
   - **Use Case**: IT support team members tasked with providing technical assistance for the platform.

Configuring Permissions in ServiceNow

Permissions in ServiceNow are granted through roles, which can be customized and assigned as needed. The permissions control what data and functionalities users can access and modify within the platform.

Defining Access Controls

ServiceNow uses Access Control Lists (ACLs) to manage permissions for specific data elements, including records and fields. Each ACL entry specifies:

- **Who**: The role or user group with the specified permission.
- **What**: The data or application component affected by the rule.
- **Operation**: The type of access allowed (e.g., read, write, delete).

Steps to Configure User Roles and Permissions

1. **Identify Role Requirements**: Review the organizational structure and determine the access needed for each user group.
2. **Create or Modify Roles**: Use ServiceNow's Role Management module to create new roles or customize existing ones to fit specific needs.
3. **Assign Roles to Users**: Assign roles directly to users or user groups based on their responsibilities within the HR department.
4. **Test Access Controls**: Verify that each role provides the appropriate level of access by testing user accounts with those roles.

Best Practices for Managing User Roles and Permissions

1. Follow the Principle of Least Privilege

Grant users only the permissions necessary to perform their job functions. This approach minimizes security risks and protects sensitive data from unauthorized access.

2. Regularly Review and Update Roles

User responsibilities may change over time, so it's important to review and update roles periodically. Ensure that former employees or users with changed responsibilities have their roles adjusted or revoked as needed.

3. Implement Role-Based Groups

Organize users into groups based on their job roles, such as HR specialists or IT support. Assign permissions to the group level, simplifying the management of roles and permissions across the organization.

4. Document Role Definitions

Maintain detailed documentation outlining the permissions associated with each role. This practice aids in compliance audits and provides a reference for onboarding new system administrators or HR leaders.

5. Use Multi-Factor Authentication (MFA)

Enhance security by requiring MFA for users accessing sensitive HR data. This additional layer of protection ensures that only authorized personnel can access critical information.

Common Challenges and Solutions

Challenge: Overlapping Role Permissions

Solution: Regularly audit role definitions to prevent users from acquiring unintended permissions due to role overlap. Use ServiceNow's built-in role audit tools to identify potential issues.

Challenge: Role Creep

Solution: Implement a robust review process to check that users have not accumulated excessive permissions over time. Remove or adjust roles to align with current responsibilities.

Challenge: Balancing Security and Usability

Solution: Ensure that roles are designed to allow necessary access without hindering productivity. Collaborate with HR leaders and IT security teams to strike the right balance between data protection and ease of use.

Conclusion

Understanding and managing user roles and permissions within ServiceNow is essential for maintaining data security, ensuring compliance, and facilitating effective HR operations. By implementing best practices and using ServiceNow's robust role management tools, organizations can create a secure and efficient environment that supports seamless HR service delivery.

Navigating the ServiceNow Interface for HR Teams

Effectively navigating the ServiceNow interface is essential for HR teams to leverage the platform's capabilities fully. ServiceNow offers a user-friendly and intuitive design that facilitates seamless interaction with HR tools, dashboards, and workflows. This chapter will walk you through the core elements of the ServiceNow interface, best practices for efficient navigation, and tips to enhance your team's productivity.

Overview of the ServiceNow Interface

The ServiceNow interface is structured to provide easy access to various functions and services through a centralized dashboard. The layout is designed to ensure that HR professionals can quickly find, manage, and complete tasks.

Key Elements of the Interface

1. **Application Navigator**
   - **Purpose**: Acts as the main menu, allowing users to access all applications, modules, and functions they have permission to use.
   - **Usage**: HR teams can search for specific applications such as HR Case Management, Lifecycle Events, and Knowledge Management.
   - **Tips**: Use the filter feature to quickly locate frequently used applications.
2. **Homepage and Dashboards**
   - **Purpose**: Serve as the central hub for viewing important information, such as active HR cases, upcoming tasks, and performance metrics.
   - **Customization**: Dashboards can be tailored to display widgets relevant to HR operations, including case status, key performance indicators (KPIs), and team workload.
   - **Best Practices**: Customize dashboards to highlight the most relevant data for your role, such as case resolution times for HR managers or open case queues for specialists.
3. **Navigation Tabs**
   - **Purpose**: Allow users to switch between active modules or tasks without losing progress. This feature enables multitasking by opening multiple records or forms in separate tabs.
   - **Tips**: Keep frequently accessed modules open for quick transitions between tasks.
4. **ServiceNow Global Search**
   - **Purpose**: Enables users to perform comprehensive searches across the entire platform, including cases, articles, employee records, and more.
   - **Usage**: Type keywords related to cases or employee names to quickly locate relevant records.
   - **Tips**: Utilize advanced search filters to narrow down results and improve search accuracy.
5. **Forms and Records**
   - **Purpose**: Central to managing and updating HR data. Forms capture specific information for cases, employee details, and service requests.
   - **Features**: Includes related lists and tabs for comprehensive data entry and viewing.
   - **Best Practices**: Complete all required fields marked with an asterisk (*) and use the "Save" option frequently to prevent data loss.
6. **Task Bar and Notifications**
   - **Purpose**: Displays assigned tasks and alerts, ensuring HR professionals are aware of pending actions.
   - **Tips**: Set up notification preferences to receive alerts for high-priority cases or updates requiring immediate attention.

Customizing the Interface for HR Needs

Personalizing Your Homepage

- **Add Widgets**: Include widgets like "My Cases," "Team Performance Metrics," and "Upcoming Employee Events" to keep essential information front and center.
- **Drag and Drop**: Rearrange elements to fit your workflow preferences.
- **Set Default Views**: Save your personalized homepage settings to ensure you start each session with the most relevant data.

Utilizing Favorites

- **Purpose**: Allows HR users to bookmark frequently used modules or reports for easy access.
- **How to Use**: Click the star icon next to any module or record to add it to your "Favorites" list.
- **Tips**: Regularly update your favorites as your role or project focus evolves to keep your list relevant.

Adjusting Settings for Optimal Use

- **Theme and Layout**: Choose a theme that enhances readability and adjust the font size for comfort.
- **Keyboard Shortcuts**: Familiarize yourself with common shortcuts, such as "Alt + G" for global search, to improve navigation speed.
- **Notification Preferences**: Set up specific alerts to stay informed on changes to HR cases, approvals, or escalations.

Best Practices for Navigating ServiceNow Efficiently

1. Use Filters and Views

Filters help streamline data display in lists and reports. Create custom filters to show cases assigned to your team, cases by priority, or cases nearing SLA deadlines.

2. Leverage the Search and Filter Navigator

Mastering the filter navigator in the Application Navigator allows HR professionals to find modules, forms, and data entries quickly. Utilize search queries like "HR Cases > My Open Cases" for efficient results.

3. Work with Related Lists and Tabs

Use related lists and tabs within forms to view comprehensive case details, such as linked knowledge articles, task assignments, and employee documents, without needing to switch screens.

4. Configure Dashboards to Reflect KPIs

Customize dashboards to include metrics that align with your HR goals. Widgets displaying metrics like "Average Case Resolution Time" or "Employee Satisfaction Rates" can help monitor performance and identify areas for improvement.

Common Navigation Challenges and Solutions

Challenge: Overwhelming Number of Options

Solution: Use the "Favorites" and filter features to streamline your interface and reduce clutter. Focus on essential applications and create simplified views for day-to-day activities.

Challenge: Frequent Switching Between Modules

Solution: Utilize navigation tabs to keep multiple modules open simultaneously, allowing for quick transitions without losing progress.

Challenge: Slow Data Entry in Forms

Solution: Pre-fill common fields using templates or leverage automation features to auto-populate data where applicable.

Training Tips for HR Teams

- **Interactive Workshops**: Conduct hands-on training sessions to familiarize HR staff with key interface elements.
- **User Guides**: Provide quick reference guides that outline the most-used navigation tips and shortcuts.
- **Practice Scenarios**: Allow users to navigate sample cases and forms to build comfort and efficiency.

Conclusion

Navigating the ServiceNow interface efficiently is a foundational skill for HR teams looking to maximize productivity and enhance service delivery. By mastering the platform's key components, customizing the user experience, and following best practices, HR professionals can streamline their workflows and provide superior support to employees.

Leveraging Dashboards and Reports in HR Modules

Dashboards and reports are essential tools for HR teams looking to gain insights, monitor performance, and make data-driven decisions. ServiceNow offers robust capabilities for creating, customizing, and utilizing dashboards and reports to track key HR metrics and visualize data effectively. This chapter will guide you through how to leverage these features to enhance HR service delivery.

Understanding Dashboards in ServiceNow

Dashboards in ServiceNow provide a visual summary of key information, displaying multiple widgets and reports in one unified view. For HR teams, dashboards can showcase metrics related to case management, employee onboarding, task completion rates, and more.

Key Components of Dashboards

1. **Widgets**
   - **Definition**: Widgets are individual elements on a dashboard that display specific data or functionality.
   - **Types**: Common widget types include charts (bar, line, pie), lists, performance indicators, and gauges.
   - **Usage**: HR managers can use widgets to display open cases, employee satisfaction scores, or SLA compliance rates.
2. **Data Sources**
   - **Purpose**: Dashboards pull data from various HR data sources such as case records, HR requests, and employee profiles.
   - **Customization**: Users can select specific data sources for each widget to tailor the dashboard to their reporting needs.
3. **User Access**
   - **Roles and Permissions**: Dashboard access can be controlled based on user roles, ensuring that only authorized HR staff can view or edit sensitive data.
   - **Customization for Roles**: Create role-specific dashboards to ensure HR specialists, managers, and administrators have relevant data at their fingertips.

Setting Up Dashboards for HR Use

1. **Determine Reporting Needs**
   - Identify which metrics are most relevant to HR goals, such as case resolution time, employee engagement levels, and onboarding progress.
2. **Create or Customize Dashboards**
   - Use ServiceNow's dashboard creation tool to design dashboards from scratch or modify existing ones.
   - Add widgets that align with your reporting objectives and ensure each displays the most critical data for your team.
3. **Enhance Visualization**
   - Select widget types that best represent the data. For instance, use bar charts for comparing performance metrics across departments or pie charts for a breakdown of case types.

Utilizing Reports in HR Modules

Reports offer detailed insights into HR data and enable users to analyze trends, identify issues, and make informed decisions. ServiceNow's reporting tools support various report types, such as lists, charts, and pivot tables.

Creating Effective HR Reports

1. **Define Report Objectives**
   - Clarify the purpose of each report. Is it to track case closure rates, monitor employee satisfaction, or assess onboarding timelines?
   - Ensure that reports align with HR KPIs for strategic value.
2. **Choose the Right Report Type**
   - **List Reports**: Ideal for displaying a detailed view of cases, employee records, or HR tasks.
   - **Chart Reports**: Useful for visual comparisons, showing trends over time, or illustrating key metrics.
   - **Pivot Reports**: Excellent for summarizing large data sets, such as HR service volumes by department or case category.
3. **Set Up Filters and Grouping**
   - Apply filters to focus on specific data subsets, like high-priority cases or onboarding requests within the last month.
   - Group data by relevant categories, such as case type or employee department, to enhance readability and insight.

Automating Report Generation

- **Scheduled Reports**: Set up reports to be automatically generated and sent to HR leaders at regular intervals (e.g., weekly, monthly).
- **Notifications**: Configure alerts for specific report outcomes, such as when case volumes exceed a certain threshold or when SLA compliance drops.

Best Practices for Using Dashboards and Reports

1. Keep Dashboards Simple and Focused

Avoid clutter by only including widgets and data that directly support HR objectives. A clear, focused dashboard is more effective than one overloaded with information.

2. Update Dashboards Regularly

Ensure that the data and widgets on dashboards are up to date and relevant to current HR needs. Periodically review and refresh dashboards to reflect any changes in HR priorities or processes.

3. Use Real-Time Data

Leverage ServiceNow's real-time data capabilities to monitor the current status of cases, tasks, and employee interactions. This helps HR teams respond quickly to trends and changes.

4. Integrate with Performance Analytics

Combine dashboard widgets with Performance Analytics metrics to gain deeper insights into long-term trends and predictive analysis. This can help HR leaders proactively address potential issues.

5. Train HR Teams on Report Customization

Empower HR teams by providing training on creating and customizing reports. This ensures that team members can generate the data they need without waiting for technical assistance.

Example Use Case: Monitoring Case Resolution Time

An HR manager wants to monitor the average resolution time for HR cases to ensure SLA compliance. Here's how they might set up their dashboard and report:

- **Dashboard Widget**: Create a line chart widget that displays average resolution times over the past six months.
- **Report**: Generate a detailed report listing all open cases exceeding SLA time limits, grouped by assigned HR specialists.
- **Automated Alert**: Set up an alert to notify the HR manager when average case resolution time exceeds the SLA threshold for more than two consecutive weeks.

Conclusion

Leveraging dashboards and reports in ServiceNow's HR modules allows HR teams to visualize key data, monitor performance, and make informed decisions. By setting up dashboards tailored to specific HR goals and creating reports that deliver actionable insights, teams can enhance productivity and optimize service delivery.

Managing Data Security and Compliance

In today's digital landscape, ensuring the security and compliance of HR data is paramount for organizations. ServiceNow provides comprehensive tools and frameworks to protect sensitive information and maintain compliance with industry regulations. This chapter will guide you through the core data security features of ServiceNow, strategies for maintaining compliance, and best practices for managing data protection within HR operations.

Importance of Data Security in HR

HR departments handle highly sensitive information, including personal and financial data of employees. Ensuring this data remains protected from unauthorized access and breaches is crucial for:

- **Building trust with employees**: Employees expect their personal data to be securely handled.
- **Maintaining legal compliance**: Adhering to data privacy laws and industry standards to avoid legal and financial penalties.
- **Safeguarding organizational reputation**: A data breach can damage an organization's reputation and lead to a loss of stakeholder confidence.

Overview of ServiceNow's Security Framework

ServiceNow employs a robust security framework designed to protect data through multiple layers of security measures:

- **Role-based Access Control (RBAC)**: Manages who can view, modify, or delete data based on their role.
- **Encryption**: Protects data at rest and in transit using advanced encryption protocols.
- **Auditing and Monitoring Tools**: Tracks user activity and changes within the system to detect and respond to potential security incidents.

Key Components of ServiceNow's Data Security

1. **Role-based Access Control (RBAC)**
   - **Purpose**: Ensures that only authorized users can access certain data or functionalities within the platform.
   - **How it works**: Permissions are assigned based on user roles, and these roles define which data or applications a user can access. For example, HR specialists may only access data relevant to their tasks, while HR managers might have broader access.
   - **Best Practice**: Regularly review and update role assignments to match current job responsibilities and prevent unnecessary access.
2. **Data Encryption**
   - **Data at Rest**: ServiceNow's platform uses industry-standard encryption techniques to secure stored data.
   - **Data in Transit**: All data transferred between users and the platform is encrypted using Transport Layer Security (TLS) to prevent interception.
   - **Encryption Keys Management**: Organizations can manage their encryption keys or use ServiceNow's built-in key management for added control.
3. **Access Control Lists (ACLs)**
   - **Definition**: ACLs determine the type of access a user has for specific data fields or records.
   - **Use Case**: Restrict access to specific fields within an HR case record so that only certain roles, such as HR managers, can view confidential details.
   - **Implementation Tip**: Use the "least privilege" principle by limiting access permissions to the minimum level required for users to perform their duties.
4. **Multi-Factor Authentication (MFA)**

- Purpose: Adds an extra layer of security by requiring users to provide two or more verification factors to access the platform.
- Benefits: Reduces the risk of unauthorized access and improves overall data security.
- Configuration Tip: Encourage HR teams to enable MFA for all logins, especially when accessing sensitive data remotely.

Maintaining Compliance with Data Privacy Regulations

Common HR Data Regulations

- **General Data Protection Regulation (GDPR)**: Enforces strict data protection and privacy laws for handling the personal data of EU citizens.
- **California Consumer Privacy Act (CCPA)**: Provides California residents with rights over their personal data and holds organizations accountable for data handling practices.
- **Health Insurance Portability and Accountability Act (HIPAA)**: Sets standards for protecting sensitive health information, relevant for organizations handling employee health data.

How ServiceNow Helps with Compliance

1. **Data Masking and Redaction**
   - Feature: Allows organizations to mask or redact sensitive data to prevent unauthorized viewing.
   - Use Case: Mask personal information in HR cases when only the general context is needed for other HR team members.
2. **Auditing and Logging**
   - Purpose: ServiceNow tracks changes made to data and records user activity, which is essential for compliance reporting and auditing.
   - Configuration Tip: Enable audit logs for high-risk actions, such as data access or record modifications, to provide a clear trail for compliance checks.
3. **Consent Management**
   - Purpose: Ensures that HR data handling aligns with consent requirements as outlined in regulations like GDPR.
   - Feature: ServiceNow can store and track employee consent records and alert HR teams when consent needs to be renewed or reviewed.

Best Practices for Compliance Management

- **Regular Training**: Educate HR teams on data protection policies and how to manage sensitive information within ServiceNow.
- **Policy Reviews**: Regularly review data security and compliance policies to stay updated with changes in legislation.
- **Data Minimization**: Collect only the data necessary for HR processes and avoid storing excessive information.

Implementing Data Security Measures in ServiceNow

Steps to Strengthen Data Security

1. **Conduct a Security Assessment**
   - Identify potential vulnerabilities and risks within your HR data management system.
   - Use ServiceNow's built-in security tools and third-party assessments to evaluate current security measures.
2. **Set Up Access Control Lists (ACLs)**
   - Define specific permissions for various data elements and assign them to appropriate user roles.
   - Test ACLs to ensure they align with HR data access requirements.

3. **Enable Advanced Security Features**
   - Activate features such as multi-factor authentication and IP whitelisting for an additional layer of protection.
4. **Monitor User Activity**
   - Use ServiceNow's monitoring tools to track data access and changes, identifying any unusual or unauthorized activity.
   - Set up alerts for suspicious actions, such as data downloads or role changes outside of business hours.

Example Use Case: Protecting Employee Data During Remote Work

As remote work becomes more common, securing HR data is a growing challenge. Here's how an HR department might leverage ServiceNow to maintain data security:

- **MFA and Secure Connections**: Require HR team members to use MFA and access ServiceNow through VPNs or secure connections.
- **IP Restrictions**: Limit access to ServiceNow from approved IP addresses to prevent unauthorized access from unknown locations.
- **Audit Logs**: Monitor access logs to identify potential breaches or policy violations.

Conclusion

Managing data security and ensuring compliance are critical responsibilities for HR teams using ServiceNow. By leveraging ServiceNow's built-in tools and following best practices, organizations can protect sensitive data, comply with regulations, and foster a culture of trust and reliability.

Section 4:
Configuring ServiceNow for HR Processes

Setting Up HR Service Portals

A well-configured HR service portal is essential for providing employees with seamless access to HR services, improving user experience, and streamlining HR processes. ServiceNow enables organizations to create and customize HR service portals that offer self-service capabilities, enhance communication, and optimize HR workflows. In this chapter, we'll explore how to set up an effective HR service portal, customize its layout, and implement best practices for usability and efficiency.

The Purpose of HR Service Portals

HR service portals act as the primary interface between employees and HR services. They offer a centralized platform where employees can:

- Submit HR requests or cases.
- Access self-service knowledge articles.
- Track the status of their ongoing HR cases.
- Communicate directly with HR representatives.

Benefits of a Well-Designed HR Service Portal

- **Improved Employee Experience**: Provides a user-friendly platform where employees can quickly find the information they need.
- **Increased Efficiency**: Reduces the workload on HR teams by enabling employees to self-solve common issues.
- **Enhanced Transparency**: Allows employees to monitor the progress of their requests and cases.
- **Streamlined Communication**: Facilitates better communication between employees and HR teams through integrated messaging and notifications.

Setting Up an HR Service Portal in ServiceNow

Step-by-Step Configuration Process

1. **Access the Service Portal Configuration**
   - Navigate to the **Service Portal Configuration** module within ServiceNow.
   - Select **HR Service Portal** or create a new portal tailored specifically for HR services.
2. **Customize the Portal Layout**
   - Choose a layout that best suits your HR needs, such as a simple home page with service categories or an interactive dashboard.
   - Utilize the drag-and-drop interface to add, remove, or rearrange widgets on the portal.
3. **Add Widgets and Functionalities**
   - **Search Bar**: Ensure the portal has a global search bar for employees to easily find relevant articles or services.
   - **HR Case Submission Form**: Include a widget that allows employees to submit new HR cases or requests.
   - **Knowledge Base Access**: Provide widgets that display popular or suggested articles from the HR knowledge base.

  - ○ **Case Tracking**: Integrate a case status widget that lets employees monitor the progress of their active cases.
4. **Incorporate Quick Links and Shortcuts**
   - ○ Add quick links to frequently used services such as leave requests, benefits information, or onboarding resources.
   - ○ Use icons and clear labels to enhance navigation and usability.
5. **Configure Personalization Options**
   - ○ Enable customization features that allow employees to personalize their portal view by adding preferred widgets or modifying the layout.
   - ○ Provide options for employees to receive notifications and updates about their cases through the portal.

Customizing the Portal for Enhanced User Experience

1. Design for Intuitive Navigation

- Organize the portal's content into clear categories, such as "Benefits," "Payroll," "Onboarding," and "Policies."
- Use a consistent naming convention and easy-to-understand terminology.

2. Employ Responsive Design

- Ensure the portal is mobile-friendly and responsive so that employees can access HR services from any device without compromising the user experience.

3. Use Visual Elements

- Add images, icons, and color schemes that align with your company's branding for a cohesive look.
- Use contrasting colors for buttons and links to make them stand out and easy to locate.

4. Integrate Feedback Mechanisms

- Include a feedback widget that allows employees to provide input on the portal's usability and suggest improvements.
- Collect feedback regularly to enhance the portal's functionality and user satisfaction.

Security and Access Control

Ensuring Data Protection

- **Role-Based Access Control (RBAC)**: Configure the portal to restrict access based on employee roles. For instance, managers may have access to view and approve leave requests, while standard employees can only submit and track their requests.
- **Secure Authentication**: Implement multi-factor authentication (MFA) for enhanced security.
- **Data Encryption**: Ensure that sensitive data transmitted through the portal is encrypted to comply with data protection regulations.

User Access Management

- Assign user roles and permissions to control which portal features are visible to specific user groups.
- Periodically review user access settings to ensure compliance with company policies and data privacy regulations.

Best Practices for Setting Up HR Service Portals

1. **Start with a Pilot Launch**

      ○ Roll out the HR service portal to a small group of users first. Gather feedback and make necessary adjustments before full-scale deployment.

2. **Provide Training and Support**
   ○ Offer training sessions or user guides to help employees become familiar with the portal's features.
   ○ Create a comprehensive FAQ section that answers common questions about using the portal.

3. **Maintain and Update Content**
   ○ Regularly update the knowledge base with new articles and revise existing ones to keep information current and useful.
   ○ Refresh the portal's layout and widgets periodically to incorporate new features and align with evolving HR needs.

4. **Monitor Usage and Performance**
   ○ Track key metrics, such as the number of submitted cases and article views, to assess the portal's effectiveness.
   ○ Use analytics to identify areas for improvement and optimize the portal accordingly.

Example Use Case: Streamlining Onboarding with an HR Portal

A company wants to streamline its onboarding process by leveraging the HR service portal. Here's how they might implement this:

- **Dedicated Onboarding Section**: Create a portal section titled "New Hires" with onboarding checklists, required documents, and direct access to HR support.
- **Automated Notifications**: Send new employees reminders for upcoming onboarding tasks and meetings.
- **Self-Service Articles**: Provide articles that guide new hires on completing onboarding procedures, accessing benefits, and understanding company policies.

Conclusion

Setting up an HR service portal in ServiceNow is a powerful way to enhance employee interactions, improve HR efficiency, and foster a culture of self-service. By carefully planning the portal's layout, incorporating user-friendly features, and maintaining a secure environment, HR teams can offer a seamless and supportive experience for employees.

Designing HR Workflows for Efficiency

Designing efficient HR workflows is key to enhancing productivity, reducing processing time, and improving employee satisfaction. ServiceNow's powerful workflow tools allow HR teams to automate and streamline processes, ensuring that tasks are completed smoothly and consistently. This chapter will guide you through the principles of designing effective HR workflows and best practices to optimize HR operations in ServiceNow.

Importance of Workflow Design in HR

HR processes often involve multiple steps and stakeholders, from case initiation to resolution. Well-structured workflows ensure:

- **Consistency**: Processes are followed in a standardized manner across the organization.
- **Efficiency**: Automation minimizes manual tasks, reducing the risk of errors and delays.
- **Transparency**: Employees and HR teams can track the status of processes and cases, improving visibility and accountability.

Key Benefits of Effective HR Workflows

- **Faster Response Times**: Automated workflows help HR teams respond to employee requests more promptly.
- **Improved Compliance**: Ensuring that all necessary steps are followed helps organizations meet legal and regulatory requirements.
- **Resource Optimization**: HR professionals can focus on strategic tasks instead of routine, repetitive work.

Steps to Design HR Workflows in ServiceNow

1. Define Workflow Objectives

- Identify the goals of the workflow, such as reducing processing time for leave approvals or standardizing onboarding procedures.
- Gather input from stakeholders to ensure the workflow meets HR team and employee expectations.

2. Map Out the Current Process

- Document the existing HR process from start to finish. Include every step, decision point, and stakeholder involved.
- Use this map as a baseline to identify inefficiencies, bottlenecks, or redundant steps.

3. Identify Areas for Automation

- Pinpoint tasks that can be automated to reduce manual effort, such as sending notifications, updating records, or generating reports.
- Consider using ServiceNow's Flow Designer to build and manage workflow automations without extensive coding.

4. Create Workflow Blueprints

- Develop a blueprint that outlines the new workflow's structure, including start and end points, tasks, approvals, and notifications.
- Use flowcharts or diagrams to visualize the workflow and ensure all participants understand the sequence of actions.

5. Configure Workflows in ServiceNow

- Use ServiceNow's **Flow Designer** to create workflows with a drag-and-drop interface.
- Set up triggers that initiate the workflow, such as a new employee request or a submitted HR form.
- Define actions and conditions for each step in the workflow, including data updates, task assignments, and notifications.

Key Elements of Efficient HR Workflows

1. Approval Processes

- **Multi-level Approvals**: Set up workflows that require approval at different stages, ensuring that requests are properly vetted before finalization.
- **Delegation and Escalation**: Enable automated delegation when approvers are unavailable and set up escalation paths for delayed approvals.

2. Notifications and Alerts

- Configure notifications for key milestones in the workflow to keep all parties informed. For instance, an employee should receive a confirmation when their request is approved or a task is completed.
- Use alerts to notify HR managers of overdue tasks or pending approvals to prevent delays.

3. Data Integration

- Integrate workflows with other HR systems, such as payroll and benefits platforms, to ensure data flows seamlessly across systems.
- Automate data entry to minimize errors and manual updates, improving overall accuracy.

4. Task Assignments

- Assign tasks to appropriate HR team members based on their roles and responsibilities. Ensure workloads are balanced to avoid bottlenecks.
- Use dynamic task assignment features to route tasks to the next available or most qualified HR representative.

5. Conditional Logic

- Implement conditions that determine the next steps in a workflow based on specific criteria. For example, if a request requires additional documentation, the workflow can automatically prompt the employee for submission.

Best Practices for Designing Efficient HR Workflows

1. Keep It Simple

- Avoid overcomplicating workflows with unnecessary steps. Simplified processes are easier to maintain and less prone to errors.
- Regularly review and streamline workflows to keep them optimized.

2. Ensure Flexibility

- Design workflows that can adapt to different scenarios. For instance, an onboarding process may vary depending on whether an employee is full-time, part-time, or remote.
- Incorporate alternative paths within the workflow for exceptions or special cases.

3. Monitor and Optimize

- Use ServiceNow's reporting tools to track the performance of HR workflows. Analyze metrics such as average completion time, number of pending tasks, and bottleneck areas.
- Make data-driven adjustments to enhance the workflow's efficiency over time.

4. Collaborate with End Users

- Involve HR staff and other end users in the workflow design process. Their insights can help identify practical needs and potential issues.
- Conduct testing sessions to gather feedback and make improvements before full deployment.

5. Ensure Compliance

- Integrate checks and documentation steps in workflows to ensure compliance with legal and company policies.
- Keep an audit trail of completed workflows to support compliance audits and reviews.

Example Use Case: Designing an Employee Onboarding Workflow

A common example of an HR workflow is the employee onboarding process. Here's how to design an efficient onboarding workflow:

1. **Trigger**: The workflow starts when HR receives a notification of a new hire.
2. **Task Assignment**: Assign tasks to the HR team, IT department, and hiring manager for necessary preparations (e.g., setting up equipment, arranging training).
3. **Approvals**: Include multi-level approvals for completed onboarding checklists.
4. **Automated Notifications**: Send updates to the new hire about their onboarding schedule and provide links to relevant resources.
5. **Integration**: Sync with payroll and benefits systems to update employee data.
6. **Completion**: Notify HR once all tasks are complete, and archive the workflow for future reference.

Conclusion

Designing efficient HR workflows in ServiceNow is essential for creating streamlined processes that save time and resources. By incorporating automation, clear task assignments, and flexible options, HR teams can enhance their service delivery and ensure a smoother experience for employees.

Creating Custom HR Services and Templates

Custom HR services and templates in ServiceNow empower HR teams to tailor processes to specific organizational needs, ensuring that workflows are streamlined, consistent, and efficient. In this chapter, we'll explore how to create custom HR services and templates, enabling organizations to manage unique HR processes with enhanced precision and flexibility.

Understanding Custom HR Services in ServiceNow

Custom HR services allow organizations to address specific HR requirements that go beyond standard out-of-the-box functionalities. These services can cover a wide range of HR needs, such as tailored leave requests, specialized onboarding programs, and unique benefit administration processes.

Key Benefits of Custom HR Services

- **Personalization**: Adapt services to meet unique organizational processes and cultural nuances.
- **Efficiency**: Streamline repetitive tasks and ensure consistent handling of similar requests.
- **Scalability**: Design services that can be modified or expanded as HR needs evolve.

Steps to Create Custom HR Services

1. Define the Service Requirements

- **Identify the Purpose**: Determine the specific HR need or challenge the service is meant to address.
- **Gather Input**: Collaborate with HR stakeholders and employees to understand pain points and desired outcomes.
- **Document Specifications**: Outline the process flow, approval hierarchy, and any notifications or integrations needed.

2. Set Up the HR Service

- Navigate to the **HR Services** module within ServiceNow.
- Select **New HR Service** to begin the configuration process.
- Fill in the basic details such as **Service Name**, **Description**, and **Service Category** (e.g., onboarding, leave management).

3. Configure Service Details

- **Assign Case Type**: Choose the appropriate case type for the service, such as a request, inquiry, or incident.
- **Define HR Criteria**: Set conditions for when this service should be available (e.g., only for full-time employees or specific departments).
- **Specify SLA (Service Level Agreement)**: Establish expected response and resolution times to maintain consistency and monitor service effectiveness.

4. Design the Workflow

- Use **Flow Designer** or **Process Automation** to map out the steps involved in the service, from initiation to completion.
- Add actions such as **task assignments**, **approval requests**, and **status updates**.
- Include conditional logic to ensure that different paths within the workflow are followed based on the provided inputs or criteria.

5. Incorporate Notifications and Alerts

- Set up automated notifications to keep employees and HR teams informed throughout the process.
- Customize alerts for important events, such as when an approval is required or a task is overdue.

Creating Custom Templates for HR Services

Templates serve as predefined formats that can be used to standardize how cases and requests are created and processed. Custom templates save time and reduce the risk of human error by ensuring consistent information input.

1. Choose a Template Type

- Determine whether the template is for a case, task, or notification.
- Access the **HR Templates** module and select **New Template**.

2. Configure Template Details

- Define the **template name**, **category**, and **description** to make it easily identifiable for users.
- Add any **predefined fields**, such as employee details, request type, or default notes, that should be auto-populated when the template is used.

3. Set Conditions for Template Use

- Specify the scenarios in which the template should be used. For instance, create conditions that trigger the use of this template only when the employee belongs to a specific department or role.
- Use **role-based access control** to limit who can apply or modify the template, ensuring that only authorized HR personnel have access.

4. Test and Validate the Template

- Test the template by applying it to a sample case to ensure it functions as intended and that all predefined fields populate correctly.
- Validate the template's performance by gathering feedback from HR users and making necessary adjustments.

Best Practices for Creating Custom HR Services and Templates

1. Start Simple

- Begin with basic templates and services before incorporating complex workflows or conditions.
- Expand and refine the service as feedback is gathered and additional needs are identified.

2. Keep Employee Experience in Mind

- Design services and templates with ease of use as a priority. Ensure that forms and processes are intuitive and do not overwhelm users with unnecessary information.
- Add help tooltips or FAQs to guide employees through filling out forms correctly.

3. Maintain Compliance

- Ensure that all custom services and templates align with data privacy regulations and company policies.
- Review templates regularly to confirm they comply with updated legal requirements or company procedures.

4. Regularly Review and Optimize

- Schedule periodic reviews of custom services and templates to assess their effectiveness and efficiency.

- Use ServiceNow's reporting tools to monitor usage patterns and make data-driven adjustments.

Example: Customizing a Leave Request Service

A company may need a leave request service that goes beyond standard annual leave to include categories such as parental leave, unpaid leave, or emergency leave. Here's how to create this service:

- **Create New Service**: Define the service as "Extended Leave Request."
- **Design Workflow**: Set up a workflow that routes requests to the employee's manager for approval, followed by HR verification.
- **Custom Template**: Design a template that includes pre-filled fields like employee ID, department, and type of leave.
- **Notifications**: Configure notifications to alert the manager and employee of the status of the leave request.
- **Integration**: Link the service to the payroll system to ensure accurate leave tracking and salary adjustments.

Conclusion

Creating custom HR services and templates in ServiceNow allows HR teams to cater to specific organizational needs while enhancing overall service delivery. By following a structured approach to designing and testing these services, HR teams can ensure processes are efficient, user-friendly, and compliant with company policies.

Automating Case Management for HR Teams

Automating case management is pivotal for HR teams aiming to enhance efficiency, streamline processes, and ensure seamless communication. With ServiceNow, HR departments can effectively handle employee queries, requests, and issues, improving overall service delivery and employee satisfaction. This chapter delves into the strategies, benefits, and best practices for automating case management using ServiceNow's robust tools.

Why Automate Case Management?

Automation in HR case management offers numerous advantages:

- **Reduced Manual Work**: Automating routine tasks allows HR staff to focus on strategic initiatives.
- **Consistent Processes**: Ensures every case follows the same standards, minimizing errors and discrepancies.
- **Improved Response Times**: Enhances HR's ability to respond quickly to employee needs, boosting morale and productivity.
- **Comprehensive Tracking**: Facilitates better oversight and reporting for HR cases, aiding in transparency and compliance.

Key Features of Automated Case Management in ServiceNow

1. Case Creation and Assignment

- **Automatic Ticket Creation**: ServiceNow can generate cases automatically when specific triggers occur, such as an employee submitting a request via an HR service portal.
- **Routing and Assignment**: Cases can be auto-assigned based on predefined criteria, such as department, issue type, or employee location, using ServiceNow's Assignment Rules and Work Assignment features.

2. Workflow Automation

- **Predefined Workflows**: Automate step-by-step workflows that guide each case from initiation to resolution. This includes task assignment, approvals, and status updates.
- **Conditional Logic**: Incorporate conditional paths to handle different scenarios within a single workflow. For example, a case may follow one path if it requires manager approval and another if no approval is needed.

3. Notifications and Alerts

- **Automated Communication**: Send notifications to employees and HR team members at critical stages, such as when a case is opened, updated, or resolved.
- **Escalation Alerts**: Configure alerts for cases that remain unresolved past a certain threshold, ensuring timely follow-up and resolution.

4. Integration with Knowledge Base

- **Quick Reference**: Enable HR agents to link relevant knowledge articles directly to cases, providing employees with quick access to information that may resolve their inquiries.
- **Self-Service Empowerment**: Empower employees to find solutions through a well-organized knowledge base, potentially reducing the number of cases filed.

Setting Up Automated Case Management in ServiceNow

1. Define Case Types and Categories

- Identify the types of HR cases commonly managed, such as payroll inquiries, benefits questions, or policy clarifications.
- Create case categories and subcategories in ServiceNow to organize and streamline the case assignment process.

2. Design Workflow Templates

- Utilize **Flow Designer** or **Workflow Editor** to create workflow templates that map out the process each case will follow.
- Include checkpoints, automated task assignments, and decision trees to handle complex case paths.

3. Configure Auto-Assignment Rules

- Set up assignment groups based on expertise, seniority, or department.
- Use ServiceNow's **Work Assignment** tool to allocate cases based on criteria such as workload balancing and agent availability.

4. Incorporate SLA Tracking

- Define Service Level Agreements (SLAs) for different types of cases to set expectations for response and resolution times.
- Implement SLA tracking and automated alerts to notify agents when deadlines are approaching or overdue.

Best Practices for Automating HR Case Management

1. Prioritize User Experience

- Simplify the case submission process with user-friendly forms and clear instructions.
- Ensure employees can easily track the status of their cases through the HR service portal.

2. Maintain Transparency

- Communicate key case updates to employees at each stage. This fosters trust and minimizes follow-up inquiries.
- Use status notifications to inform employees when their case has been escalated or when additional information is needed.

3. Integrate with Existing Systems

- Seamlessly integrate ServiceNow with other HR systems such as payroll, time tracking, and benefits management tools to pull relevant data into cases automatically.
- Automate data exchange between platforms to reduce manual entry and potential errors.

4. Regularly Review and Optimize Workflows

- Periodically analyze workflow performance using ServiceNow's reporting tools to identify areas for improvement.
- Update workflows based on feedback from HR agents and employees to ensure they remain effective and relevant.

5. Ensure Data Security and Compliance

- Protect employee data by ensuring that automated processes comply with data protection regulations and company policies.
- Restrict access to sensitive case information based on user roles and responsibilities.

Example Scenario: Automating Employee Leave Requests

An employee initiates a leave request through the HR portal. Here's how automation can streamline the process:

- **Case Creation**: The request triggers an automated creation of a case in ServiceNow.
- **Routing**: The case is auto-assigned to the employee's HR representative.
- **Approval Workflow**: The case follows a workflow that requires manager approval before HR finalizes it.
- **Notifications**: The employee receives automatic updates when the request is submitted, approved, and finalized.
- **Integration**: The system syncs with the payroll platform to adjust the employee's leave balance accordingly.

Challenges and Solutions

Challenge: Resistance to Change

- **Solution**: Provide training and resources to HR teams to ensure a smooth transition to automated systems. Highlight the time-saving benefits and improved accuracy to encourage adoption.

Challenge: Complexity of Custom Cases

- **Solution**: Start by automating simple, repetitive cases and gradually build workflows for more complex scenarios. Work with ServiceNow developers or specialists to create sophisticated automations when needed.

Conclusion

Automating case management in ServiceNow helps HR teams enhance efficiency, reduce manual work, and improve service quality. By leveraging automation tools and best practices, HR departments can streamline their processes, ensure consistent case handling, and create a better experience for employees.

Integrating ServiceNow with Existing HR Systems

Seamless integration between ServiceNow and existing HR systems is essential for creating a unified digital ecosystem that maximizes efficiency, enhances data flow, and streamlines HR operations. This chapter outlines strategies, tools, and best practices for integrating ServiceNow with other HR platforms and tools to enhance workflow automation and improve data consistency.

The Importance of Integration

Integrating ServiceNow with existing HR systems provides significant benefits, including:

- **Centralized Data Management**: Reduces data silos and promotes a comprehensive view of HR data.
- **Enhanced Process Efficiency**: Automates workflows across multiple platforms, minimizing manual work.
- **Consistent Data Flow**: Ensures that employee data remains synchronized across systems, reducing errors.
- **Improved User Experience**: Allows employees and HR professionals to access and manage data seamlessly without switching between multiple interfaces.

Key Integration Considerations

1. Understanding System Compatibility

- **Platform Support**: Verify that the existing HR systems support integration with ServiceNow. Common systems include SAP SuccessFactors, Workday, ADP, and Oracle HCM.
- **Data Formats**: Ensure compatibility in data formats (e.g., JSON, XML) for data transfer.

2. Defining Integration Objectives

- **Purpose of Integration**: Identify the main objectives such as data synchronization, workflow automation, or report generation.
- **Scope**: Define which data points and processes need integration, such as employee onboarding, leave management, or payroll updates.

3. Security and Compliance

- **Data Protection**: Implement security protocols to safeguard employee data during transfers.
- **Compliance Checks**: Ensure integrations comply with data protection regulations like GDPR or local labor laws.

Integration Methods

1. APIs (Application Programming Interfaces)

- **ServiceNow REST and SOAP APIs**: Utilize ServiceNow's robust REST and SOAP APIs to create connections with external HR systems.
- **Third-Party API Platforms**: Consider middleware solutions like MuleSoft or Dell Boomi for simplified integration.

2. Integration Hub

- **Built-In Capabilities**: ServiceNow's Integration Hub provides pre-built spokes and connectors for common HR systems.
- **Custom Spokes**: Create custom spokes to meet unique integration needs, enhancing connectivity and process automation.

3. Data Import/Export Tools

- **Scheduled Imports/Exports**: Use ServiceNow's import/export tools to schedule data transfers at regular intervals.
- **Transform Maps**: Utilize transform maps to map incoming data to appropriate fields within ServiceNow.

Step-by-Step Integration Process

Step 1: Assess Existing Infrastructure

- **Inventory Existing Systems**: List the current HR systems and their integration capabilities.
- **Evaluate Connectivity**: Check whether these systems support direct API calls or require middleware.

Step 2: Plan the Integration Strategy

- **Choose Integration Method**: Select between direct API use, Integration Hub, or middleware based on system complexity.
- **Create Data Mapping Plans**: Define how data fields from external HR systems correspond to those in ServiceNow.

Step 3: Set Up and Configure Connections

- **Configure API Access**: Set up API keys, authentication, and endpoint details for secure access.
- **Create Data Sources**: Use ServiceNow to define data sources that pull information from connected systems.

Step 4: Test the Integration

- **Pilot Test**: Run a pilot test with limited data sets to evaluate performance and accuracy.
- **Resolve Errors**: Monitor the integration logs and troubleshoot any issues related to data transfer or workflow alignment.

Step 5: Launch and Monitor

- **Deploy Gradually**: Implement the integration in phases to minimize potential disruptions.
- **Continuous Monitoring**: Use ServiceNow's monitoring tools to ensure the integration is running smoothly and make adjustments as needed.

Common Challenges and Solutions

Challenge 1: Data Inconsistencies

- **Solution**: Implement validation checks to identify and resolve data mismatches before they impact workflows.

Challenge 2: Security Concerns

- **Solution**: Use encryption protocols and secure authentication methods (e.g., OAuth 2.0) to protect data during transfers.

Challenge 3: System Downtime

- **Solution**: Schedule integrations during low-usage periods and have a rollback plan in case of failures.

Example Use Case: Integrating ServiceNow with Workday for Onboarding

When a new employee is onboarded in Workday, an integration with ServiceNow can automate the following:

- **Case Creation**: Automatically generate a new onboarding case in ServiceNow.
- **Task Assignment**: Assign tasks related to IT provisioning, document collection, and training schedules.
- **Notifications**: Send automated alerts to relevant HR team members and the new hire, updating them on progress.
- **Data Synchronization**: Sync employee data between Workday and ServiceNow to ensure HR teams have updated records across platforms.

Best Practices for Effective Integration

1. **Start with High-Impact Processes**: Prioritize integrations that deliver the most significant ROI, such as onboarding and payroll.
2. **Maintain Clear Documentation**: Keep thorough documentation of the integration process and configuration settings.
3. **Collaborate Across Departments**: Work closely with IT and HR teams to align goals and ensure a seamless integration experience.
4. **Regular Updates**: Schedule periodic reviews of the integration setup to accommodate software updates or business process changes.

Conclusion

Integrating ServiceNow with existing HR systems is essential for creating a streamlined, cohesive HR technology environment. By leveraging ServiceNow's tools, APIs, and Integration Hub, organizations can enhance their HR operations, reduce manual work, and provide a more connected experience for employees and HR professionals alike.

Configuring Knowledge Management for HR Needs

Effective knowledge management is essential for HR departments to provide employees with timely and accurate information. With ServiceNow, organizations can create a centralized knowledge base that empowers HR teams to manage and disseminate critical resources seamlessly. This chapter delves into how to set up and optimize knowledge management in ServiceNow specifically for HR needs.

The Role of Knowledge Management in HR

Knowledge management within an HR context involves curating, organizing, and sharing information that supports HR functions and enhances the employee experience. Key benefits include:

- **Faster Issue Resolution**: Employees can access a knowledge base to find solutions without needing to contact HR directly.
- **Consistent Information Delivery**: Standardizes HR communications and procedures.
- **Increased HR Efficiency**: Reduces repetitive queries, allowing HR professionals to focus on more complex tasks.

Configuring Knowledge Management in ServiceNow

1. Setting Up the Knowledge Base

- **Creating Knowledge Bases**: Start by creating a dedicated HR knowledge base within ServiceNow. Navigate to the *Knowledge Management* module and select *Create New* under *Knowledge Bases*. Name the base (e.g., "HR Policies and Procedures").
- **Defining Categories**: Organize content into logical categories like *Employee Benefits*, *Leave Policies*, *Onboarding*, and *Compliance* to help users find information quickly.
- **Permissions and Access**: Configure user roles and permissions to ensure only authorized personnel can create, edit, or access sensitive content. For example, general HR policy documents might be public to all employees, while detailed compliance protocols are restricted to HR staff.

2. Authoring and Publishing Content

- **Content Creation Tools**: Use the built-in rich text editor in ServiceNow to author articles. Ensure that articles are concise, well-structured, and use HR-friendly language.
- **Templates and Consistency**: Implement article templates to maintain uniformity across the knowledge base. A consistent format makes it easier for employees to consume information.
- **Approval Workflows**: Establish an approval process where new content goes through HR review before publication. This helps maintain accuracy and relevancy.

3. Enhancing Search Functionality

- **Keywords and Tags**: Add relevant keywords and tags to articles to improve searchability. For example, an article on "Parental Leave" can be tagged with "maternity," "paternity," and "leave policy."
- **Search Filters**: Enable search filters such as category, date, or most viewed to assist users in narrowing down results.
- **Feedback Mechanism**: Include a feedback option so users can rate the helpfulness of articles, allowing continuous improvement of content.

4. Integrating Knowledge Management with HR Services

- **Embedding Knowledge in HR Portals**: Link the knowledge base directly to the HR service portal, enabling employees to find relevant information as they submit requests or seek assistance.

- **Automated Article Suggestions**: Configure the system to suggest articles when users start typing their queries in the HR portal. For example, if an employee types "leave application," the system might suggest articles related to leave policies and processes.
- **Case Deflection**: Implement case deflection to automatically display related knowledge articles when employees raise support tickets. This helps resolve common issues without further HR intervention.

Best Practices for HR Knowledge Management

1. Regular Content Audits

- Conduct periodic reviews of the knowledge base to ensure information is up-to-date and relevant. Remove outdated articles and update those with policy changes or new regulations.

2. Encouraging User Engagement

- Promote the use of the knowledge base by educating employees on how to find and use it effectively. Incorporate training sessions or quick guides during onboarding.
- Gather employee feedback on content usefulness and make adjustments based on their input.

3. Ensuring Data Security

- Protect sensitive HR information by applying strict access controls. Use ServiceNow's role-based permissions to manage who can access, modify, or share knowledge articles.
- Employ data encryption for articles containing confidential employee information or company-sensitive policies.

Monitoring and Measuring Success

1. Key Performance Indicators (KPIs)

- **Usage Metrics**: Track metrics such as the number of article views, unique users accessing the knowledge base, and the frequency of article searches.
- **Resolution Time**: Measure the reduction in HR support response time after implementing knowledge management.
- **Feedback Scores**: Analyze feedback and ratings for articles to identify which content requires updates or additional detail.

2. Continuous Improvement

- Regularly update the knowledge base based on trends in HR requests and feedback to improve the comprehensiveness of the information.
- Use insights from reports and analytics to identify knowledge gaps and add relevant content to fill those needs.

Example Use Case: Streamlining Onboarding with Knowledge Articles

When new employees join, they often have a host of questions about company policies, procedures, and resources. By integrating ServiceNow's knowledge management with the onboarding process, HR teams can:

- **Automate Distribution**: Provide automatic access to an "Onboarding" knowledge category for all new hires.
- **Preempt Queries**: Address frequently asked questions related to onboarding, such as "How to access payroll?" or "What benefits am I eligible for?" through pre-written knowledge articles.
- **Guide Self-Service**: Empower new employees to find answers quickly, freeing HR to focus on more personalized support when necessary.

Conclusion

Configuring knowledge management in ServiceNow for HR purposes enhances efficiency, ensures consistent information dissemination, and empowers employees to resolve common issues independently. Properly structured and integrated knowledge bases facilitate smoother HR operations and provide significant long-term value to both HR professionals and employees.

Section 5:
HR Service Delivery Modules in Depth

Employee Document Management and Compliance

Managing employee documents effectively is a cornerstone of HR operations. From contracts and tax forms to performance reviews and certifications, an efficient document management system ensures that critical records are accessible, secure, and compliant with regulations. ServiceNow's HR Service Delivery modules offer a comprehensive solution for document management that aligns with these needs.

The Importance of Document Management in HR

In the HR domain, accurate and secure handling of documents is essential for:

- **Compliance**: Adhering to labor laws, data protection regulations, and company policies.
- **Accessibility**: Ensuring that HR personnel and employees can quickly access relevant documents.
- **Efficiency**: Reducing manual paperwork and the time spent searching for and organizing records.
- **Security**: Safeguarding sensitive information through controlled access and data protection protocols.

Setting Up Document Management in ServiceNow

1. Creating a Centralized Document Repository

- **Repository Structure**: Use ServiceNow's document repository to create structured folders based on document types, such as *Employee Contracts*, *Performance Reviews*, and *Compliance Records*.
- **Classification and Tagging**: Tag documents with relevant metadata, such as employee ID, department, and document type, to make searching and sorting easier.
- **Access Controls**: Implement role-based permissions to ensure only authorized personnel can access sensitive documents. For instance, contracts may only be accessible to HR managers and above.

2. Automating Document Workflows

- **Document Upload and Approval**: Set up automated workflows for document uploads and approvals. For example, an employee contract can be uploaded, automatically routed to an HR manager for approval, and stored in the appropriate folder.
- **Notifications and Reminders**: Configure alerts to remind HR staff of document expiry dates or required updates, ensuring that compliance records remain current.

3. Integrating Document Management with HR Services

- **Employee Self-Service Portals**: Enable employees to access their documents through the self-service portal. This can include viewing pay stubs, contracts, or submitting documents required for specific HR processes like benefits enrollment.
- **Case Integration**: Link documents directly to HR cases for easy reference. For instance, if an employee opens a case regarding their performance review, the associated review document can be attached to the case.

Ensuring Compliance with Regulatory Standards

1. Understanding Applicable Regulations

- **GDPR**: For organizations within the EU or handling EU citizens' data, the General Data Protection Regulation mandates stringent data privacy and document management practices.
- **HIPAA**: For companies in the healthcare sector, the Health Insurance Portability and Accountability Act requires the secure handling of employee health information.
- **Other Local Regulations**: Be aware of labor laws and industry-specific requirements that might affect document storage and access.

2. Implementing Compliance Features

- **Audit Trails**: Use ServiceNow's audit trail features to maintain a record of document access and modifications. This ensures that HR can trace who viewed or edited a document and when.
- **Data Retention Policies**: Set automated retention policies to delete or archive documents after a specified period, in line with compliance requirements.
- **Encryption and Security**: Ensure all documents are encrypted both at rest and in transit to protect sensitive information from unauthorized access.

Best Practices for Effective Document Management

1. Standardizing Document Formats

- Use standardized templates for commonly used documents, such as employee contracts and performance reviews, to maintain consistency and facilitate faster processing.

2. Training HR Staff

- Provide training to HR staff on how to use the document management features of ServiceNow efficiently, including uploading documents, setting access permissions, and linking documents to cases.

3. Regular Audits

- Schedule regular audits of the document repository to verify compliance with company policies and regulations. Ensure that documents are filed correctly, up-to-date, and stored securely.

Monitoring and Reporting

1. Dashboard Monitoring

- Set up dashboards to monitor the status of document management activities, such as outstanding approvals, expiring documents, and compliance checks.
- **Metrics to Track**:
  - Number of documents uploaded per month.
  - Time taken to process and approve documents.
  - Compliance checks completed within a reporting period.

2. Reporting Tools

- Use ServiceNow's reporting tools to generate reports on document access history, approval workflows, and audit trails. This provides HR with valuable insights into document management processes and helps demonstrate compliance during audits.

Example Scenario: Streamlining Onboarding Documents

During the onboarding process, new employees must submit various documents, including identity proofs and signed contracts. With ServiceNow's document management:

- **Automation**: The system sends automated reminders to new employees for submitting required documents.
- **Centralized Access**: HR can quickly verify submitted documents, approve them, and securely store them in the respective employee's folder.
- **Self-Service**: New hires can access their onboarding checklist and upload necessary documents directly through the HR portal, streamlining the process.

Conclusion

Employee document management is an integral aspect of HR operations, influencing compliance, accessibility, and efficiency. By leveraging ServiceNow's robust document management capabilities, HR teams can streamline workflows, ensure regulatory compliance, and enhance the overall employee experience.

Managing Employee Onboarding and Offboarding

The onboarding and offboarding processes are critical to an employee's lifecycle within an organization. Effective onboarding sets the tone for new hires, ensuring they integrate smoothly and become productive members of the team. Conversely, a structured offboarding process safeguards the company's assets, maintains compliance, and leaves a positive last impression. ServiceNow provides robust tools to manage both processes, streamlining them into efficient workflows that enhance the HR team's productivity and improve employee experience.

The Significance of Streamlined Onboarding and Offboarding

1. Onboarding

A well-orchestrated onboarding process supports new employees by providing them with the resources and information they need to succeed. Key benefits include:

- **Accelerated Productivity**: New hires reach full productivity faster when they are properly introduced to their role, colleagues, and company culture.
- **Increased Retention**: Effective onboarding has been linked to improved job satisfaction and lower turnover rates.
- **Consistency**: Standardized onboarding processes ensure that all employees receive the same level of preparation and support.

2. Offboarding

A smooth offboarding process ensures that departing employees leave on a positive note while safeguarding company interests. Key aspects include:

- **Security and Compliance**: Ensures the proper handling of sensitive information and deactivation of accounts.
- **Knowledge Transfer**: Facilitates the transfer of responsibilities to avoid disruptions in workflow.
- **Exit Insights**: Structured exit interviews can provide feedback for future organizational improvements.

Setting Up Onboarding Workflows in ServiceNow

1. Creating Customized Onboarding Checklists

ServiceNow allows HR teams to create tailored onboarding checklists that cover all necessary steps, such as:

- Document submission (e.g., tax forms, identification).
- Provisioning of equipment (e.g., laptops, security badges).
- Scheduling initial training sessions and orientation meetings.
- Assigning mentors or onboarding buddies to guide new employees through their first few weeks.

2. Automated Task Assignment

The automated workflow engine in ServiceNow ensures that tasks are automatically assigned to relevant departments, such as IT, security, and training teams. For example:

- **IT Support**: Tasked with setting up user accounts and provisioning necessary software.
- **Facilities Management**: Responsible for preparing workspace or remote work resources.
- **HR Team**: Reviews submitted documentation and schedules introductory sessions.

3. Communication and Notifications

ServiceNow's integrated communication tools ensure that both new employees and HR staff stay informed:

- **Automated Welcome Messages**: Sent to new hires, providing them with an overview of what to expect.
- **Notifications**: Alert HR staff and other relevant stakeholders of upcoming tasks and deadlines.
- **Progress Tracking**: HR teams can track the status of onboarding tasks in real time to prevent delays.

Configuring Offboarding Processes

1. Initiating the Offboarding Workflow

An offboarding workflow in ServiceNow typically starts with the submission of an HR case or an automated trigger based on an employee's planned departure. The workflow may include:

- **Exit Interview Scheduling**: Ensures HR captures valuable feedback and insights.
- **Final Paycheck and Benefits Management**: Facilitates the preparation of final compensation and benefits settlements.
- **Access Revocation**: Triggers IT to deactivate user accounts, reclaim company assets, and remove system access.

2. Knowledge Transfer and Handover Tasks

To maintain workflow continuity, offboarding can be configured to include:

- **Task Assignment**: Ensures critical responsibilities are reassigned to colleagues or interim staff.
- **Document Handover**: Centralized access to relevant documentation for ongoing projects.
- **Checklist Completion**: Verifies that the departing employee has returned company property and completed any required knowledge transfer activities.

3. Exit Surveys and Feedback

Offboarding should not end when an employee's tenure concludes. ServiceNow allows HR to send automated exit surveys to gather feedback, which can inform future policy improvements and enhance employee retention strategies.

Best Practices for Effective Onboarding and Offboarding

1. Standardization with Flexibility

Ensure that the onboarding and offboarding processes are standardized but adaptable for different roles and situations. For instance, remote workers may need virtual orientation sessions, while in-office employees might benefit from in-person onboarding activities.

2. Maintaining Compliance

Both processes should be aligned with relevant compliance standards. ServiceNow supports:

- **Data Privacy Regulations**: By securing personal information and maintaining access logs.
- **Audit Trails**: By providing detailed records of completed tasks and communication during the onboarding and offboarding process.

3. Continuous Process Improvement

Use feedback from onboarding and exit interviews to continually enhance the process. Analyze data from ServiceNow dashboards to identify bottlenecks or areas for improvement.

Monitoring and Reporting

1. Progress Dashboards

HR teams can use ServiceNow's dashboards to monitor onboarding and offboarding progress in real-time, ensuring that no steps are missed and that the process stays on schedule.

2. Metrics to Track

Some key performance indicators (KPIs) include:

- Average time taken to complete onboarding/offboarding.
- Satisfaction scores from new hire and exit surveys.
- Number of compliance checks completed.

3. Report Generation

ServiceNow's reporting tools allow HR to create comprehensive reports on onboarding and offboarding activities, helping teams to demonstrate compliance and performance to management.

Example Scenario: Onboarding a New Remote Employee

For a new remote employee, ServiceNow's onboarding process might include:

- **Digital Document Submission**: The employee uploads required documents through the HR portal.
- **Virtual Equipment Provisioning**: IT ships a company laptop and sets up remote access credentials.
- **Orientation via Video Call**: HR schedules a virtual orientation session and sends calendar invites.
- **Assigned Buddy System**: An experienced remote team member is assigned as the new hire's mentor for the first month.

Conclusion

The management of onboarding and offboarding processes can significantly influence an employee's experience and the overall efficiency of the HR department. ServiceNow's HR Service Delivery modules provide the tools necessary to automate, track, and enhance these critical processes, ensuring that both new and departing employees are well-supported.

Case and Knowledge Management Best Practices

Effective HR service delivery relies heavily on well-structured case and knowledge management practices. With ServiceNow's comprehensive HR Service Delivery (HRSD) module, HR teams can streamline case management and empower employees with self-service capabilities. By integrating best practices for case and knowledge management, organizations can enhance HR operations, reduce response times, and foster a knowledge-driven culture that supports continuous improvement.

The Importance of Case and Knowledge Management in HR

1. Streamlined Employee Support

Case management allows HR teams to manage employee queries, requests, and issues in an organized and efficient manner. A robust system ensures:

- **Timely Resolution**: Cases are tracked and managed to resolution, enhancing the employee experience.
- **Accountability and Transparency**: Clear case tracking ensures that HR staff remain accountable, and employees have transparency into the status of their requests.

2. Enhanced Knowledge Sharing

Effective knowledge management empowers employees to find answers to common questions independently, reducing the volume of repetitive inquiries and freeing HR resources for more complex issues. Key benefits include:

- **Self-Service Efficiency**: Employees can access HR policies, how-to guides, and answers to frequently asked questions through an organized knowledge base.
- **Continuous Learning**: A knowledge base that evolves with company updates ensures that employees and HR staff alike remain informed and up-to-date.

Configuring Case Management in ServiceNow

1. Creating and Classifying Cases

ServiceNow allows HR teams to create cases that can be classified and prioritized based on the type of inquiry or request. Best practices include:

- **Defining Case Categories and Subcategories**: Classify cases (e.g., payroll, benefits, onboarding) to streamline assignment and resolution.
- **Establishing Service Level Agreements (SLAs)**: Define SLAs to set expectations for response and resolution times, ensuring timely follow-ups.
- **Automated Assignment Rules**: Use predefined rules to route cases to the appropriate HR specialists based on the category or type.

2. Workflow Automation

Automating workflows helps maintain consistency in handling cases. Effective workflow automation includes:

- **Triggers and Notifications**: Set up triggers that notify HR staff and employees when certain actions are required or when cases progress to different stages.
- **Standardized Responses**: Use templates and quick responses for common inquiries to maintain consistent communication.
- **Approval Processes**: Configure automated approval workflows for cases that require managerial or multi-departmental sign-off.

Best Practices for Managing HR Cases

1. Ensure Accurate Case Logging

Train HR staff to log cases with complete and accurate details. Important fields include:

- **Employee Information**: Details of the requesting employee (e.g., name, department).
- **Case Description**: Clear and concise descriptions of the issue or request.
- **Attachments**: Relevant documents or screenshots that may aid in resolving the case.

2. Monitor Case Status and Metrics

Regularly track case metrics to identify trends and improve performance. Key performance indicators (KPIs) to monitor include:

- **First Response Time**: The time taken to initially respond to a case.
- **Resolution Time**: The total time taken to resolve cases.
- **Case Reopen Rate**: The percentage of cases that are reopened, indicating potential gaps in the resolution process.

3. Collaborate Across Departments

Complex cases may require input from other departments. ServiceNow supports cross-functional collaboration through:

- **Case Comments**: Facilitate real-time communication between HR and other involved parties.
- **Case Escalation Protocols**: Clearly define escalation paths for cases that require urgent attention or senior-level involvement.

Building an Effective HR Knowledge Base

1. Curating Knowledge Articles

Knowledge articles should be tailored to address common employee queries and HR procedures. Tips for curating articles include:

- **Use Clear Language**: Write articles in plain language that employees can easily understand.
- **Keep Content Concise**: Focus on delivering essential information without unnecessary jargon.
- **Update Regularly**: Periodically review articles to ensure they remain relevant and accurate.

2. Organize Content for Easy Access

A well-structured knowledge base is critical for effective use. Best practices include:

- **Categorize by Topic**: Group articles by relevant HR topics such as benefits, leave policies, and payroll.
- **Use Tags and Keywords**: Implement tags and keywords for improved search functionality.
- **Include Multimedia**: Add images, charts, and videos to enhance comprehension and engagement.

3. Empower Employees with Self-Service

Encourage employees to use the knowledge base for self-service by:

- **Promoting Self-Service Tools**: Highlight the knowledge base in onboarding materials and HR communications.
- **User-Friendly Portals**: Ensure that the HR portal provides an intuitive user experience with easy navigation.

- **Feedback Mechanism**: Implement a feedback feature so employees can suggest updates or new articles for the knowledge base.

Integrating Case and Knowledge Management

One of the most powerful features of ServiceNow is its ability to integrate case and knowledge management seamlessly. This integration allows HR staff to:

- **Link Knowledge Articles to Cases**: Provide employees with relevant articles as part of the case response, aiding faster resolution.
- **Create Knowledge from Cases**: Convert resolved cases into knowledge articles if they address unique or recurring issues.
- **Track Knowledge Use**: Analyze which articles are frequently referenced in cases to determine their effectiveness and update them as needed.

Training HR Teams for Effective Use

For case and knowledge management to be effective, HR teams should be trained in:

- **Navigating the ServiceNow Platform**: Ensure all team members are comfortable using ServiceNow's case and knowledge management modules.
- **Standardized Procedures**: Train staff on standardized workflows for handling different case types.
- **Continuous Learning**: Encourage regular training sessions to update HR staff on new features and enhancements.

Leveraging Analytics for Continuous Improvement

ServiceNow's analytics tools provide valuable insights for refining case and knowledge management practices:

- **Case Volume Reports**: Identify high-volume case types to determine where additional resources or process improvements are needed.
- **Knowledge Base Utilization**: Track which articles are most accessed to understand common pain points and areas that may need additional content.
- **Employee Feedback Analysis**: Use feedback data to make targeted improvements to both case management and the knowledge base.

Conclusion

An integrated approach to case and knowledge management within ServiceNow enables HR teams to manage employee interactions efficiently and proactively. By adhering to best practices, automating processes, and leveraging analytics, HR can provide exceptional service while empowering employees through self-service solutions. This approach not only improves productivity but also fosters a positive employee experience, reinforcing HR's role as a strategic partner in organizational success.

HR Ticketing System and Workflow Optimization

An optimized HR ticketing system is fundamental for effective and efficient service delivery within an organization. ServiceNow's HR Service Delivery (HRSD) platform is designed to streamline and enhance the way HR teams manage, track, and resolve employee requests. By leveraging ServiceNow's capabilities, HR departments can create workflows that not only support timely ticket resolution but also improve employee satisfaction and operational efficiency.

The Value of an Optimized HR Ticketing System

1. Centralized Request Management

A robust HR ticketing system allows for a centralized platform where all employee requests and cases can be managed. Benefits include:

- **Single Point of Contact**: Employees have a dedicated place to submit requests, reducing confusion and delays.
- **Visibility and Transparency**: HR teams and employees alike can track the status of tickets in real-time.

2. Enhanced Communication

Clear communication between HR teams and employees is crucial for the successful resolution of requests. An optimized system ensures:

- **Automated Notifications**: Employees receive updates on the status of their requests.
- **Consistent Responses**: Standardized templates and pre-written responses enhance communication efficiency.

3. Prioritization and Efficient Case Management

ServiceNow enables HR teams to prioritize tickets based on urgency and importance. This helps in:

- **Managing Workload**: High-priority issues can be resolved quickly while ensuring that no tickets are overlooked.
- **Tracking Performance**: Managers can monitor case resolution times and identify bottlenecks in the workflow.

Best Practices for HR Ticketing System Optimization

1. Define Clear Ticket Categories

Categorizing tickets is essential for streamlining HR workflows. Best practices include:

- **Segmenting by Request Type**: Organize tickets into categories such as payroll inquiries, benefits requests, onboarding, and policy clarifications.
- **Subcategories for Specificity**: Include subcategories to make ticket classification more precise, aiding in quicker resolution.

2. Develop Standardized Processes

To enhance consistency and efficiency:

- **Create Standard Operating Procedures (SOPs)**: Document detailed SOPs for handling each type of request.
- **Workflow Templates**: Use pre-configured workflows for frequently occurring cases to save time and maintain uniformity.

3. Automate Routine Workflows

Automation can greatly enhance the speed and accuracy of HR service delivery:

- **Trigger-Based Actions**: Set up automated actions, such as ticket routing to the appropriate HR specialist or sending automatic updates to employees.
- **Approvals and Escalations**: Automate approval workflows for requests that require managerial input or escalate tickets that exceed their SLA.

4. Leverage Self-Service Portals

Implementing self-service tools as part of the ticketing system reduces the number of basic inquiries directed to HR. Key strategies include:

- **Knowledge Base Integration**: Embed knowledge articles within the self-service portal to guide employees toward self-resolution for common questions.
- **Intelligent FAQs**: Use AI-driven FAQs that provide instant answers to routine questions, deflecting tickets that don't require human intervention.

Optimizing HR Workflows for Improved Efficiency

1. Identify Bottlenecks and Redundant Processes

Regularly audit HR workflows to pinpoint steps that delay ticket resolution:

- **Workflow Mapping**: Visually map out each HR process to identify and eliminate redundant or non-value-adding steps.
- **Feedback Loops**: Collect feedback from HR staff and employees to discover inefficiencies and make necessary adjustments.

2. Integrate Cross-Functional Collaboration

Complex HR cases often involve input from multiple departments. Effective integration enables:

- **Seamless Communication**: Utilize ServiceNow's collaborative tools to facilitate communication between HR, IT, finance, and other departments.
- **Shared Responsibility**: Define clear roles and permissions within workflows so team members understand their responsibilities.

3. Use Data Analytics for Workflow Improvement

ServiceNow's analytics capabilities can be used to gather insights and optimize workflows:

- **Track Key Metrics**: Monitor metrics such as average resolution time, first response time, and employee satisfaction scores.
- **Continuous Improvement**: Use the data to implement workflow enhancements that improve efficiency and reduce case resolution time.

Real-Life Example: HR Ticketing Workflow Implementation

Consider a mid-sized company that implemented ServiceNow's HRSD for its onboarding process. Initially, onboarding requests were handled manually, leading to delays and inconsistencies. After deploying a structured HR ticketing workflow:

- **Onboarding tickets were automatically routed** to the relevant HR specialists and integrated with IT for provisioning employee accounts.
- **Notifications were automated**, informing new hires about the status of their onboarding process and required next steps.

- **The HR team noticed a 40% reduction** in onboarding time, significantly improving the experience for new employees and allowing HR staff to focus on strategic tasks.

Training HR Teams for Optimized Workflow Management

1. Comprehensive Training Programs

Ensure that HR staff are well-versed in managing the ticketing system and workflows:

- **Initial Onboarding**: Provide in-depth training for new HR team members on navigating ServiceNow's ticketing features.
- **Ongoing Workshops**: Regular workshops to update the team on new ServiceNow functionalities and workflow enhancements.

2. Role-Specific Training

Tailor training programs to the specific roles within the HR team:

- **Case Managers**: Focus on in-depth workflow navigation, ticket escalation, and reporting features.
- **HR Specialists**: Emphasize quick response techniques, use of knowledge base resources, and communication best practices.

3. Creating a Supportive Culture

Encourage an open environment where HR staff can:

- **Share Best Practices**: Hold regular team meetings to discuss and share what is working well in ticket management.
- **Collaborate on Improvements**: Collaborate on finding solutions for common challenges encountered in managing HR tickets.

Leveraging Technology to Drive Workflow Excellence

Technology enhancements can play a crucial role in maintaining optimized HR workflows:

- **AI and Machine Learning**: Utilize machine learning algorithms to predict ticket categories and suggest relevant knowledge articles for HR staff.
- **Mobile Access**: Ensure that HR staff can manage and track tickets from mobile devices, providing flexibility and quick response capabilities.
- **Integration with Other Systems**: Integrate ServiceNow with other HR tools like payroll, benefits management, and learning platforms to create a seamless experience.

Conclusion

Implementing and optimizing HR ticketing systems and workflows is essential for effective service delivery. By leveraging ServiceNow's powerful HRSD features and adhering to best practices in workflow optimization, HR teams can enhance their service capabilities, ensure timely resolutions, and create a seamless experience for employees. The result is an HR department that not only manages cases efficiently but also proactively supports the organization's strategic goals.

Automating HR Requests and Approvals

The automation of HR requests and approvals is a transformative aspect of ServiceNow's HR Service Delivery (HRSD) platform. By leveraging automation, HR teams can streamline workflows, reduce manual tasks, and improve overall efficiency. This chapter provides an in-depth guide on how to automate HR requests and approvals within ServiceNow, focusing on best practices and practical steps to enhance workflow management.

The Importance of Automation in HR Requests and Approvals

1. Reducing Manual Workload

Automating routine HR tasks helps free up HR staff to focus on strategic initiatives:

- **Time Savings**: Automating repetitive tasks such as processing leave requests and benefits approvals reduces the time HR teams spend on manual entry.
- **Reduced Errors**: Automated workflows minimize the risk of human error, ensuring greater accuracy in data processing and task execution.

2. Enhancing Employee Experience

Automation contributes to a seamless and user-friendly experience:

- **Quick Response Time**: Employees receive faster responses to their requests, leading to improved satisfaction and engagement.
- **Transparency**: Automated notifications keep employees informed about the status of their requests in real-time.

3. Ensuring Consistency and Compliance

Automated workflows ensure that every request follows the same approval path, helping maintain consistency and compliance:

- **Standardized Processes**: Automation enforces adherence to company policies and regulations.
- **Audit Trails**: Every automated step is documented, providing an easy-to-access history for compliance checks.

Key Features of ServiceNow for Automating HR Processes

1. Workflow Automation Engine

The Workflow Automation Engine in ServiceNow is designed to manage complex HR processes:

- **Pre-Built Templates**: Utilize templates for common HR processes like leave requests, expense approvals, and performance review cycles.
- **Drag-and-Drop Builder**: Simplify workflow creation with an intuitive interface that doesn't require coding expertise.

2. Approval Rules and Routing

ServiceNow's rule-based engine ensures that requests are routed to the appropriate approvers:

- **Conditional Logic**: Customize approval paths based on the type of request, department, or employee role.
- **Escalation Paths**: Define escalation routes for requests that require additional review or have surpassed defined response times.

3. Integration with HR Systems

ServiceNow can be integrated with existing HR management systems to facilitate seamless data flow:

- **Data Synchronization**: Automatically pull employee data and approvals from connected systems.
- **Unified Interfaces**: Present users with a cohesive view of HR services without navigating multiple platforms.

Implementing Automation for Common HR Requests

1. Leave and Time-Off Requests

Automating leave requests ensures quick processing and up-to-date tracking of leave balances:

- **Self-Service Portals**: Employees can submit leave requests through a user-friendly portal that triggers an automated approval workflow.
- **Integrated Calendars**: Sync approved leave requests with the company's calendar system to avoid scheduling conflicts.

2. Expense Approvals

Automating expense approvals speeds up reimbursement processes and improves accuracy:

- **Document Submission**: Employees upload receipts and documents, which are automatically routed to the appropriate approvers.
- **Policy Checks**: Embedded policy rules ensure expenses comply with company guidelines before reaching the approval stage.

3. Job Offer and Onboarding Approvals

For HR teams managing recruitment:

- **Automated Offer Letters**: Generate customized offer letters and route them for approval before sending them to candidates.
- **Onboarding Workflows**: Automate onboarding steps like account setup, document verification, and role-based training assignments.

Best Practices for Automating HR Approvals

1. Map Out Workflows in Advance

Understand the full process before automating:

- **Process Mapping**: Identify all steps involved in an HR request and approval process.
- **Stakeholder Input**: Collaborate with HR, IT, and department managers to ensure the workflow meets business needs.

2. Set Clear Approval Thresholds

Not all requests require the same level of scrutiny:

- **Tiered Approvals**: Define which types of requests can be automatically approved versus those that need multiple levels of approval.
- **Delegation Options**: Establish clear delegation rules for cases when primary approvers are unavailable.

3. Utilize Notifications and Alerts

Keep all involved parties informed throughout the process:

- **Automated Alerts**: Set up email or in-platform notifications to inform approvers and requestors of updates or delays.
- **Follow-Up Reminders**: Use reminders to prompt approvers who haven't responded within a set timeframe.

4. Regularly Monitor and Refine Workflows

Maintain optimal performance by regularly reviewing automated workflows:

- **Performance Dashboards**: Track workflow efficiency and identify areas for improvement using ServiceNow's analytics tools.
- **Feedback Loops**: Collect feedback from HR staff and employees to make adjustments to automated processes.

Challenges and How to Address Them

1. Handling Exceptions

Not all cases fit within a standard workflow:

- **Customizable Rules**: Build workflows that can handle exceptions by routing unique cases to specialized teams.
- **Manual Overrides**: Allow HR personnel to manually intervene in automated workflows when needed.

2. Employee Adoption

Ensuring employees use the automated systems effectively:

- **Training and Support**: Provide comprehensive training and user guides to educate employees on how to submit requests and track their status.
- **Feedback Mechanism**: Implement a feedback system to understand employee concerns and refine the automation process.

Example Case Study: Automating Approvals for Professional Development Requests

A company introduced an automated approval process for professional development requests to streamline the allocation of training budgets:

- **Submission Portal**: Employees submitted training requests through an online portal.
- **Policy Integration**: The system automatically checked if the training aligned with company policy and budget.
- **Multi-Level Approvals**: Requests were routed to department heads and HR managers for approval.
- **Outcome**: The company reported a 50% faster approval process, reduced errors, and improved satisfaction among employees seeking professional growth opportunities.

Conclusion

Automating HR requests and approvals in ServiceNow enhances efficiency, accuracy, and employee satisfaction. By implementing best practices, leveraging ServiceNow's advanced tools, and continuously optimizing workflows, HR departments can streamline processes and focus more on strategic HR functions. The key to successful automation lies in detailed planning, stakeholder collaboration, and continuous improvement.

Benefits Administration with ServiceNow

Effective benefits administration is a critical aspect of human resources management, impacting employee satisfaction, retention, and overall well-being. ServiceNow's HR Service Delivery (HRSD) platform provides a comprehensive approach to managing and automating benefits processes, allowing HR teams to streamline administration while ensuring compliance and accuracy. This chapter will explore how to leverage ServiceNow for benefits administration, detailing the key features, best practices, and implementation strategies to optimize HR operations.

The Importance of Streamlined Benefits Administration

1. Enhancing Employee Satisfaction

A seamless benefits experience can significantly improve employee morale and retention:

- **Accessibility**: Employees can easily view, enroll in, and manage their benefits through an intuitive self-service portal.
- **Transparency**: Automated notifications keep employees informed about their benefits status, reducing confusion and the need for manual inquiries.

2. Improving HR Efficiency

Automating benefits processes helps HR teams reduce time spent on manual tasks:

- **Centralized Management**: ServiceNow offers a single platform for managing various benefits programs, eliminating the need for disparate systems.
- **Reduced Errors**: Automation minimizes human error, ensuring accurate benefits data and compliance with policies.

3. Ensuring Compliance

Keeping up with regulatory requirements is essential for HR departments:

- **Automated Compliance Checks**: ServiceNow can be configured to align with local and international regulations, such as GDPR, HIPAA, and benefits-specific laws.
- **Audit Trails**: Detailed records of benefits transactions and communications provide transparency and readiness for audits.

Key Features of ServiceNow for Benefits Administration

1. Employee Self-Service Portals

ServiceNow's self-service portals empower employees to manage their benefits with ease:

- **Benefits Enrollment**: Employees can browse and enroll in available benefit plans during open enrollment periods or qualifying life events.
- **Status Tracking**: Real-time updates allow employees to track the status of their benefit applications.

2. Workflow Automation for Benefits Approvals

Automate benefits-related workflows to streamline approval processes:

- **Configurable Workflows**: Customizable workflows ensure benefits requests are routed to the appropriate approvers for review and approval.
- **Notifications and Reminders**: Automated alerts notify employees and HR staff of pending tasks and deadlines.

3. Integration with Payroll and External Systems

ServiceNow supports seamless integration with payroll systems and third-party benefits providers:

- **Data Synchronization**: Sync benefits data with payroll systems for accurate deductions and processing.
- **Third-Party Integrations**: Connect with external providers for services such as health insurance, retirement plans, and other benefits.

4. Reporting and Analytics Tools

Gain insights into benefits usage and trends:

- **Benefits Utilization Reports**: Analyze which benefits are most popular and identify areas for potential cost savings or expansion.
- **Custom Dashboards**: Create dashboards to monitor enrollment, changes, and overall benefits performance.

Implementing Benefits Administration in ServiceNow

1. Setting Up Benefits Plans

Create and configure various benefits plans within ServiceNow to match company offerings:

- **Plan Details**: Include all necessary details, such as coverage options, eligibility criteria, and enrollment periods.
- **Tiered Plans**: Offer employees different levels of coverage (e.g., basic, premium, or family plans).

2. Automating the Enrollment Process

Ensure a smooth enrollment experience through automation:

- **Open Enrollment Setup**: Schedule open enrollment periods with automatic notifications sent to eligible employees.
- **Eligibility Verification**: Configure the system to check employee eligibility for specific plans based on factors like tenure and employment status.

3. Managing Changes and Life Events

Employees may need to update their benefits due to life changes (e.g., marriage, birth of a child):

- **Life Event Workflows**: Automate the process for submitting life event changes, routing them to the necessary approvers, and updating records accordingly.
- **Document Uploads**: Allow employees to submit required documentation directly through the portal.

4. Integrating with Payroll and Providers

Ensure benefits data is accurately transferred to payroll and third-party providers:

- **Secure Data Transfer**: Utilize encrypted channels for data synchronization to maintain data privacy and security.
- **API Integrations**: Use ServiceNow's APIs to establish direct connections with external systems for real-time updates.

Best Practices for Benefits Administration

1. Maintain Up-to-Date Plan Information

Keep all plan details current to avoid confusion:

- **Regular Updates**: Review and update plan information regularly to reflect changes in policy or provider offerings.
- **Employee Communication**: Inform employees of any updates or new benefits options through automated announcements.

2. Ensure Comprehensive Training for HR Teams

Provide training for HR teams to manage benefits processes effectively:

- **Workshops and Guides**: Conduct training sessions on navigating the benefits module and handling exceptions.
- **Documentation**: Create user manuals and FAQs to support HR staff and employees in understanding the system.

3. Collect Feedback for Continuous Improvement

Employee feedback helps refine benefits administration:

- **Surveys and Polls**: Send periodic surveys to gather feedback on the benefits enrollment and management process.
- **Iterative Improvements**: Use the feedback to make adjustments that enhance the user experience and workflow efficiency.

4. Regularly Audit the System

Perform audits to ensure compliance and identify areas for improvement:

- **Compliance Checks**: Schedule periodic compliance reviews to align with regulatory requirements.
- **System Health Audits**: Monitor system performance to address any issues that could impact the benefits process.

Overcoming Common Challenges

1. Managing High Enrollment Volumes

Large organizations may experience high enrollment traffic, especially during open enrollment:

- **Load Balancing**: Use ServiceNow's capabilities to manage server load and prevent downtime during peak periods.
- **Scalable Solutions**: Implement scalable workflows that can handle increased demand without performance degradation.

2. Addressing Data Privacy Concerns

Protecting employee data is a top priority:

- **Data Encryption**: Ensure data at rest and in transit is encrypted to maintain privacy.
- **Access Controls**: Implement role-based access to limit data visibility to authorized personnel only.

3. Navigating Integration Complexities

Integrating ServiceNow with existing HR systems can be complex:

- **Step-by-Step Integration Plan**: Develop a comprehensive plan that outlines each step of the integration process, including testing and validation phases.

- **Collaborate with IT Teams**: Work closely with IT professionals to address technical challenges and ensure smooth integration.

Conclusion

Automating benefits administration with ServiceNow transforms HR processes by enhancing efficiency, improving employee experiences, and ensuring compliance. By leveraging ServiceNow's advanced capabilities, HR teams can manage benefits with confidence, allowing them to focus on strategic initiatives that contribute to overall organizational success. Implementing best practices, staying compliant, and continuously refining workflows will lead to a robust and scalable benefits administration system.

Section 6:
Advanced Customization and Integration

Customizing HR Workflows with Flow Designer

Effective customization of HR workflows is essential for aligning ServiceNow's capabilities with an organization's unique needs. The Flow Designer, a powerful tool within the ServiceNow platform, provides an intuitive and flexible way to create, modify, and automate workflows without extensive coding knowledge. This chapter explores the process of using Flow Designer to build and customize HR workflows, offering insights into best practices and strategies for maximizing efficiency and consistency in HR operations.

The Role of Flow Designer in Workflow Customization

1. Intuitive Interface and No-Code Approach

Flow Designer empowers HR professionals and administrators by providing a no-code environment:

- **Drag-and-Drop Interface**: Users can design workflows by dragging and dropping components, making it accessible even for those without programming expertise.
- **Pre-Built Actions**: The platform includes numerous pre-configured actions and templates that can be used or modified to suit specific HR needs.

2. Seamless Integration with HR Modules

Flow Designer integrates smoothly with ServiceNow's HR Service Delivery (HRSD) modules:

- **Unified Workflow Management**: Create workflows that interact with various HR modules, such as onboarding, case management, and benefits administration.
- **Data Synchronization**: Ensure consistency across different HR processes by linking data between connected modules.

3. Automation Capabilities

Automating repetitive tasks with Flow Designer helps streamline operations and improve response times:

- **Triggered Actions**: Automate actions based on specific triggers, such as form submissions or employee status changes.
- **Scheduled Flows**: Set workflows to run at specified intervals to maintain regular updates and ensure timely task completion.

Key Components of Flow Designer

1. Flows

Flows are the core structure of any workflow in ServiceNow:

- **Flow Triggers**: Initiate the workflow based on events such as HR requests, approvals, or task completions.
- **Flow Actions**: Define the tasks that the system should perform, from notifying HR staff to updating records.

2. Subflows

Subflows are reusable sets of actions that can be embedded into multiple workflows:

- **Consistency and Reusability**: Reduce repetitive configurations by using subflows across different HR workflows.
- **Modularity**: Enhance workflow modularity and make future updates simpler.

3. Actions and Conditions

Actions perform specific tasks within a flow, while conditions help control the flow's path:

- **Custom Actions**: Design tailored actions to meet unique HR needs, such as sending tailored notifications or generating reports.
- **Conditional Logic**: Add conditions to branch workflows based on data inputs, ensuring workflows adapt dynamically to varying scenarios.

Designing Custom HR Workflows with Flow Designer

1. Mapping Out the Workflow

Before using Flow Designer, outline the steps required in the workflow:

- **Identify Objectives**: Clarify the goal of the workflow, whether it is for automating an onboarding process or handling HR service requests.
- **Break Down Processes**: Divide the workflow into logical steps, mapping triggers, actions, and outcomes.

2. Creating a Flow

To create a new flow in Flow Designer:

- **Access Flow Designer**: Navigate to the Flow Designer application within the ServiceNow platform.
- **Add a New Flow**: Select "Create New" and provide a name and description for the flow.
- **Set Triggers**: Define the event that will activate the flow, such as the submission of an HR service request.

3. Building the Flow

- **Add Actions**: Use pre-built or custom actions to define tasks, such as sending confirmation emails or updating HR records.
- **Incorporate Conditions**: Use "If" statements or switch logic to guide the flow based on different input variables.
- **Embed Subflows**: Include subflows where applicable to enhance efficiency and maintain consistency across multiple workflows.

4. Testing and Validation

Ensure that the workflow functions as intended by:

- **Running Test Flows**: Use sample data to simulate the flow and verify its functionality.
- **Debugging**: Identify and resolve errors or inefficiencies in the flow logic.

Best Practices for Customizing HR Workflows

1. Keep Flows Simple and Maintainable

Complex workflows can be difficult to manage and troubleshoot:

- **Modular Design**: Break down large processes into smaller subflows to make the overall workflow more manageable.
- **Documentation**: Maintain clear documentation for each flow to facilitate future updates and onboarding of new HR administrators.

2. Involve Key Stakeholders in the Design Process

Ensure the customized workflows align with HR policies and needs by involving relevant stakeholders:

- **Collaborative Development**: Engage HR team members to provide insights and feedback during the workflow design phase.
- **User Acceptance Testing**: Have end-users test the flows to confirm they meet their expectations and requirements.

3. Regularly Review and Update Workflows

HR processes and policies evolve over time, necessitating updates to workflows:

- **Scheduled Reviews**: Periodically review workflows to identify areas for improvement or adjustments.
- **Feedback Integration**: Collect feedback from users and incorporate suggestions to refine workflows for better performance.

4. Ensure Compliance and Security

Custom workflows must adhere to internal policies and regulatory requirements:

- **Data Handling**: Implement data privacy measures to protect sensitive employee information.
- **Access Controls**: Limit access to specific flows to authorized HR personnel to prevent unauthorized modifications.

Examples of HR Workflows Customizable with Flow Designer

1. Onboarding and Offboarding Processes

Create comprehensive onboarding and offboarding flows that handle multiple tasks, such as:

- **New Employee Setup**: Automate IT service requests, account creation, and HR orientation scheduling.
- **Exit Process**: Streamline final paycheck processing, equipment return, and exit interviews.

2. HR Case Escalation

Develop workflows that manage case escalations based on priority:

- **Automatic Routing**: Route urgent cases to senior HR staff for immediate attention.
- **Response Tracking**: Monitor case resolution timeframes and send reminders for pending actions.

3. Leave and Absence Management

Customize workflows for managing employee leave requests:

- **Approval Chains**: Set up multi-level approval workflows to ensure requests are reviewed by appropriate parties.
- **Notifications**: Notify employees and managers of approved or denied leave requests automatically.

Conclusion

Flow Designer in ServiceNow is an invaluable tool for customizing and automating HR workflows, making processes more efficient and responsive to the needs of both HR teams and employees. By leveraging Flow Designer's capabilities, organizations can create tailored solutions that simplify complex workflows, enhance compliance, and support strategic HR objectives. Implementing best practices such as modular design, regular updates, and stakeholder involvement ensures these workflows remain effective and adaptable to changing business needs.

Advanced Scripting for HR Use Cases

The ability to customize and extend the functionality of ServiceNow is a vital aspect of optimizing HR workflows to meet specific business needs. Advanced scripting provides HR teams and administrators the flexibility to create tailored solutions, automate complex processes, and enhance the overall efficiency of ServiceNow implementations. This chapter will explore the different types of scripting available in ServiceNow, practical examples of HR use cases that benefit from scripting, and best practices for leveraging these capabilities securely and effectively.

1. Overview of Scripting in ServiceNow

1.1. Client-Side and Server-Side Scripting

ServiceNow supports both client-side and server-side scripting to handle different functional requirements:

- **Client-Side Scripting**: Executed on the user's browser and primarily used for enhancing user interface interactions and validations. This includes scripts such as:
  - **Client Scripts**: Validate form inputs, display alerts, and dynamically update field values.
  - **UI Policies**: Control form behaviors without writing extensive code.
- **Server-Side Scripting**: Executed on the ServiceNow server and used for background processing, automation, and complex business logic. This includes:
  - **Business Rules**: Triggered when records are created, updated, or deleted to enforce business policies.
  - **Script Includes**: Contain reusable functions for use in various scripts and processes.
  - **Scheduled Jobs**: Run scripts at specified intervals for automated tasks.

1.2. Benefits of Scripting in HR Workflows

- **Enhanced Automation**: Automate complex HR processes that standard workflows cannot cover.
- **Improved User Experience**: Customize form fields, validations, and behaviors to align with HR policies.
- **Data Integrity**: Enforce rules to ensure accurate and complete data entry.
- **Integration Capabilities**: Facilitate seamless data exchange with third-party HR systems through scripted APIs.

2. Common Scripting Use Cases in HR

2.1. Automating Approval Processes

HR often involves multi-tier approval workflows for actions like leave requests, job changes, or payroll adjustments. Scripting can automate these processes:

- **Business Rules**: Automatically assign approval tasks to specific managers based on department or job level.
- **Client Scripts**: Validate form inputs and provide real-time feedback to users submitting requests.

Example Script Snippet for Business Rule:

```
if (current.hr_request_type == 'Leave Request' && current.days_requested > 10) {
    current.approver = gs.getUserIDByName('HR Manager');
    current.state = 'Awaiting Approval';
}
```

2.2. Dynamic Form Customization

HR forms may need to dynamically display or hide fields based on user inputs to simplify the user experience and reduce errors:

- **Client Scripts**: Hide or show fields based on the type of request selected.
- **UI Policies**: Make fields mandatory or read-only based on specific conditions.

Example of a Client Script:

```
function onChange(control, oldValue, newValue, isLoading) {
    if (newValue == 'Onboarding') {
        g_form.setVisible('welcome_package', true);
    } else {
        g_form.setVisible('welcome_package', false);
    }
}
```

2.3. Data Validation and Cleanup

Ensuring the accuracy and quality of HR data is critical. Server-side scripting can automate data validation and periodic cleanup tasks:

- **Scheduled Jobs**: Run scripts that identify and correct data discrepancies or remove outdated records.
- **Business Rules**: Validate data before records are saved to prevent entry errors.

Scheduled Job Example:

```
var hrDataCleanup = new GlideRecord('hr_employee');
hrDataCleanup.addQuery('status', 'Inactive');
hrDataCleanup.query();
while (hrDataCleanup.next()) {
    hrDataCleanup.deleteRecord();
}
```

2.4. Integration with External HR Systems

ServiceNow can connect to external HR systems through scripted APIs and web services, enabling data exchange and process synchronization:

- **Scripted REST APIs**: Create custom endpoints to expose ServiceNow data to other systems.
- **Outbound HTTP Calls**: Integrate ServiceNow with payroll systems, employee management software, or recruitment platforms.

Scripted REST API Example:

```
(function process(/*RESTAPIRequest*/ request, /*RESTAPIResponse*/ response) {
    var employeeID = request.queryParams.employee_id;
    var employeeRecord = new GlideRecord('hr_employee');
    employeeRecord.addQuery('employee_number', employeeID);
    employeeRecord.query();

    if (employeeRecord.next()) {
        response.setBody(JSON.stringify({
            name: employeeRecord.name.toString(),
            department: employeeRecord.department.toString()
        }));
    } else {
        response.setStatus(404);
    }
```

```
}) (request, response);
```

3. Best Practices for Scripting in HR

3.1. Ensure Code Efficiency

- **Avoid Redundant Code**: Use reusable Script Includes for commonly used functions.
- **Minimize Client-Side Load**: Limit client-side scripting to avoid slowing down the user interface.
- **Use GlideRecord and GlideAjax Wisely**: Reduce database calls and avoid unnecessary server load by combining queries.

3.2. Prioritize Security

- **Input Validation**: Always validate and sanitize user inputs to prevent cross-site scripting (XSS) and other vulnerabilities.
- **Access Controls**: Ensure that scripts respect ServiceNow's role-based access control to protect sensitive HR data.
- **Logging and Monitoring**: Implement logs for critical actions to help with auditing and troubleshooting.

3.3. Maintain Clear Documentation

- **Comment Your Code**: Add comments to explain complex logic for easier maintenance.
- **Follow Naming Conventions**: Use clear and descriptive names for scripts, variables, and functions.
- **Version Control**: Maintain version histories of scripts to track changes and revert if needed.

3.4. Testing and Debugging

- **Use the Script Debugger**: ServiceNow's built-in debugger can help identify issues in server-side scripts.
- **Test in a Development Instance**: Always test scripts in a sandbox environment before deploying them to production.
- **User Feedback**: Gather feedback from HR teams to identify areas for script refinement.

4. Example HR Use Case: Custom Employee Onboarding Workflow

Objective:

Create an automated onboarding workflow that assigns tasks, sends notifications, and sets up access for new employees based on their role.

Workflow Steps:

1. **Initiation**: HR submits a new hire form that triggers the onboarding process.
2. **Role-Based Actions**: A Business Rule assigns specific tasks to IT, Facilities, and HR based on the new hire's job role.
3. **Notifications**: Client scripts send welcome emails and task notifications.
4. **Access Provisioning**: Script Includes handle account creation and access permissions.

Example Business Rule:

```
if (current.job_role == 'Manager') {
    current.addTask('IT Setup', 'Setup laptop and email');
    current.addTask('Facilities', 'Prepare office space');
    gs.eventQueue('hr.onboarding.welcome', current, current.hr_user,
gs.getUserID());
}
```

Conclusion

Advanced scripting in ServiceNow allows HR departments to go beyond standard workflows and create customized solutions that enhance productivity, data integrity, and user satisfaction. By following best practices and leveraging the wide array of scripting tools available, HR teams can tailor processes to meet specific needs, ensure compliance, and drive strategic initiatives.

Integrating ServiceNow with Third-Party HR Applications

In today's interconnected HR ecosystem, seamless integration between various tools and platforms is essential to ensure cohesive operations and data continuity. ServiceNow, with its powerful integration capabilities, can serve as the hub for managing diverse HR processes. This chapter delves into how to integrate ServiceNow with third-party HR applications to enhance functionality, streamline processes, and drive operational efficiency.

1. The Importance of Integrating HR Applications

Integrating ServiceNow with third-party HR applications brings numerous benefits:

- **Centralized Data Management**: Consolidates HR data into a single source of truth.
- **Enhanced Process Automation**: Connects workflows across systems, reducing manual intervention.
- **Improved Data Accuracy**: Ensures real-time data synchronization and consistency across applications.
- **Streamlined Employee Experience**: Provides a seamless interaction for employees accessing HR services.

HR departments commonly integrate ServiceNow with applications like payroll systems, applicant tracking systems (ATS), learning management systems (LMS), and benefits management platforms.

2. Integration Techniques in ServiceNow

ServiceNow offers multiple methods for integration, each suited to different needs and levels of complexity:

2.1. IntegrationHub

IntegrationHub is ServiceNow's comprehensive tool for building integrations with other systems through no-code or low-code solutions. It offers pre-built spokes for popular HR platforms and enables rapid deployment of integrations.

Key Features:

- Drag-and-drop flow designer for integration logic.
- Pre-built connectors for popular HR services.
- Capable of handling both inbound and outbound data transfers.

2.2. REST and SOAP APIs

ServiceNow supports both **REST** and **SOAP** web services for integration with external platforms. These APIs allow HR teams to develop custom integrations tailored to specific needs.

REST API Integration Use Case: Integrating an HR benefits platform to update employee benefits information in real-time.

```
var client = new sn_ws.RESTMessageV2();
client.setEndpoint('https://api.hr-benefits-platform.com/employee');
client.setHttpMethod('POST');
client.setRequestBody(JSON.stringify({ employeeId: current.employee_id, benefits:
current.benefits }));
var response = client.execute();
```

2.3. Scripted Web Services

Scripted web services enable you to create custom API endpoints in ServiceNow that external applications can call. This approach is useful when existing API capabilities don't meet the integration requirements.

2.4. Middleware and iPaaS Solutions

For complex integrations involving multiple platforms, middleware or integration Platform as a Service (iPaaS) solutions such as **MuleSoft**, **Zapier**, or **Boomi** can be used. These tools simplify integration by providing connectors and data transformation capabilities.

3. Step-by-Step Guide to Integrating a Third-Party HR Application

3.1. Initial Planning and Assessment

- **Identify Business Objectives**: Define what HR goals you aim to achieve with the integration, such as automating employee onboarding or synchronizing payroll data.
- **Assess Data Flow**: Map the data flow between ServiceNow and the third-party HR system. Identify data sources, data types, and synchronization frequency.
- **Evaluate Security Protocols**: Ensure that both ServiceNow and the third-party application support secure data transfer methods, such as OAuth 2.0 or mutual TLS.

3.2. Setting Up IntegrationHub Spoke

1. **Install the Relevant Spoke**:
   - Navigate to the **IntegrationHub** module in ServiceNow and search for the spoke that corresponds to the third-party HR system.
2. **Configure Connection Details**:
   - Enter API credentials and endpoint URLs provided by the third-party system.
3. **Design Integration Flow**:
   - Use the **Flow Designer** to create a flow that triggers when certain conditions are met (e.g., an employee record is updated).

3.3. Developing Custom REST API Integrations

1. **Create REST Message**:
   - Go to **System Web Services > REST Message** and configure the HTTP method and endpoint.
2. **Set Up Authentication**:
   - Add authentication profiles for secure API access.
3. **Test and Validate**:
   - Use **REST API Explorer** to test the message and ensure data transfer is successful.

3.4. Building a Scripted Web Service

1. **Navigate to Scripted REST APIs**:
   - Go to **System Web Services > Scripted REST APIs**.
2. **Create a New API**:
   - Define the API name, path, and HTTP method.
3. **Write Custom Logic**:
   - Implement logic to process incoming requests and respond accordingly.

Example Script:

```
(function process(/*RESTAPIRequest*/ request, /*RESTAPIResponse*/ response) {
    var requestBody = JSON.parse(request.body.data);
```

```
    var employeeRecord = new GlideRecord('hr_employee');
    employeeRecord.addQuery('employee_number', requestBody.employeeId);
    employeeRecord.query();

    if (employeeRecord.next()) {
        // Update employee record logic
        employeeRecord.benefits_plan = requestBody.benefitsPlan;
        employeeRecord.update();
        response.setBody(JSON.stringify({ status: 'Success', message: 'Record
updated.' }));
    } else {
        response.setStatus(404);
        response.setBody(JSON.stringify({ status: 'Error', message: 'Employee not
found.' }));
    }
})(request, response);
```

4. Common Challenges and How to Overcome Them

4.1. Data Mapping and Transformation

Challenge: Ensuring consistent data formats between ServiceNow and external systems. **Solution**: Use data transformation scripts or middleware tools that map and convert data structures automatically.

4.2. Security Concerns

Challenge: Maintaining secure data exchange, especially when dealing with sensitive HR data. **Solution**: Implement industry-standard security protocols and ensure all API communications are encrypted.

4.3. Error Handling and Monitoring

Challenge: Managing errors and failures during data synchronization. **Solution**: Implement error-handling mechanisms and set up logging to monitor integration flows. Use ServiceNow's **IntegrationHub** for built-in error notifications and flow auditing.

5. Best Practices for Integrating ServiceNow with HR Applications

- **Start with a Pilot**: Test integrations on a subset of data before a full-scale rollout.
- **Document the Integration Process**: Keep detailed records of configuration settings and API documentation.
- **Continuous Monitoring**: Regularly monitor data flows and integration performance for any discrepancies or issues.
- **Version Control**: Maintain version histories of scripts and configurations to easily revert changes if needed.
- **Collaborate with IT and HR Teams**: Ensure ongoing communication between technical teams and HR staff to align on expectations and troubleshoot issues efficiently.

6. Real-World Example: Automating Payroll Data Sync

Use Case:

Integrating ServiceNow with an external payroll system to automate the updating of salary and benefits information as HR changes occur.

Solution:

- Configure a scheduled flow in **IntegrationHub** to push updates from ServiceNow to the payroll system every night.

- Use REST APIs for real-time updates when immediate changes are needed.

Outcome:

- Reduced manual entry, minimized errors, and maintained up-to-date payroll information.

Conclusion

Integrating ServiceNow with third-party HR applications empowers HR departments to streamline processes, improve efficiency, and deliver a unified employee experience. Whether using pre-built IntegrationHub spokes or custom API scripts, ServiceNow offers the flexibility and power to meet a variety of integration needs.

Using APIs for Enhanced HR Functionality

In modern HR operations, enhancing digital workflows often involves integrating various systems and automating data exchanges. ServiceNow's robust API capabilities allow organizations to extend the platform's functionality, create custom applications, and integrate third-party systems seamlessly. This chapter explores how HR teams can leverage ServiceNow's APIs for customized solutions, efficient data management, and improved employee services.

1. Introduction to ServiceNow's API Ecosystem

ServiceNow provides an extensive set of APIs that enable developers and HR teams to build custom applications, automate workflows, and integrate with other HR systems. The most commonly used APIs include:

- **REST API**: A widely adopted protocol used for building seamless integrations and custom solutions that communicate with external applications.
- **SOAP API**: Used for more complex integrations, typically in legacy systems where REST is not supported.
- **Scripted REST APIs**: Customized API endpoints within ServiceNow that allow specific business logic and data management.

2. Benefits of Using APIs for HR Processes

APIs open up a wide range of possibilities for HR operations:

- **Automated Data Synchronization**: Keep data synchronized between ServiceNow and external HR systems, such as payroll and benefits platforms.
- **Custom HR Applications**: Build specialized applications to meet unique HR needs without being confined to out-of-the-box solutions.
- **Enhanced Employee Self-Service**: Create customized service portals and integrate them with other tools to enhance user experience.
- **Improved Reporting and Analytics**: Use APIs to pull data from various sources, enabling comprehensive HR reporting and analytics.

3. Key API Use Cases for HR

3.1. Integrating with Payroll Systems

HR teams often need to ensure payroll systems are updated with accurate, real-time data regarding employee status, benefits, and deductions. By using ServiceNow's REST API, teams can automate these data exchanges, minimizing manual input and reducing errors.

Example Scenario: Automatically update payroll systems whenever there is a change in an employee's salary or benefits.

3.2. Employee Onboarding and Offboarding

APIs facilitate the automation of onboarding and offboarding workflows by integrating with external systems like identity management and IT provisioning tools. This helps create a seamless process where access credentials, equipment requests, and welcome communications are triggered by status changes in ServiceNow.

Key Steps:

1. Use REST API calls to initiate external service requests.
2. Implement custom notifications and task triggers through ServiceNow workflows.

3.3. Custom HR Reporting Dashboards

By using APIs to pull data from ServiceNow and other HR tools into a unified dashboard, HR teams can create comprehensive reports that provide deeper insights into workforce metrics and performance.

API Method:

- Use REST API GET requests to extract data from the HR table.
- Utilize JavaScript or data visualization tools to process and display the data.

4. Step-by-Step Guide: Implementing API Integrations

4.1. Setting Up REST API in ServiceNow

1. **Navigate to REST API Explorer**:
   - Go to **System Web Services > REST API Explorer**.
2. **Create a New API**:
   - Configure the HTTP method (e.g., GET, POST) and endpoint URL.
3. **Set Parameters and Authentication**:
   - Specify query parameters and headers.
   - Choose an authentication method, such as OAuth 2.0 or Basic Auth, for secure data exchanges.
4. **Test the API Call**:
   - Use the built-in testing tools to validate the functionality and output of your API.

4.2. Developing Scripted REST APIs

Scripted REST APIs allow HR teams to create tailored endpoints that handle specific data manipulations or workflow triggers.

Creating a Scripted REST API:

1. Navigate to **System Web Services > Scripted REST APIs** and create a new API.
2. Define the API path and HTTP methods.
3. Write server-side scripts to handle incoming requests and customize responses.

Example Script:

```
(function process(/*RESTAPIRequest*/ request, /*RESTAPIResponse*/ response) {
    var requestBody = request.body.data;
    var employee = new GlideRecord('hr_employee');
    employee.get('employee_number', requestBody.employeeId);

    if (employee.isValidRecord()) {
        employee.status = 'Active';
        employee.update();
        response.setStatus(200);
        response.setBody(JSON.stringify({ message: 'Employee status updated successfully' }));
    } else {
        response.setStatus(404);
        response.setBody(JSON.stringify({ error: 'Employee not found' }));
    }
})(request, response);
```

4.3. Integrating with External Systems

To integrate with external HR applications, establish secure connections using ServiceNow's built-in connection tools and API authentication options.

Tips:

- Use **OAuth 2.0** for secure, token-based authentication when connecting with external platforms.
- Schedule API calls to run at specific intervals for batch data processing.

5. Best Practices for API Management

5.1. Ensure Data Security and Compliance

- Implement authentication methods such as OAuth 2.0 to protect data transfers.
- Regularly audit API usage to maintain compliance with data privacy regulations, including GDPR.

5.2. Monitor and Log API Usage

- Use ServiceNow's monitoring tools to log API calls, measure response times, and identify any failures.
- Implement alert mechanisms for quick troubleshooting.

5.3. Version Control and Documentation

- Maintain clear documentation for all custom APIs, detailing endpoints, parameters, and sample payloads.
- Utilize version control to track changes and roll back if necessary.

6. Troubleshooting Common API Challenges

6.1. Authentication Failures

Ensure that authentication tokens are valid and properly configured. For OAuth 2.0, refresh tokens periodically to maintain uninterrupted access.

6.2. Data Formatting Errors

API calls may fail due to mismatched data formats. Use data transformation scripts to align incoming and outgoing data structures.

6.3. Rate Limiting and Performance Bottlenecks

Monitor API usage to prevent rate-limiting issues, especially when dealing with high-frequency calls. Optimize API logic to improve performance and minimize data retrieval times.

7. Real-World Example: Automated Leave Management Integration

Scenario: An HR team wants to synchronize leave requests between ServiceNow and their HR management system.

Approach:

1. Develop a REST API that triggers whenever a leave request is created or updated in ServiceNow.
2. Send API calls to the HR management system to update leave balances in real time.
3. Implement error handling to ensure data consistency across both platforms.

Conclusion

APIs provide a powerful tool for HR teams to enhance their digital workflows, integrate with external systems, and create customized HR solutions. By following best practices for API management and leveraging ServiceNow's scripting capabilities, HR teams can achieve greater efficiency and automation.

Incorporating AI and Machine Learning in HR Processes

The rapid advancements in technology have revolutionized how HR departments operate, and ServiceNow's integration capabilities with AI and Machine Learning (ML) are at the forefront of these innovations. By incorporating AI and ML into HR processes, organizations can enhance their efficiency, improve decision-making, and deliver personalized employee experiences. This chapter will explore the ways ServiceNow leverages AI and ML to optimize HR workflows and deliver tangible benefits to HR teams and employees alike.

1. The Role of AI and Machine Learning in Modern HR

AI and ML have become essential tools in HR, providing predictive insights and automating routine tasks. These technologies enable HR teams to:

- **Predict Workforce Trends**: Analyze historical data to forecast turnover rates and identify patterns that indicate potential challenges.
- **Automate Routine Processes**: Streamline repetitive tasks, such as responding to common HR queries or managing simple workflows, through chatbots and intelligent automation.
- **Personalize Employee Interactions**: Tailor communication and solutions to individual employees based on their preferences and previous interactions.
- **Improve Data-Driven Decision Making**: Leverage data analysis tools to enhance strategic decisions related to recruitment, training, and employee retention.

2. ServiceNow's AI Capabilities for HR

ServiceNow provides built-in AI and ML functionalities that HR teams can harness for improved service delivery. Key capabilities include:

- **Virtual Agents**: AI-driven chatbots that can handle common employee queries, provide instant responses, and reduce the workload on HR teams.
- **Predictive Intelligence**: Machine learning algorithms that analyze data trends and recommend actions, such as routing HR cases to the most appropriate team or suggesting relevant articles to employees.
- **Intelligent Workflows**: AI-powered workflows that automate repetitive HR processes, such as benefits enrollment, leave management, and employee onboarding.

2.1. Virtual Agents for HR Support

ServiceNow's virtual agents are designed to interact with employees, providing answers to frequently asked questions and guiding them through self-service tasks. These agents are customizable, allowing HR teams to tailor responses and integrate them with other HR systems.

Benefits:

- 24/7 support for employees.
- Reduced volume of HR service desk tickets.
- Consistent and accurate responses.

Implementation Tip: To maximize the effectiveness of virtual agents, HR teams should map out common employee queries and train the AI models using relevant data.

2.2. Predictive Intelligence for Case Management

Predictive intelligence in ServiceNow helps HR teams automatically classify and assign cases based on historical data. This technology ensures that cases are routed to the right personnel, reducing response times and enhancing employee satisfaction.

Example Use Case: When an employee submits a case related to payroll, predictive intelligence can recognize the keywords and route the case to the payroll specialist team, bypassing manual triage.

Configuration Steps:

1. Access the **Predictive Intelligence Workbench**.
2. Define training data sets and input historical HR cases.
3. Train the model and test its predictive accuracy.
4. Deploy the model into live HR case management workflows.

3. Enhancing HR Workflows with Machine Learning

Machine learning models within ServiceNow can identify patterns and make data-driven recommendations for process optimization. HR departments can leverage ML to:

- **Optimize Recruitment Processes**: Screen resumes more effectively by using ML algorithms that match candidate skills with job requirements.
- **Enhance Training Programs**: Analyze employee performance data to recommend targeted training modules and development paths.
- **Reduce Response Times**: Use historical data to forecast HR service request volumes and allocate resources more efficiently.

ML Integration Example: A company uses ServiceNow's ML tools to predict spikes in leave requests during peak holiday seasons. This insight allows HR to allocate support staff proactively, minimizing delays and maintaining service quality.

4. Implementing AI and ML in ServiceNow HR

4.1. Steps to Get Started with AI and ML

1. **Identify HR Processes for Automation**: Start by listing the HR processes that can benefit from AI and ML, such as employee onboarding, document verification, and case routing.
2. **Set Up Data Sources**: Ensure that data used for AI and ML models is clean, comprehensive, and up-to-date. Integrate data from various HR systems if necessary.
3. **Configure AI Models**: Use ServiceNow's **AI Model Builder** to configure and train custom models tailored to specific HR needs.
4. **Monitor Performance**: Continuously monitor AI and ML model performance, using feedback loops to fine-tune algorithms and improve accuracy.

4.2. Best Practices for Successful Implementation

- **Start with High-Impact Areas**: Focus initial efforts on processes that will provide the most significant return on investment, such as employee support through virtual agents.
- **Maintain Data Privacy**: Ensure that data used in AI and ML models complies with privacy regulations and is anonymized where necessary.
- **Train HR Staff**: Provide training to HR teams on how to interpret and act on AI-generated insights and reports.

5. Challenges and Solutions

5.1. Data Quality Issues

AI and ML models are only as good as the data they rely on. Poor data quality can lead to inaccurate predictions and reduced effectiveness.

Solution: Implement robust data governance practices and periodically audit data sources to ensure consistency and accuracy.

5.2. User Adoption

Employees and HR professionals may be hesitant to adopt AI-driven tools due to unfamiliarity or fear of job displacement.

Solution: Emphasize the complementary nature of AI and human work, highlighting how these tools assist rather than replace HR professionals. Offer training and onboarding sessions for new tools.

5.3. Balancing Automation and Personalization

While automation improves efficiency, it's crucial to maintain a personal touch in HR services.

Solution: Utilize AI and ML for initial responses and routine tasks while reserving more complex or sensitive interactions for HR professionals.

6. Future of AI and ML in HR

The potential for AI and ML in HR continues to expand as technology advances. Emerging trends include:

- **Emotion Recognition**: AI tools capable of understanding the emotional tone of employee interactions to tailor responses.
- **Proactive Support**: Predictive models that anticipate employee needs and proactively offer assistance.
- **Advanced Analytics**: Enhanced data analytics that offer deep insights into employee engagement, retention risks, and workforce planning.

Conclusion

Integrating AI and Machine Learning into HR processes on the ServiceNow platform opens up a realm of possibilities for automation, enhanced decision-making, and personalized service delivery. As HR technology evolves, these tools will become indispensable in creating more efficient, data-driven, and employee-centric HR operations.

Optimizing Mobile Access for HR Services

As modern HR teams evolve, ensuring that employees can access HR services seamlessly from any location has become a necessity. The shift towards a mobile-first approach has been driven by the need for real-time information, flexibility, and improved user experience. ServiceNow provides robust tools for optimizing mobile access, empowering HR teams to deliver services efficiently and enabling employees to access vital HR functionalities from their mobile devices.

This chapter covers strategies for enhancing mobile access to HR services within ServiceNow, exploring best practices, configuration techniques, and benefits to employees and HR teams alike.

1. The Importance of Mobile Access in HR

In today's fast-paced work environment, employees often require immediate access to HR services and support. Whether they are in the office, traveling, or working remotely, mobile access allows employees to:

- **Submit HR Requests on the Go**: From submitting leave requests to reporting workplace incidents, mobile access facilitates real-time interaction with HR systems.
- **Stay Updated**: Receive notifications and updates related to HR cases or new policy changes directly on mobile devices.
- **Access Self-Service Tools**: Empower employees to find answers and resolve common issues themselves through mobile-friendly self-service portals.

Benefits to HR Teams:

- Increased employee engagement and satisfaction.
- Reduced load on HR departments by streamlining simple processes through self-service features.
- Enhanced data collection and process transparency.

2. Configuring Mobile Access in ServiceNow

ServiceNow offers a dedicated mobile app and web-based mobile configurations that HR departments can tailor to fit their needs. Configuring these features ensures that employees can interact with HR services efficiently and securely.

2.1. Setting Up the ServiceNow Mobile App

The ServiceNow mobile app is a key tool for delivering mobile access. HR teams can customize the app to reflect the specific needs of the organization.

Steps to Configure the Mobile App:

1. **Download and Install the App**: Ensure that employees have the ServiceNow mobile app installed on their devices.
2. **Enable Mobile Views**: Use the ServiceNow platform to create mobile-specific views for different HR services and workflows.
3. **Configure Quick Actions**: Set up shortcuts for frequently used services such as leave requests, policy lookups, and HR case submissions.
4. **Test and Optimize**: Test the app for usability and performance, making adjustments as necessary to enhance user experience.

2.2. Creating Mobile-Friendly HR Portals

ServiceNow allows for the creation of custom portals optimized for mobile devices. These portals ensure that employees have quick and intuitive access to HR services.

Key Considerations:

- **Responsive Design**: Ensure that the portal layout adapts to various screen sizes for a seamless experience on smartphones and tablets.
- **Intuitive Navigation**: Simplify the navigation to make it easy for employees to find what they need without excessive scrolling or clicks.
- **Accessible Features**: Prioritize important HR functionalities, such as case submission, document access, and self-help resources, in the portal's design.

Best Practices:

- Use icons and concise labels for quick identification of features.
- Incorporate a search function to help employees find information easily.

3. Mobile Workflow Automation

ServiceNow's mobile capabilities extend beyond access; they support automated HR workflows that employees can initiate and complete through their mobile devices. This includes:

- **Approvals and Sign-Offs**: Managers can approve leave requests or expense claims directly from their mobile devices.
- **Automated Notifications**: Employees receive automatic notifications regarding the status of their cases or upcoming deadlines.
- **Document Uploads**: Allow employees to upload necessary documents or photos via their mobile devices for HR processes such as onboarding or benefits enrollment.

3.1. Setting Up Automated Mobile Workflows

1. **Design the Workflow**: Use ServiceNow's workflow designer to map out the steps of the HR process, specifying mobile accessibility.
2. **Configure Triggers**: Set up triggers for mobile notifications or actions based on events (e.g., approval requests).
3. **Test Workflow Compatibility**: Ensure that the automated workflow functions seamlessly on mobile devices.

4. Security Considerations for Mobile Access

Ensuring data security is paramount when enabling mobile access to HR services. HR data often contains sensitive employee information, so it is critical to implement robust security protocols.

4.1. Implementing Mobile Security Best Practices

- **Authentication**: Use multi-factor authentication (MFA) to verify user identity and secure access.
- **Data Encryption**: Ensure that all data transmitted between the mobile device and the ServiceNow platform is encrypted.
- **Session Management**: Implement automatic logout features and session timeouts to protect data from unauthorized access.

4.2. Employee Training for Mobile Security

Educate employees on safe practices when using mobile devices for HR processes, including:

- Using strong, unique passwords.
- Avoiding public Wi-Fi for accessing HR systems.
- Reporting lost or stolen devices promptly to the HR department or IT team.

5. Enhancing the Employee Experience through Mobile Access

Mobile access isn't just about convenience—it's about creating a positive user experience that enhances employee satisfaction and productivity.

5.1. Personalized Mobile Dashboards

Custom dashboards tailored to individual roles or departments can help employees quickly access relevant HR services. For example:

- **New Hires**: A dashboard that highlights onboarding tasks and resources.
- **Managers**: A dashboard with tools for approving requests and managing team documents.

5.2. Feedback Mechanisms

Incorporate feedback tools within the mobile interface, allowing employees to rate their experience and provide suggestions. This feedback helps HR teams refine mobile services to better meet employee needs.

6. Challenges and Solutions in Mobile Access Implementation

6.1. Limited Connectivity

Challenge: Employees in areas with limited internet access may experience difficulties using mobile HR services. **Solution**: Implement offline capabilities for essential features so employees can continue using the platform and sync data once connected.

6.2. Device Compatibility

Challenge: Ensuring that the mobile platform works across different devices and operating systems. **Solution**: Regularly test and update the mobile configurations to align with device compatibility standards.

Conclusion

Optimizing mobile access for HR services is a strategic investment that benefits both employees and HR departments. With ServiceNow's mobile tools, organizations can create a seamless, efficient, and secure environment for HR interactions, enabling employees to stay connected and engaged from anywhere.

Section 7:
Change Management and User Training

Managing Change Effectively During Implementation

Implementing ServiceNow for HR processes involves more than just technological changes; it requires managing the human aspect of transformation to ensure a smooth transition and widespread adoption. Change management is critical to the successful rollout of any new system, and its importance becomes even more pronounced in the context of HR processes that directly impact every employee in an organization. This chapter will explore best practices for managing change during the implementation of ServiceNow, addressing strategies that help build trust, minimize resistance, and promote a culture that embraces digital workflows.

1. The Importance of Change Management

Change management involves preparing, equipping, and supporting employees to successfully adopt change to drive organizational success. Effective change management can result in:

- **Higher Adoption Rates**: Employees are more likely to embrace new processes if they are informed and prepared.
- **Reduced Resistance**: Proactive management can help address concerns, alleviate fears, and reduce resistance to new systems.
- **Improved Morale and Productivity**: A well-handled transition ensures that employees feel supported and confident in their roles, maintaining productivity levels.
- **Long-Term Sustainability**: Ensuring that the change is integrated smoothly helps establish long-lasting improvements.

2. Building a Change Management Strategy

A structured approach to change management is essential for the successful implementation of ServiceNow. The following strategies can help build an effective change management plan:

2.1. Communicate Early and Often

Key Principle: Transparent and continuous communication builds trust and engagement.

Action Steps:

- **Develop a Communication Plan**: Outline what information needs to be shared, when, and through which channels.
- **Tailor Messages to Different Audiences**: Address the unique concerns and needs of HR teams, managers, and employees.
- **Highlight the Benefits**: Emphasize the advantages that the new system will bring, such as time savings, easier access to services, and improved HR support.

2.2. Involve Key Stakeholders

Key Principle: Including stakeholders in the process fosters a sense of ownership and commitment.

Action Steps:

- **Identify Key Stakeholders**: Include HR leadership, team managers, IT professionals, and influential employees.
- **Gather Feedback**: Use workshops, surveys, and meetings to collect input that can inform the implementation plan.
- **Create a Change Network**: Designate change ambassadors within different departments who can champion the new system and provide support to their peers.

2.3. Provide Clear Training and Support

Key Principle: Comprehensive training reduces uncertainty and builds competence.

Action Steps:

- **Develop Training Programs**: Design training that suits various learning styles, including hands-on workshops, tutorials, and virtual training sessions.
- **Create a Resource Library**: Provide accessible documentation, FAQs, and video guides.
- **Set Up a Help Desk**: Ensure that employees have a dedicated support channel to address any questions or issues.

2.4. Plan for Gradual Implementation

Key Principle: A phased rollout helps manage the scale of change and allows for adjustments along the way.

Action Steps:

- **Pilot Program**: Launch the system with a small group to identify potential issues and collect initial feedback.
- **Iterative Rollout**: Gradually expand implementation to other parts of the organization, using lessons learned to refine processes.
- **Monitor Progress**: Use data and feedback to track the rollout's success and make adjustments as needed.

3. Addressing Resistance to Change

Resistance to change is natural, and HR leaders must be prepared to address it proactively. The following strategies can help mitigate resistance:

3.1. Understand Common Concerns

Employee Concerns:

- Fear of job displacement or increased workload.
- Uncertainty about mastering a new system.
- Concerns about data security and privacy.

Response Strategies:

- **Provide Reassurance**: Communicate that the change aims to enhance roles and streamline work, not replace human expertise.
- **Highlight Security Measures**: Ensure employees know about the robust data security protocols in place.
- **Acknowledge and Validate Feelings**: Recognize that change can be challenging and show empathy to employees' concerns.

3.2. Create Feedback Loops

Key Principle: Continuous feedback helps address issues early and fosters a sense of involvement.

Action Steps:

- **Regular Check-Ins**: Schedule team meetings to gather input and address questions.
- **Anonymous Feedback Channels**: Allow employees to share concerns without fear of repercussion.
- **Act on Feedback**: Demonstrate that feedback is valued by implementing changes or addressing concerns when possible.

4. Maintaining Momentum Post-Implementation

Sustaining change is just as crucial as the initial rollout. Organizations should focus on the following practices to maintain momentum:

4.1. Celebrate Milestones

Key Principle: Recognizing progress boosts morale and reinforces positive attitudes toward the new system.

Action Steps:

- **Acknowledge Achievements**: Highlight successful case studies and stories within the organization.
- **Incentivize Early Adopters**: Reward individuals or teams that show outstanding adaptation to the new system.

4.2. Foster Continuous Learning

Key Principle: Learning should be ongoing to ensure that employees stay up to date with system improvements and best practices.

Action Steps:

- **Offer Refresher Courses**: Provide periodic training sessions to cover updates and advanced features.
- **Update Resource Libraries**: Keep training materials and guides current with new information.
- **Promote Peer Support**: Encourage a culture where employees help each other learn and grow.

5. Case Study: Successful Change Management in Practice

Example: An international company rolled out ServiceNow for HR with a phased approach that involved:

- **Pilot Testing**: Testing the new system in one regional office.
- **Stakeholder Engagement**: Involving key HR leaders in planning and rollout.
- **Comprehensive Training**: Offering live sessions, recorded tutorials, and an FAQ database.
- **Feedback Integration**: Actively adjusting the system based on user feedback from the pilot group.

Results:

- **High Adoption Rates**: Employees reported increased satisfaction and confidence in accessing HR services.
- **Reduced Resistance**: Clear communication and training minimized pushback.
- **Improved Efficiency**: The HR team experienced a notable decrease in repetitive administrative tasks.

Conclusion

Managing change effectively during the implementation of ServiceNow for HR processes is a multifaceted effort that prioritizes communication, training, and support. By addressing potential resistance, involving stakeholders, and celebrating progress, HR leaders can facilitate a successful transition that leads to sustained productivity and improved employee experience.

Training HR Teams to Use ServiceNow Effectively

Training HR teams is a crucial component of successfully implementing ServiceNow for HR processes. Proper training ensures that HR professionals are equipped with the necessary skills to maximize the platform's capabilities, foster user confidence, and reduce potential disruptions during the transition. This chapter outlines practical strategies and best practices for designing comprehensive training programs that empower HR teams to use ServiceNow effectively and efficiently.

1. The Importance of Comprehensive Training

Effective training helps bridge the gap between the introduction of a new system and its optimal use in daily HR activities. The benefits of a thorough training program include:

- **Increased Productivity**: Skilled HR teams can navigate the platform with ease, completing tasks faster and more accurately.
- **Reduced Resistance**: Training alleviates the apprehension associated with new technology, encouraging team buy-in.
- **Enhanced User Confidence**: Well-trained HR professionals feel more confident in their roles, promoting smoother adoption.
- **Long-Term Efficiency**: Continuous learning ensures HR teams remain adept as new features and updates are introduced.

2. Designing an Effective Training Program

A successful training program should cater to the diverse needs of HR team members and align with the specific functions they perform. Below are key steps to consider when designing an HR training program for ServiceNow.

2.1. Assess Training Needs

Key Principle: Identify the specific knowledge gaps and skill levels within the HR team.

Action Steps:

- **Conduct a Needs Assessment**: Use surveys, interviews, and skills evaluations to understand the current level of familiarity with digital tools.
- **Define Training Objectives**: Tailor training goals to match the HR team's roles, from data management to advanced reporting.

2.2. Develop Customized Training Content

Key Principle: Training content should be relevant, practical, and easy to understand.

Action Steps:

- **Create Role-Based Modules**: Design modules that focus on different HR functions, such as employee onboarding, case management, and benefits administration.
- **Incorporate Real-World Scenarios**: Use examples and scenarios that HR professionals encounter daily to make training relatable.
- **Include Interactive Elements**: Utilize hands-on practice sessions, quizzes, and interactive workshops for better engagement and retention.

2.3. Choose the Right Training Methods

Key Principle: Combine various training methods to accommodate different learning preferences.

Training Formats:

- **Instructor-Led Training (ILT)**: Conduct in-person or virtual sessions led by an experienced trainer for real-time interaction and feedback.
- **E-Learning Modules**: Offer self-paced digital courses that HR teams can complete on their own schedule.
- **Workshops and Labs**: Organize hands-on workshops that allow HR professionals to practice using ServiceNow in a controlled environment.
- **On-the-Job Training**: Implement shadowing and mentoring programs where experienced users guide newer team members.

2.4. Provide Comprehensive Resources

Key Principle: Ensure that resources are easily accessible for continuous learning.

Resources to Include:

- **User Guides and Manuals**: Provide step-by-step written guides with screenshots and detailed instructions.
- **Video Tutorials**: Create short, topic-specific videos demonstrating key processes.
- **FAQs and Troubleshooting Tips**: Compile a list of common questions and solutions to help HR teams address issues independently.
- **Helpdesk Support**: Offer access to a dedicated support team that can provide assistance as needed.

3. Encouraging Engagement and Participation

Training is most effective when HR team members are actively engaged. Here are strategies to enhance participation:

3.1. Foster a Collaborative Learning Environment

Key Principle: Create a sense of community where HR team members can learn from one another.

Action Steps:

- **Peer Learning Groups**: Form small groups that can collaborate, share insights, and discuss challenges during training.
- **Feedback Loops**: Regularly solicit feedback to improve training sessions and address any gaps or areas of difficulty.
- **Recognition and Incentives**: Acknowledge employees who complete training milestones with certificates or incentives to encourage participation.

3.2. Implement Continuous Training

Key Principle: Training should not be a one-time event but an ongoing process.

Action Steps:

- **Refresher Courses**: Schedule periodic refresher sessions to reinforce learning and introduce updates to the platform.
- **Advanced Training Workshops**: Provide advanced training for HR team members who want to deepen their knowledge and expertise.
- **Learning Paths for New Employees**: Integrate ServiceNow training into the onboarding process for new HR staff to ensure consistency.

4. Measuring Training Effectiveness

It's essential to evaluate the effectiveness of training programs to make necessary adjustments and enhance future training efforts.

4.1. Collect Feedback

Action Steps:

- **Post-Training Surveys**: Collect feedback from participants to assess the clarity, relevance, and usefulness of the training.
- **One-on-One Reviews**: Conduct individual reviews with team members to understand their comfort level with the platform.

4.2. Track Performance Metrics

Key Metrics:

- **User Adoption Rates**: Monitor how quickly and effectively HR teams begin using ServiceNow in their workflows.
- **Task Completion Time**: Evaluate whether tasks are being completed more efficiently after training.
- **Error Rates**: Track any reduction in errors when performing HR functions using ServiceNow.

4.3. Adjust and Improve

Key Principle: Use insights gained from feedback and performance metrics to refine future training initiatives.

Action Steps:

- **Identify Areas for Improvement**: Adjust training materials and methods based on the feedback received.
- **Update Content Regularly**: Ensure training content remains current with ServiceNow's latest updates and features.
- **Celebrate Successes**: Share success stories from training programs to motivate and inspire the HR team.

5. Case Study: A Successful Training Implementation

Example: A multinational company implemented ServiceNow for HR services and designed a comprehensive training program that included:

- **Role-Based Training Modules** tailored to different HR functions.
- **Live Workshops and Webinars** for in-depth learning and Q&A sessions.
- **Follow-Up Support** with a dedicated helpdesk and peer support groups.

Results:

- **High Adoption Rate**: 90% of the HR team reported feeling confident in using ServiceNow within the first two months.
- **Improved Efficiency**: The team experienced a 30% reduction in time spent on routine HR tasks.
- **Positive Feedback**: The training program received high ratings for clarity, engagement, and practical relevance.

Conclusion: Training HR teams to use ServiceNow effectively is a multifaceted process that requires thoughtful planning, customization, and continuous improvement. By investing in comprehensive training programs, HR leaders can ensure their teams are well-prepared to leverage the full potential of ServiceNow, enhancing both employee and organizational outcomes.

Designing User Guides and Training Materials

Creating comprehensive user guides and training materials is an essential step in ensuring that HR teams can effectively use ServiceNow in their daily operations. Well-designed documentation empowers users to become self-sufficient, encourages the adoption of new workflows, and helps maintain consistency across HR processes. This chapter will guide you through best practices for developing effective user guides and training resources tailored to HR needs.

1. The Importance of User Guides and Training Materials

User guides and training materials serve as critical reference points for HR professionals navigating ServiceNow. Proper documentation:

- **Reduces Dependency on Support Teams**: Detailed guides help users resolve common issues independently, decreasing the load on IT and support teams.
- **Enhances Knowledge Retention**: Written and visual materials reinforce learning from initial training sessions.
- **Ensures Consistent Application**: Uniform documentation helps maintain consistency in how processes are applied throughout the HR department.
- **Supports New Staff Onboarding**: Well-crafted guides provide a seamless way for new employees to get up to speed quickly.

2. Key Components of Effective User Guides

To create user guides that are clear, comprehensive, and easy to follow, consider including the following components:

2.1. Introduction and Purpose

Key Principle: Begin each guide by explaining its purpose and which HR processes it covers.

Action Steps:

- Clearly define the guide's objective.
- State the target audience (e.g., HR managers, general HR staff, IT support).

2.2. Step-by-Step Instructions

Key Principle: Provide detailed, sequential instructions for completing tasks in ServiceNow.

Action Steps:

- Break down processes into smaller, manageable steps.
- Use numbered lists or bullet points for easy reading.
- Highlight important actions or decisions that may require user input.

Example: *Creating a Case in ServiceNow* might include steps such as:

1. Navigate to the "HR Cases" module.
2. Click on "New Case."
3. Enter the relevant employee information.
4. Select the appropriate case type from the dropdown menu.

2.3. Screenshots and Visual Aids

Key Principle: Visual elements support textual instructions and enhance comprehension.

Action Steps:

- Include screenshots for each major step, showing the interface and relevant actions.
- Use annotations, such as arrows or highlights, to draw attention to key areas.
- Ensure screenshots are clear and up to date, reflecting the current version of ServiceNow.

2.4. Troubleshooting Tips

Key Principle: Anticipate common questions or issues that users may face and provide solutions.

Action Steps:

- Add a "Troubleshooting" section at the end of the guide.
- Include frequently asked questions (FAQs) related to the process.
- Offer clear resolutions for typical problems, such as login issues or navigation errors.

3. Developing Comprehensive Training Materials

Training materials should complement user guides and cater to different learning styles. Below are strategies for creating engaging training resources:

3.1. Formats of Training Materials

Key Principle: Use a mix of formats to appeal to various learning preferences.

Training Formats:

- **Written Manuals**: Ideal for step-by-step learning and as reference materials.
- **Video Tutorials**: Great for visual learners and demonstrating complex actions.
- **Interactive Presentations**: Engaging for group training sessions.
- **Quick Reference Cards**: Concise summaries for frequently used tasks.

3.2. Structuring Training Content

Key Principle: Organize training materials in a logical flow that builds upon foundational knowledge.

Action Steps:

- Start with basic navigation and fundamental tasks in ServiceNow.
- Gradually progress to more advanced functions, such as workflow automation and reporting.
- Use real-world HR scenarios to make training relatable and practical.

3.3. Incorporating Hands-On Practice

Key Principle: Hands-on practice is essential for skill retention and confidence building.

Action Steps:

- Create sandbox environments where HR teams can practice without risk.
- Include exercises and mock cases for trainees to complete.
- Provide feedback on practice sessions to reinforce learning.

4. Tips for Ensuring Effective Documentation and Training

4.1. Keep Content Updated

Key Principle: Regularly review and update user guides and training materials to reflect new features and system updates.

Action Steps:

- Schedule periodic reviews of documentation.
- Update screenshots and instructions following system updates or workflow changes.
- Communicate changes to HR teams promptly.

4.2. Make Materials Accessible

Key Principle: Ensure that documentation and training resources are easily accessible to all HR staff.

Action Steps:

- Store guides and training content on a centralized, easily accessible platform, such as the company intranet or a knowledge base.
- Offer digital and printed formats to suit different preferences.

4.3. Gather Feedback and Iterate

Key Principle: Collect feedback from HR teams to improve the relevance and clarity of documentation and training.

Action Steps:

- Conduct post-training surveys to gather feedback on the usefulness of the materials.
- Encourage HR staff to suggest areas for further detail or clarity.
- Regularly incorporate feedback into updates.

5. Case Study: Successful Implementation of Training Materials

Example: A medium-sized enterprise that implemented ServiceNow developed role-specific user guides for HR functions, complemented by video tutorials and interactive workshops. The result was a marked increase in HR process efficiency and a significant decrease in support tickets related to basic navigation and task execution.

Results:

- **User Satisfaction**: 95% of HR team members reported being satisfied with the training resources provided.
- **Improved Efficiency**: Average task completion time decreased by 25%.
- **Reduced Support Dependence**: Support requests related to system use dropped by 40% within the first three months.

Conclusion

Designing user guides and training materials tailored to your HR team's needs ensures a seamless and confident adoption of ServiceNow. These resources not only empower team members to perform their roles more effectively but also foster a culture of continuous learning and self-reliance.

Ensuring User Adoption and Engagement

Implementing ServiceNow for HR is only the beginning of digital transformation. The real challenge lies in ensuring that HR teams not only use the new system but engage with it effectively and consistently. User adoption and engagement are critical for maximizing the return on investment (ROI) in ServiceNow and achieving sustainable improvements in HR processes. This chapter will outline practical strategies for driving adoption and fostering continuous engagement among HR users.

1. The Importance of User Adoption and Engagement

User adoption and engagement are essential for realizing the benefits of a new system. Without proper adoption:

- **Productivity May Decline**: If HR staff are not confident using ServiceNow, productivity may suffer.
- **Resistance to Change**: A lack of engagement can lead to a preference for legacy systems or outdated processes.
- **Missed Opportunities for Improvement**: Engaged users are more likely to suggest optimizations and identify opportunities to streamline HR operations.

2. Strategies for Maximizing User Adoption

2.1. Effective Communication

Key Principle: Open, transparent communication helps build trust and eases the transition to new tools.

Action Steps:

- **Announce Changes Early**: Inform HR teams about the upcoming implementation well in advance. Explain the reasons for the change and the expected benefits.
- **Regular Updates**: Provide regular progress updates to keep users informed about the implementation status.
- **Two-Way Communication**: Encourage feedback and questions. Address concerns proactively to alleviate anxiety.

2.2. Comprehensive Training Programs

Key Principle: Training is a cornerstone of successful user adoption.

Action Steps:

- **Tailored Training Sessions**: Customize training programs based on user roles (e.g., HR managers, general HR staff, administrators).
- **Interactive Workshops**: Incorporate interactive elements such as Q&A sessions and hands-on practice.
- **Follow-Up Training**: Offer periodic refresher courses to reinforce learning and introduce new system features.

2.3. Demonstrating Value Early

Key Principle: Users are more likely to engage when they see immediate benefits.

Action Steps:

- **Quick Wins**: Identify and showcase features that provide quick, noticeable improvements to HR workflows.

- **Success Stories**: Share examples of team members who have benefited from the system, highlighting improvements in their tasks or productivity.

2.4. Assigning System Champions

Key Principle: Designating system champions helps encourage wider adoption and provides a point of reference for other users.

Action Steps:

- **Choose Advocates**: Select tech-savvy and enthusiastic HR team members to act as champions and mentors.
- **Empower with Knowledge**: Provide champions with additional training so they can support their colleagues effectively.
- **Recognition**: Acknowledge and reward champions for their role in facilitating user adoption.

3. Techniques for Sustaining Engagement

3.1. Continuous Support and Resources

Key Principle: Ensuring that users have ongoing support sustains long-term engagement.

Action Steps:

- **Accessible Support Channels**: Offer multiple support options, such as an internal helpdesk, chat support, or peer support groups.
- **Resource Library**: Maintain a repository of user guides, video tutorials, and FAQs.
- **Scheduled Office Hours**: Hold regular office hours where HR staff can drop in to ask questions and get assistance.

3.2. Encouraging Feedback and Iteration

Key Principle: Gathering user feedback fosters a sense of ownership and facilitates continuous improvement.

Action Steps:

- **Surveys and Polls**: Periodically survey users to gauge their satisfaction and gather suggestions for enhancements.
- **Feedback Loops**: Act on feedback by making adjustments and communicating the changes back to users.
- **Feedback Forums**: Create spaces for users to share their experiences and ideas, such as monthly meetings or digital forums.

3.3. Keeping Users Informed About Updates

Key Principle: Users are more likely to remain engaged if they know the system is evolving to meet their needs.

Action Steps:

- **Update Briefings**: Hold regular briefings to inform users about new ServiceNow features or updates.
- **Highlight Benefits**: Clearly explain how new features will improve their day-to-day tasks.
- **Change Announcements**: Notify users well in advance when updates or significant changes are planned.

4. Measuring Success in User Adoption

4.1. Key Performance Indicators (KPIs)

Key Principle: Establishing KPIs helps track adoption progress and engagement levels.

Suggested KPIs:

- **System Usage Rate**: Measure how frequently HR teams use ServiceNow compared to legacy systems.
- **Training Completion Rates**: Track how many users have completed training programs.
- **Support Ticket Volume**: Monitor the number and types of support requests to identify common issues.
- **User Satisfaction Scores**: Use post-training surveys and periodic polls to assess user satisfaction and engagement.

4.2. Analyzing Data for Continuous Improvement

Key Principle: Regular analysis of adoption data enables the refinement of engagement strategies.

Action Steps:

- **Review Usage Reports**: Analyze usage data to identify underutilized features and address potential gaps in training.
- **Feedback Analysis**: Review feedback and suggestions from users to identify recurring themes.
- **Adjust Strategies**: Modify training, support, or communication strategies based on data insights.

5. Case Study: Achieving High Adoption Rates

Example: A multinational corporation implemented ServiceNow for HR and saw impressive user adoption rates by employing a comprehensive approach that included extensive communication, role-specific training, and the establishment of system champions. They measured success through KPIs such as user satisfaction scores and system usage metrics, achieving a 90% adoption rate within six months.

Results:

- **Improved Efficiency**: HR processes became 20% faster due to better engagement.
- **Reduced Support Dependency**: A 30% drop in support tickets related to process navigation.
- **High Satisfaction**: 85% of users reported being confident in using ServiceNow for their daily tasks.

Conclusion

Ensuring user adoption and engagement is not a one-time effort but an ongoing process. By combining effective training, continuous support, and active communication, HR teams can be empowered to fully leverage ServiceNow's capabilities, leading to more efficient operations and a positive impact on the entire organization.

Continuous Feedback Loops for User Experience Improvement

Ensuring that HR teams not only adopt ServiceNow but also continually improve how they use it requires a focus on continuous feedback. A well-established feedback loop is vital for fostering engagement, identifying challenges early, and enhancing user experience. This chapter outlines strategies for setting up and maintaining effective feedback mechanisms to drive long-term improvement and user satisfaction.

1. The Importance of Continuous Feedback

Continuous feedback allows organizations to:

- **Identify Gaps and Pain Points**: Pinpoint areas where users encounter difficulties or inefficiencies.
- **Adapt to User Needs**: Modify and refine workflows based on user input, making the system more aligned with real-world HR needs.
- **Boost User Engagement**: Involving users in the process gives them a sense of ownership and encourages active participation.
- **Maintain High Adoption Rates**: Addressing user concerns promptly ensures the system remains a preferred tool for HR processes.

2. Setting Up Effective Feedback Channels

2.1. Surveys and Questionnaires

Key Principle: Structured surveys provide quantitative insights into user satisfaction and areas for improvement.

Best Practices:

- **Keep It Short and Specific**: Design concise surveys that target specific aspects of the user experience.
- **Schedule Regularly**: Conduct surveys at consistent intervals (e.g., quarterly) to track changes over time.
- **Anonymity Option**: Offer users the choice to provide feedback anonymously to encourage honest input.

2.2. Feedback Forums and Meetings

Key Principle: Real-time discussions help gather qualitative feedback and build a community of practice.

Approach:

- **Host Regular Meetings**: Organize monthly or bi-monthly meetings where HR team members can voice their feedback.
- **Include All User Levels**: Ensure that feedback meetings include a mix of end-users, administrators, and decision-makers.
- **Action-Oriented Discussions**: Focus on actionable insights and solutions during these sessions.

2.3. Integrated Feedback Tools

Key Principle: Embedding feedback tools directly into ServiceNow simplifies the process for users to provide ongoing input.

Implementation Tips:

- **User-Friendly Interface**: Ensure feedback tools are easy to use and accessible within the ServiceNow platform.
- **Immediate Feedback Prompts**: Include prompts after completing major tasks or processes to gather immediate responses.
- **Track and Display Progress**: Show users how their feedback has been acted upon to reinforce that their input is valued.

3. Analyzing and Acting on Feedback

3.1. Collecting and Categorizing Feedback

Key Principle: Organize feedback to identify common themes and prioritize improvements.

Methods:

- **Categorize by Theme**: Group feedback into themes such as system performance, usability, and specific workflow issues.
- **Use Analytics Tools**: Leverage data analysis tools to process and visualize feedback trends.
- **Create a Feedback Dashboard**: Build a dashboard within ServiceNow that tracks feedback trends and highlights critical issues.

3.2. Developing a Response Plan

Key Principle: Act on feedback in a structured and transparent manner.

Steps:

- **Prioritize by Impact**: Address feedback that affects a significant portion of users or has the greatest potential for improvement.
- **Create Action Plans**: For each major feedback point, outline a plan that includes timelines, responsible parties, and expected outcomes.
- **Communicate Progress**: Update users on how their feedback is being implemented, reinforcing their engagement and trust in the process.

3.3. Iterative Improvements

Key Principle: Continuous improvement involves revisiting workflows and processes regularly.

Cycle Approach:

- **Implement Changes**: Roll out improvements in phases to minimize disruption.
- **Monitor Outcomes**: Track user response to the changes and assess their impact on overall satisfaction.
- **Refine Further**: Use follow-up feedback to make iterative enhancements until the desired level of user experience is achieved.

4. Encouraging a Culture of Feedback

4.1. Leadership Involvement

Key Principle: Senior leadership should set an example by actively participating in feedback loops.

Strategies:

- **Leadership Presence**: Encourage leaders to attend feedback forums and acknowledge valuable user input.
- **Public Recognition**: Recognize and thank contributors whose feedback has led to substantial improvements.

4.2. Training on Giving Constructive Feedback

Key Principle: Equip users with the skills to provide constructive, actionable feedback.

Training Tips:

- **Guidelines for Feedback**: Train HR teams on how to provide feedback that is specific, relevant, and actionable.
- **Encourage Positivity**: Foster a feedback culture that balances identifying challenges with recognizing what works well.

5. Measuring the Success of Feedback Loops

5.1. Key Performance Indicators (KPIs)

Suggested KPIs:

- **Feedback Participation Rate**: Track the percentage of users contributing feedback regularly.
- **Implementation Rate**: Measure the proportion of feedback points that result in actionable changes.
- **User Satisfaction**: Monitor satisfaction scores pre- and post-implementation of feedback-based changes.

5.2. Adjusting Feedback Strategies

Key Principle: Continuously refine feedback collection and analysis methods to ensure they remain effective.

Review Practices:

- **Annual Reviews**: Assess the effectiveness of feedback loops annually and make adjustments as needed.
- **Benchmarking**: Compare feedback-related KPIs with industry standards to identify areas for growth.

Conclusion

Continuous feedback loops are vital for maintaining high user engagement and optimizing HR processes with ServiceNow. By establishing effective feedback channels, acting on user input, and fostering a culture of open communication, organizations can ensure their investment in ServiceNow delivers long-term value. This proactive approach not only enhances user satisfaction but also creates a dynamic HR environment ready to adapt and thrive in the face of change.

Section 8:
Monitoring and Performance Optimization

Performance Metrics for HR Workflow Efficiency

To ensure the effectiveness and continuous improvement of HR processes within ServiceNow, it is essential to establish and monitor performance metrics. These metrics help identify areas of success, potential bottlenecks, and opportunities for optimization. This chapter provides an in-depth look at key performance indicators (KPIs) and best practices for evaluating HR workflow efficiency.

1. The Importance of Measuring HR Workflow Efficiency

Why Measure Performance?

- **Data-Driven Decision-Making**: Metrics enable HR teams to make informed decisions based on real-time data rather than assumptions.
- **Continuous Improvement**: Regular performance evaluations help in refining and improving HR workflows.
- **Resource Allocation**: Metrics highlight where resources are effectively utilized and where adjustments may be necessary.
- **User Satisfaction**: Tracking performance can help identify areas where user experience can be improved.

2. Key Performance Indicators (KPIs) for HR Workflows

2.1. Process Completion Time

Definition: The average time taken to complete HR tasks or workflows from start to finish.

Why It Matters: A shorter completion time indicates an efficient workflow, leading to higher productivity and better employee experiences.

How to Measure:

- Track the time stamps of workflow initiation and completion.
- Calculate averages across different workflow types, such as onboarding, approvals, or case resolutions.

2.2. First-Time Resolution Rate

Definition: The percentage of HR cases or tasks resolved without the need for rework or follow-up actions.

Why It Matters: A high first-time resolution rate reflects well-designed and comprehensive workflows, minimizing delays and repeated efforts.

How to Measure:

- Compare the number of cases resolved in the first attempt to the total number of cases.
- Identify trends in rework and analyze common factors contributing to repeated tasks.

2.3. User Satisfaction Score

Definition: A metric based on feedback from HR team members and employees who use the workflows.

Why It Matters: High user satisfaction correlates with streamlined and user-friendly processes that meet employee needs.

How to Measure:

- Use surveys or quick post-workflow feedback forms embedded in ServiceNow.
- Calculate average satisfaction scores over time to identify changes.

2.4. Workflow Error Rate

Definition: The number of errors encountered during workflow executions relative to the total number of workflows processed.

Why It Matters: A low error rate indicates well-configured and reliable workflows. High error rates may signal a need for better workflow design or additional user training.

How to Measure:

- Monitor error logs and feedback reports within ServiceNow.
- Track the types of errors and their frequency to identify root causes.

2.5. Case Escalation Rate

Definition: The proportion of HR cases that require escalation to higher-level support or management for resolution.

Why It Matters: High escalation rates may indicate complex or unclear workflows, while low rates suggest processes are well-understood and manageable by HR teams.

How to Measure:

- Track the number of escalated cases compared to the total cases.
- Analyze escalation trends to determine if specific workflows require simplification or additional support mechanisms.

3. Setting Baseline Metrics and Goals

3.1. Establishing Baselines

Approach:

- Monitor workflows over a specific period (e.g., three months) to establish average performance metrics.
- Use baseline data as a reference point for future improvements and comparisons.

3.2. Defining Performance Goals

Best Practices:

- **SMART Goals**: Ensure goals are Specific, Measurable, Achievable, Relevant, and Time-bound.
- **Alignment with Business Objectives**: Metrics should tie into the broader organizational goals, such as reducing onboarding time or improving overall HR service quality.

4. Tools for Monitoring Performance Metrics

ServiceNow's Built-In Analytics:

- **Performance Analytics**: A tool within ServiceNow that allows HR teams to set, track, and visualize key performance indicators.
- **Dashboards and Reports**: Create custom dashboards to display real-time and historical data for quick assessments.

Third-Party Integrations:

- Integrate ServiceNow with external reporting tools like Power BI or Tableau for more complex data analysis and visualization.

5. Best Practices for Optimizing HR Workflow Performance

5.1. Regular Performance Reviews

Routine Assessments:

- Schedule monthly or quarterly performance reviews.
- Adjust workflows based on data insights to ensure continuous alignment with efficiency goals.

5.2. Engaging Stakeholders

Collaboration:

- Involve key stakeholders, including HR leaders and IT administrators, in reviewing performance data.
- Foster open discussions about challenges and successes to align on future improvements.

5.3. Leveraging Automation

Automated Enhancements:

- Implement automation features in ServiceNow to reduce manual interventions in repetitive tasks.
- Use AI and machine learning tools to identify workflow optimizations automatically.

6. Addressing Performance Gaps

6.1. Identifying Bottlenecks

Analysis:

- Use process flow diagrams and data points to spot stages where workflows slow down or stall.
- Investigate whether delays are due to technical issues, resource constraints, or user behavior.

6.2. Implementing Solutions

Strategies:

- **Process Redesign**: Simplify overly complex workflows that contribute to delays.
- **Training**: Provide targeted training to HR teams where gaps in knowledge are identified.
- **Resource Allocation**: Ensure that critical workflows have sufficient resources to operate smoothly.

6.3. Continuous Improvement Plan

Cycle:

- Follow the Plan-Do-Check-Act (PDCA) model to maintain an ongoing cycle of monitoring, reviewing, and improving HR workflows.
- Regularly incorporate feedback from users to refine KPIs and ensure they reflect current operational needs.

Conclusion

By leveraging performance metrics, HR teams can transform data into actionable insights, driving significant improvements in workflow efficiency. With well-chosen KPIs and a commitment to continuous monitoring and adjustment, organizations can ensure that ServiceNow becomes a pillar of HR operational success. This proactive approach supports a dynamic, efficient, and user-focused HR environment that meets and exceeds business goals.

Regular Audits and System Health Checks

Maintaining a high-functioning and efficient HR environment within ServiceNow requires more than just initial setup and occasional updates. Regular audits and system health checks are critical practices that ensure the platform continues to meet operational goals, remains secure, and runs smoothly. This chapter explores how to conduct effective audits and health checks and why they are essential for sustaining optimal performance in HR workflows.

1. The Importance of Regular Audits and System Health Checks

1.1. Sustaining Performance and Efficiency

Routine audits help maintain the performance levels expected from ServiceNow by:

- Identifying and addressing potential issues before they impact HR operations.
- Ensuring that workflows remain optimized as processes evolve.
- Providing insights into where additional enhancements or updates may be needed.

1.2. Compliance and Risk Mitigation

Regular checks contribute to compliance with industry standards and data protection regulations by:

- Validating that data handling practices align with policies such as GDPR.
- Confirming that user access controls are enforced and up to date.
- Reducing the risk of data breaches or unauthorized access through proactive monitoring.

1.3. Enhancing User Experience

By maintaining a well-audited system, HR teams can ensure:

- A seamless user experience with minimal interruptions or errors.
- High levels of trust and satisfaction among employees who interact with HR workflows.

2. Core Components of an Effective Audit

2.1. Data Integrity and Accuracy

Purpose: Ensure that all HR data stored and processed is accurate and up to date.

Best Practices:

- Periodically review data records for inconsistencies or duplicates.
- Implement automated checks to alert administrators to potential data issues.

2.2. Security and Access Controls

Purpose: Verify that user permissions are correctly configured to safeguard sensitive HR data.

Best Practices:

- Conduct regular reviews of user roles and permissions.
- Confirm that access levels align with the principle of least privilege, where users only have access necessary for their role.

2.3. Workflow and Process Validation

Purpose: Confirm that workflows function as intended and that any updates or changes have not disrupted existing processes.

Best Practices:

- Test key workflows and processes using sample data to identify potential issues.
- Track any modifications made to workflows and ensure they are documented for future reference.

3. Conducting System Health Checks

3.1. Performance Monitoring

Goals: Detect performance bottlenecks or degradation in system response times.

Steps:

- Use ServiceNow's built-in Performance Analytics tool to review system health metrics.
- Monitor key indicators such as page load times, transaction speeds, and server response times.
- Compare current performance data with historical benchmarks to detect anomalies.

3.2. Data Storage and Usage Audits

Goals: Ensure that storage is used efficiently and does not hinder system performance.

Steps:

- Regularly review storage capacity and usage reports.
- Identify and archive or remove obsolete records and files.
- Implement data lifecycle management policies to automate data archival processes.

3.3. Application and Plugin Review

Goals: Verify that all installed applications and plugins are current and secure.

Steps:

- Ensure that plugins are updated to their latest, secure versions.
- Review plugin usage to confirm that they still serve a necessary purpose within HR workflows.

4. Tools and Techniques for Audits and Health Checks

4.1. ServiceNow Performance Analytics

Utilize the **Performance Analytics** module to:

- Track and report on workflow KPIs.
- Generate automated reports for review by HR and IT teams.
- Set up alerts for potential performance issues.

4.2. System Log Review

Purpose: Identify unusual activity or errors that may indicate performance or security issues.

Best Practices:

- Regularly check system logs for signs of repeated errors or warnings.
- Use automated tools to filter and flag critical log entries for further investigation.

4.3. User Feedback

Purpose: Collect user insights to complement technical audits and identify issues not visible through system metrics.

Methods:

- Conduct regular surveys with HR staff and end-users about their experiences.
- Implement a feedback mechanism where users can report issues in real-time.

5. Best Practices for Scheduling Audits and Health Checks

5.1. Routine Audits

Frequency: Conduct audits at least quarterly or bi-annually to keep systems running smoothly and compliant.

5.2. Health Check Schedule

Daily Checks:

- Review performance dashboards and logs for immediate issues.

Weekly Checks:

- Validate recent workflow changes and process updates.

Monthly Checks:

- Comprehensive security and access control reviews.
- Detailed analysis of workflow metrics and process efficiency.

6. Addressing Findings from Audits and Health Checks

6.1. Creating Action Plans

Steps:

- Categorize findings based on their impact level (e.g., critical, high, medium, low).
- Develop an action plan that prioritizes addressing high-impact issues.

6.2. Implementing Fixes

Approach:

- Collaborate with IT and HR teams to apply fixes in a controlled environment before rolling out to the live system.
- Document changes made during the resolution process for future reference.

6.3. Follow-Up Reviews

Purpose: Ensure that fixes have been effective and that no new issues have been introduced.

Method:

- Schedule follow-up audits focused on previously identified issues to confirm they have been resolved.

Conclusion

Regular audits and system health checks are essential practices to ensure the continued success of ServiceNow HR workflows. They help identify and mitigate potential risks, maintain compliance, and optimize performance for a seamless user experience. By following a structured approach to audits and leveraging available tools, organizations can ensure that their HR operations remain efficient, secure, and aligned with their goals.

Fine-Tuning HR Service Delivery Processes

Enhancing the efficiency and effectiveness of HR service delivery is crucial to ensure that ServiceNow continues to meet the evolving needs of HR teams and the organization at large. Fine-tuning these processes helps maximize the potential of digital workflows, improves response times, and enhances employee satisfaction. This chapter explores the steps and strategies for refining HR service delivery processes within the ServiceNow platform.

1. The Importance of Continuous Process Optimization

1.1. Adapting to Changing Business Needs

HR processes are not static; they evolve with changing business objectives, workforce dynamics, and regulatory requirements. Regular fine-tuning helps ensure that HR services remain aligned with these shifts, keeping the organization agile and responsive.

1.2. Enhancing Employee Experience

Streamlined service delivery directly impacts the employee experience, reducing delays and making interactions with HR seamless. This boosts employee trust and engagement.

1.3. Improving Operational Efficiency

Efficient service delivery processes reduce repetitive tasks and resource consumption, allowing HR teams to focus on strategic activities instead of administrative duties.

2. Identifying Areas for Improvement

2.1. Analyzing Workflow Performance

Review key performance indicators (KPIs) such as task completion times, service level agreement (SLA) adherence, and user feedback to identify bottlenecks.

Best Practices:

- Use the **Performance Analytics** module in ServiceNow to gather and visualize data.
- Set regular review meetings with HR and IT stakeholders to discuss workflow performance.

2.2. Gathering Employee Feedback

Engage employees to understand their experience with existing HR processes. Their insights can reveal areas where improvements are needed.

Methods:

- Conduct periodic surveys focused on the ease of using HR services.
- Create feedback loops that allow employees to report issues or suggest improvements in real-time.

2.3. Benchmarking Against Best Practices

Compare current HR service delivery processes with industry best practices to identify potential enhancements.

Steps:

- Participate in industry workshops or webinars on HR technology trends.

- Review case studies and reports from organizations that have optimized their HR processes using ServiceNow.

3. Techniques for Fine-Tuning HR Service Delivery

3.1. Streamlining Workflows

Simplify overly complex workflows by:

- Removing redundant steps that do not add value.
- Consolidating similar tasks into unified workflows.
- Automating decision points using ServiceNow's **Flow Designer** and **Business Rules**.

3.2. Enhancing Automation

Leverage automation to improve efficiency by:

- Implementing automated notifications and reminders for HR tasks that require follow-up.
- Using machine learning algorithms to predict service outcomes and suggest next steps.

3.3. Optimizing SLA Management

Review and adjust SLAs to ensure they are realistic and aligned with the organization's objectives.

Tips:

- Monitor SLA breaches and investigate root causes.
- Adjust SLA timelines based on data insights from past service performance.

3.4. Implementing Dynamic Forms and Data Collection

Ensure that the data collection forms used in HR processes are intuitive and adapt to user inputs.

Techniques:

- Use **ServiceNow Form Design** tools to create dynamic, user-friendly forms.
- Employ conditional logic to display relevant questions based on prior answers, reducing unnecessary input fields.

4. Utilizing ServiceNow Tools for Optimization

4.1. Performance Analytics

Purpose: Track and analyze workflow metrics over time to identify trends and areas for improvement.

Features:

- Real-time dashboards for visualizing HR process efficiency.
- Automated reports that highlight performance changes.

4.2. Predictive Intelligence

Purpose: Use AI-powered features to streamline HR service delivery and decision-making.

Applications:

- Predict case assignment and prioritization based on historical data.
- Automate task routing for quicker case resolution.

4.3. Workflow Editor

Purpose: Adjust existing workflows or create new ones that are more efficient.

Best Practices:

- Regularly review workflows to ensure they are not outdated.
- Involve HR staff in testing and validating workflow changes before deployment.

5. Case Study: Successful Process Fine-Tuning

Background

A global company using ServiceNow for HR services identified delays in their onboarding process. Employee feedback highlighted repetitive data entry as a significant pain point.

Solution

The HR team analyzed onboarding workflow metrics and discovered redundant verification steps. By optimizing the process, removing duplicative tasks, and implementing automated data population, they reduced onboarding time by 30%.

Outcome

- Faster onboarding improved new hire satisfaction.
- The HR team could allocate time to more strategic tasks.

6. Monitoring and Continuous Improvement

6.1. Setting Up Continuous Monitoring

Establish a schedule for ongoing reviews to assess the impact of fine-tuning efforts.

Tools:

- **ServiceNow Health Scan** for checking the platform's configuration.
- Scheduled data refreshes in **Performance Analytics** to maintain updated insights.

6.2. Adapting to New Requirements

Ensure the HR team is trained to identify when new business needs or regulatory changes may require workflow adjustments.

Tips:

- Stay informed about updates in HR policies or ServiceNow capabilities.
- Include process improvement discussions in HR department meetings.

Conclusion

Fine-tuning HR service delivery processes is an ongoing commitment that pays off through improved efficiency, better employee experiences, and enhanced operational performance. Leveraging the capabilities of ServiceNow, HR teams can refine workflows and processes to stay agile and responsive to business needs. Regularly reviewing KPIs, incorporating employee feedback, and applying targeted optimizations are essential steps for maintaining a competitive and effective HR service delivery model.

Managing System Updates and Upgrades

Staying current with system updates and upgrades is essential for ensuring that your HR processes in ServiceNow remain efficient, secure, and aligned with the latest technological advancements. This chapter provides a comprehensive guide to planning, executing, and monitoring updates and upgrades in ServiceNow, focusing on best practices that minimize disruption and optimize performance.

1. Understanding the Importance of System Updates and Upgrades

1.1. Enhancing Platform Capabilities

Regular updates introduce new features, improvements, and enhancements that can streamline HR workflows and improve the overall user experience. By staying updated, HR teams can leverage new functionalities that enhance efficiency and productivity.

1.2. Security and Compliance

Updates often include critical security patches that protect HR data and systems from vulnerabilities. Keeping the platform current helps ensure compliance with industry standards and reduces the risk of data breaches.

1.3. Performance Improvements

System upgrades can optimize performance, reducing response times and ensuring that the platform remains responsive even as usage grows.

2. Planning for Updates and Upgrades

2.1. Establishing an Update Schedule

Developing a regular update and upgrade schedule is essential for proactive system management.

Tips:

- Align updates with lower-usage periods to minimize disruptions.
- Plan for major upgrades during annual or biannual periods to coincide with broader IT updates.

2.2. Preparing for Upgrades

Preparation is key to a seamless upgrade process.

Steps:

- Conduct a **pre-upgrade assessment** to identify any potential compatibility issues with custom scripts, integrations, or configurations.
- Communicate with HR and IT stakeholders about the timeline and expected impact of the update.
- Ensure that all documentation is up-to-date, detailing current customizations and integrations.

2.3. Testing Before Implementation

Create a testing environment that mirrors the production system to test updates before deployment.

Best Practices:

- Use **ServiceNow's Upgrade Preview** feature to simulate the upgrade in a sandbox environment.
- Test critical HR workflows to verify functionality post-upgrade.
- Ensure that key stakeholders participate in testing to identify any unforeseen issues.

3. Executing System Updates and Upgrades

3.1. Backup and Risk Management

Before executing any updates, back up all essential data and configurations to safeguard against unexpected failures.

Checklist:

- Perform a full system backup.
- Document all current configurations and customizations.
- Have a rollback plan in place to revert to the previous version if needed.

3.2. Implementing the Upgrade

Follow a structured approach when applying the update:

Steps:

- Apply the update to the testing environment first and run pre-defined test cases.
- Review logs and reports generated during testing for any errors or warnings.
- Once testing is successful, schedule the upgrade for the production environment.

3.3. Monitoring During and After the Upgrade

Active monitoring during and immediately after the update helps ensure a smooth transition.

Tips:

- Use **ServiceNow's System Logs** and **Performance Monitoring Tools** to track the upgrade process.
- Engage the IT team to monitor for anomalies or system performance issues post-upgrade.
- Maintain open communication with HR teams to address any user-reported issues quickly.

4. Post-Upgrade Best Practices

4.1. Validating System Performance

Conduct a post-upgrade validation to ensure that all HR workflows and modules are functioning as expected.

Checklist:

- Test key HR processes, such as case management, onboarding, and knowledge base access.
- Validate integrations with third-party systems to ensure they are working properly.

4.2. Updating User Training and Documentation

Ensure that any new features or changes introduced in the upgrade are reflected in training materials and user documentation.

Steps:

- Update user manuals and training guides to include information on new features or interface changes.
- Organize training sessions or workshops for HR teams to get acquainted with new functionalities.

4.3. Gathering Feedback

Solicit feedback from HR users to understand their experience with the upgraded system and identify any additional adjustments needed.

Approaches:

- Use surveys to gather input on new features and overall system performance.
- Schedule follow-up meetings with key HR stakeholders to discuss their observations and concerns.

5. Leveraging ServiceNow Tools for Update Management

5.1. Upgrade Center

The **Upgrade Center** within ServiceNow provides comprehensive tools and resources to manage upgrades effectively.

Features:

- Access to upgrade schedules and notifications.
- Insights into changes included in the latest updates.
- Recommendations for managing any detected issues.

5.2. Automated Testing Framework (ATF)

ATF allows HR teams and IT administrators to automate testing processes, making it easier to identify and address potential issues before they impact the production environment.

Benefits:

- Saves time by automating repetitive tests.
- Ensures comprehensive testing coverage across critical HR processes.

5.3. Release Notes and Documentation

Refer to ServiceNow's release notes for detailed information about updates and changes.

Best Practices:

- Review release notes to identify relevant changes that may affect customizations or HR-specific modules.
- Stay informed about deprecated features to plan for necessary adjustments.

6. Case Study: Successful Management of a ServiceNow Upgrade

Background

A mid-sized company using ServiceNow for HR services was preparing for a significant platform upgrade that introduced new AI-powered workflow enhancements. The IT and HR teams collaborated closely to ensure a smooth transition.

Process

- The company set up a test environment replicating their production system.
- HR stakeholders participated in testing and identified a minor issue with custom scripts.
- Adjustments were made, and the upgrade was scheduled during a low-activity period.

Outcome

- The upgrade was implemented successfully without disruption to HR services.
- New features, such as predictive task routing, enhanced overall workflow efficiency.

- Positive feedback was received from HR teams and employees, highlighting improved response times and user experience.

Conclusion

Managing system updates and upgrades is a critical component of maintaining a robust and effective HR service delivery platform. By planning updates strategically, testing comprehensively, and using ServiceNow's built-in tools, organizations can ensure a seamless transition that enhances both system performance and user satisfaction. Regular updates and proactive upgrade management pave the way for a resilient and innovative HR infrastructure.

Troubleshooting Common Issues in HR Workflows

Even with a robust platform like ServiceNow, HR teams may encounter occasional challenges that disrupt workflows or affect system performance. This chapter provides practical guidance on identifying, diagnosing, and resolving common issues that may arise in HR workflows to maintain seamless operations and high user satisfaction.

1. Common Issues in HR Workflows and Their Causes

1.1. Workflow Delays and Bottlenecks

Potential Causes:

- Inefficient process design leading to redundant steps.
- Insufficient system resources causing slow response times.
- Incorrect configurations or errors in business rules.

Signs to Look For:

- Increased processing time for HR requests.
- Frequent complaints from users about delayed approvals or case resolutions.

1.2. Errors in Automation and Scripting

Potential Causes:

- Outdated or incorrect scripts causing automation failures.
- Misconfigured triggers or conditions within workflows.

Signs to Look For:

- Failure of automated tasks or incomplete workflow execution.
- Error messages related to script executions.

1.3. Data Inconsistencies

Potential Causes:

- Integration issues with external HR systems leading to data mismatches.
- Human errors during manual data entry.

Signs to Look For:

- Discrepancies between data records in different modules.
- Reports highlighting inconsistent or missing data points.

1.4. User Access Issues

Potential Causes:

- Misconfigured roles and permissions preventing users from accessing necessary features.
- Changes in user profiles without corresponding updates to access settings.

Signs to Look For:

- Users unable to access certain dashboards, reports, or process steps.
- Increase in help desk tickets related to access problems.

2. Diagnosing and Resolving Issues

2.1. Using ServiceNow Diagnostic Tools

Approach:

- **System Logs**: Review system logs for detailed error reports and traces of failed transactions.
- **Performance Analytics**: Identify slow-running processes and pinpoint where bottlenecks occur.
- **Automated Test Framework (ATF)**: Run automated tests to identify issues in workflows, especially after updates or new customizations.

2.2. Checking Workflow Configurations

Steps:

1. **Review Workflow Designs**: Ensure that each step is configured correctly and there are no unnecessary loops or branches.
2. **Examine Business Rules and Conditions**: Check for conflicts or misconfigurations that could be halting workflow progression.
3. **Audit Scripting**: Ensure scripts are up-to-date and free of errors by running them in a testing environment.

2.3. Troubleshooting Data Integration Problems

Approach:

- **Verify Data Mapping**: Confirm that data fields from integrated systems align with those in ServiceNow.
- **Monitor Data Transfer**: Use integration logs to trace data flow between ServiceNow and third-party applications.
- **Re-sync Data**: In cases of data mismatches, consider performing a data sync to update records.

2.4. Addressing User Access Issues

Approach:

- **Audit User Permissions**: Regularly audit user roles and permissions to align them with current job functions.
- **Review Recent Changes**: Look at recent changes to user profiles or access controls that may have inadvertently limited access.
- **Communicate Changes**: Inform HR teams of updates to access configurations to prevent confusion.

3. Preventative Measures to Avoid Common Issues

3.1. Implementing Regular System Audits

Routine audits can help detect and address potential issues before they affect workflows.

Best Practices:

- Schedule monthly or quarterly audits of workflow configurations and scripts.
- Involve IT and HR stakeholders in reviewing audit findings to prioritize fixes.

3.2. Continuous Training and Knowledge Sharing

Ensure that HR teams and administrators are well-trained to handle common troubleshooting tasks.

Tips:

- Conduct training sessions focused on troubleshooting workflows and handling basic issues.
- Maintain a knowledge base with step-by-step guides for common troubleshooting scenarios.

3.3. Establishing a Feedback Loop

Encourage HR teams to report issues and provide feedback on workflow efficiency.

Benefits:

- Identifies problems early through user observations.
- Allows for quick adjustments based on real-time feedback.

4. Case Study: Resolving a Common HR Workflow Issue

Background

A mid-sized enterprise using ServiceNow for HR experienced delays in their employee onboarding process. HR teams reported that onboarding workflows were stalling at the approval step, impacting new hires' ability to start work on time.

Diagnosis

The IT team reviewed the workflow configuration and discovered that a recent change to business rules caused a conflict, leading to a delay in task automation.

Resolution

The team:

- Rolled back the conflicting business rule and adjusted it to align with the new workflow requirements.
- Added a pre-check step to test changes in a sandbox environment before deploying to production.

Outcome

The workflow resumed normal operation, with HR teams reporting faster onboarding times. The case underscored the importance of thorough testing before implementing workflow changes.

5. Leveraging ServiceNow Support and Community Resources

5.1. Utilizing ServiceNow Support

Engage with ServiceNow's support team for complex issues that require expert assistance.

5.2. Participating in ServiceNow Community Forums

Join community forums and user groups to exchange troubleshooting tips and solutions.

Benefits:

- Gain insights from other organizations facing similar challenges.
- Access resources and documentation that can aid in faster problem resolution.

Conclusion

Effective troubleshooting in ServiceNow HR workflows is critical for maintaining seamless operations and ensuring a positive user experience. By proactively identifying common issues, utilizing available diagnostic tools, and implementing preventive strategies, HR teams can minimize disruptions and maintain efficient processes. Addressing issues swiftly and thoroughly supports a resilient HR infrastructure that leverages ServiceNow's full potential.

Section 9:
Scaling and Expanding ServiceNow Capabilities

Expanding HR Services to Global Operations

Expanding HR services to support global operations is a strategic move that enhances a company's reach, talent acquisition, and employee experience across borders. However, scaling these services introduces complexities that require robust, adaptable solutions. ServiceNow's platform, with its flexible and customizable capabilities, provides the ideal foundation for HR teams looking to scale operations globally while maintaining efficiency, compliance, and a consistent user experience.

1. Challenges of Scaling HR Services Globally

1.1. Diverse Regulatory Requirements

Operating across multiple countries means complying with a variety of labor laws and data protection regulations. Each region may have specific rules regarding employee data storage, reporting, benefits, and contractual obligations.

Key Considerations:

- Adapt workflows to meet local employment regulations.
- Ensure that data storage and processing adhere to country-specific privacy laws such as GDPR, CCPA, or regional equivalents.

1.2. Cultural and Linguistic Barriers

HR processes need to cater to diverse cultural norms and linguistic preferences. This includes tailoring communication styles, service options, and documentation to reflect local practices and languages.

Key Considerations:

- Provide multi-language support for HR portals and documentation.
- Adjust templates and communication strategies to resonate with cultural expectations.

1.3. Time Zone Differences and Operational Hours

Supporting a global workforce requires round-the-clock HR service availability to account for varying time zones.

Key Considerations:

- Implement 24/7 support mechanisms, such as chatbots and self-service portals, to provide continuous assistance.
- Create escalation workflows that accommodate different working hours for HR teams in various regions.

2. Leveraging ServiceNow for Global Expansion

2.1. Multi-Language and Multi-Currency Capabilities

ServiceNow's platform is designed with global scalability in mind. It allows HR departments to set up multi-language support and integrate currency conversion functionalities directly into workflows.

How to Implement:

- Configure HR service portals to offer content in multiple languages based on user location or preferences.
- Integrate currency management tools for payroll and benefits administration, ensuring accurate compensation in different currencies.

2.2. Customizable Workflows for Regional Needs

ServiceNow's flexibility enables HR teams to create custom workflows that comply with region-specific requirements while maintaining a unified global standard.

Steps to Customize:

1. **Assess Regional Requirements**: Identify the unique HR needs and legal mandates of each country or region.
2. **Configure Conditional Workflows**: Use ServiceNow's Workflow Editor to design conditional branches that adapt processes to meet local needs.
3. **Test Region-Specific Scenarios**: Utilize the Automated Test Framework (ATF) to validate workflows for each country before deployment.

2.3. Centralized Knowledge Base

Maintaining a centralized yet accessible knowledge base for global HR practices ensures that employees and HR staff have consistent access to information, regardless of location.

Benefits:

- Streamlines access to policies, procedures, and training materials.
- Enables localized knowledge articles while retaining a core global repository.

Implementation Tips:

- Use categories and tags to organize articles by region and language.
- Regularly update content to reflect changes in global and regional policies.

3. Enhancing Collaboration Across Borders

3.1. Cross-Regional Collaboration Tools

ServiceNow's collaboration features, such as chat and integrated communication tools, foster teamwork among HR professionals across different regions.

Features to Utilize:

- **Collaborative Workspaces**: Set up shared workspaces for HR teams to coordinate efforts and share updates.
- **Integrated Messaging**: Use ServiceNow's chat capabilities to facilitate real-time communication between global HR units.

3.2. Unified Reporting and Analytics

To ensure effective management and decision-making, HR teams need insights that span the entire organization. ServiceNow's advanced reporting and analytics tools offer this capability, providing centralized visibility into global HR metrics.

How to Optimize:

- Customize dashboards to display key performance indicators (KPIs) relevant to different regions.
- Use built-in analytics tools to monitor workflow efficiency and employee satisfaction on a global scale.

4. Case Study: Successful Global HR Service Expansion

Company Overview: A multinational tech firm with offices in over 20 countries aimed to unify its HR operations under a single digital platform. They implemented ServiceNow to streamline workflows, improve compliance, and provide consistent HR services worldwide.

Challenges Faced:

- Navigating various regulatory landscapes.
- Bridging cultural and linguistic differences among employees.
- Maintaining HR service consistency across multiple time zones.

Solutions Implemented:

- **Localized Workflows**: Customized processes for benefits, leave management, and onboarding to meet local compliance needs.
- **Multi-Language Portals**: Deployed HR service portals in the primary languages spoken in each region.
- **24/7 Support**: Integrated AI-driven chatbots for immediate support outside regular business hours.

Outcome: The company reported a 30% improvement in HR efficiency and a significant reduction in compliance-related issues. Employee satisfaction surveys highlighted the positive impact of consistent and accessible HR services.

5. Best Practices for Expanding HR Services Globally

5.1. Engage Regional HR Leaders

Collaborate with local HR managers to understand the nuances of regional laws and cultural expectations. This partnership ensures that workflows are both compliant and culturally appropriate.

5.2. Regularly Review and Update Workflows

Global regulations and workforce expectations change over time. Regularly reviewing and updating workflows helps maintain compliance and effectiveness.

5.3. Leverage User Feedback

Gather feedback from employees and HR teams in various regions to identify areas for improvement. Continuous feedback loops help refine global HR processes and enhance user experience.

Conclusion

Expanding HR services to global operations is a complex yet rewarding endeavor that can greatly enhance an organization's competitiveness and operational effectiveness. ServiceNow's platform provides the tools and flexibility needed to tailor HR services to diverse regional needs while maintaining a cohesive global strategy. By leveraging ServiceNow's multi-language support, customizable workflows, and collaborative tools, HR teams can deliver consistent, efficient, and compliant services across all regions.

Supporting Multi-Language and Multi-Currency Needs

As organizations expand their operations across borders, the ability to support multi-language and multi-currency functionalities becomes a crucial aspect of effective HR service delivery. ServiceNow, with its adaptable platform, offers robust features to help HR departments cater to the diverse needs of an international workforce. This chapter explores how to leverage ServiceNow to manage language diversity and multi-currency processing efficiently, ensuring that HR services remain consistent, compliant, and user-friendly across all regions.

1. The Importance of Multi-Language and Multi-Currency Support

1.1. Enhancing Employee Experience

Providing HR services in employees' native languages and handling currency in their respective formats significantly enhances their experience and satisfaction. Employees are more likely to engage with HR processes when they feel understood and supported.

Key Benefits:

- Improved accessibility and engagement.
- Reduction in language and currency-related misunderstandings.
- Enhanced global workforce satisfaction and productivity.

1.2. Ensuring Compliance and Accuracy

Different countries have unique legal requirements for currency and language in employment documents, payroll, and communication. Supporting multi-language and multi-currency capabilities helps HR teams comply with these regulations and maintain accurate records.

Key Points:

- Compliance with regional language and financial laws.
- Accuracy in financial transactions and documentation.

2. Leveraging ServiceNow's Multi-Language Capabilities

2.1. Configuring Language Settings

ServiceNow's platform can be configured to support multiple languages, making it easy for HR teams to localize content, communications, and workflows.

Steps for Implementation:

1. **Activate Language Packs**: ServiceNow provides a variety of language packs that can be activated to enable multi-language support.
2. **Translate Key Content**: Use the translation feature within ServiceNow to localize essential HR documents, notifications, and service catalog items.
3. **Dynamic Language Selection**: Configure the system to automatically detect and display content in the user's preferred language.

2.2. Best Practices for Localization

Ensuring content quality and consistency across languages requires thorough planning and execution.

Recommendations:

- **Professional Translations**: Collaborate with professional translators to maintain the accuracy and cultural relevance of HR materials.
- **Standardized Terminology**: Create a glossary of terms to ensure consistent translation of HR jargon across all languages.
- **Review and Feedback**: Implement a process for native-speaking employees to review translated content and provide feedback.

3. Implementing Multi-Currency Capabilities

3.1. Setting Up Currency Support

ServiceNow's platform allows for the integration of multi-currency functionality, making it easier to manage payroll, reimbursements, and financial transactions globally.

How to Implement Multi-Currency:

1. **Enable Currency Configuration**: Navigate to the ServiceNow platform settings and enable multi-currency options.
2. **Set Default and Regional Currencies**: Define the default currency for global operations and configure specific currencies for different regions.
3. **Automate Currency Conversion**: Use ServiceNow's integration capabilities to link with external financial systems or APIs for real-time currency exchange rates.

3.2. Benefits of Automated Currency Management

Automating currency conversion and management reduces the potential for errors and ensures that HR transactions remain transparent and accurate.

Advantages:

- Accurate financial reporting across regions.
- Streamlined payroll and benefits processing.
- Simplified budget allocation for international operations.

4. Ensuring a Seamless User Experience

4.1. Unified Interface for All Users

ServiceNow's platform provides a unified interface that adapts to language and currency preferences without altering the core structure of HR workflows.

Features to Utilize:

- **Localized Dashboards**: Create dashboards that display data in the appropriate language and currency for each region.
- **Adaptive Design**: Ensure that portals and service pages adjust based on the language and currency settings of the user.

4.2. Training and Support for HR Teams

Supporting a multi-language and multi-currency HR system requires training and support to ensure that HR teams can manage and troubleshoot issues effectively.

Training Recommendations:

- Conduct workshops on how to update and maintain multi-language content.
- Train HR teams on currency management tools and financial reporting.

- Provide a centralized knowledge base with guides for handling multi-language and multi-currency configurations.

5. Overcoming Common Challenges

5.1. Maintaining Consistency Across Languages

Ensuring that translations are consistent and reflect the same quality as the original content is a common challenge.

Solutions:

- Use translation memory tools to maintain consistency in commonly used phrases and terms.
- Schedule regular audits to review the quality and relevance of localized content.

5.2. Real-Time Currency Fluctuations

Currency values can change rapidly, affecting payroll and financial transactions.

How to Address:

- Integrate ServiceNow with real-time currency conversion APIs to update rates automatically.
- Implement alerts and notifications for significant currency fluctuations that may impact HR operations.

6. Case Study: Multi-National Company Success with ServiceNow

Background: A global manufacturing company faced challenges in providing consistent HR services across 15 countries. Differences in language and currency processing were leading to inefficiencies and employee dissatisfaction.

Solution Implemented:

- Activated ServiceNow's language packs and customized HR workflows for local languages.
- Integrated the platform with a currency conversion tool for real-time financial management.
- Provided training sessions for HR teams to ensure smooth adoption and effective management of the new capabilities.

Results:

- Enhanced employee satisfaction due to personalized and localized HR support.
- Reduced errors in payroll and financial reporting.
- Streamlined HR processes, leading to a 25% increase in process efficiency.

7. Best Practices for Long-Term Success

7.1. Regular Updates and Maintenance

Ensure that language packs and currency integrations are updated regularly to align with global standards and practices.

7.2. Gathering Feedback for Continuous Improvement

Collect feedback from both HR teams and employees to identify any gaps in the multi-language and multi-currency features and make iterative improvements.

Conclusion: Supporting multi-language and multi-currency needs is essential for organizations operating on a global scale. ServiceNow's comprehensive tools and adaptable platform make it possible to implement these capabilities effectively, providing a seamless experience for employees and HR teams alike. By following best practices and leveraging ServiceNow's features, companies can enhance global HR services and ensure compliance and employee satisfaction across regions.

Advanced HR Reporting and Analytics

In the modern HR landscape, data-driven decision-making has become essential for organizations striving to remain competitive and effective. ServiceNow's advanced reporting and analytics capabilities empower HR professionals to monitor, analyze, and enhance HR processes with actionable insights. This chapter explores the ways in which ServiceNow's HR Service Delivery platform can be leveraged for sophisticated reporting and data analysis to optimize HR operations and drive strategic initiatives.

1. The Importance of Advanced HR Reporting and Analytics

1.1. Enhancing HR Decision-Making

HR analytics provide a clear, data-driven view of HR performance and workforce trends. By leveraging these insights, HR teams can make informed decisions that align with organizational goals.

Key Benefits:

- Improved decision-making based on real-time data.
- Identification of workforce trends and areas for improvement.
- Enhanced strategic planning and resource allocation.

1.2. Aligning HR Metrics with Business Objectives

Advanced analytics allow HR leaders to align key HR metrics with broader business objectives, demonstrating the impact of HR initiatives on organizational success.

Core Metrics to Track:

- Employee engagement and satisfaction scores.
- Time-to-hire and onboarding effectiveness.
- Case resolution time and service efficiency.

2. Leveraging ServiceNow's Reporting Capabilities

2.1. Built-In Reports and Dashboards

ServiceNow's platform offers a variety of built-in reports and customizable dashboards tailored to HR functions. These tools allow HR professionals to visualize and track key performance indicators (KPIs).

How to Utilize Built-In Reports:

- Access pre-configured HR reports that cover common metrics, such as case resolution times and service request volumes.
- Customize dashboards to reflect department-specific goals and priorities.
- Use visualizations like graphs, charts, and tables for easy interpretation of complex data.

2.2. Creating Custom Reports

While built-in reports are beneficial, custom reports offer the flexibility to focus on specific metrics or performance areas unique to an organization's needs.

Steps for Creating Custom Reports:

1. **Navigate to Report Designer**: Use the report designer tool within ServiceNow to create and customize reports.
2. **Select Data Sources**: Identify and select relevant data sources, such as case management logs or employee satisfaction surveys.

3. **Design the Report Layout**: Choose the appropriate visualization format, such as bar charts, line graphs, or heatmaps, for optimal data representation.
4. **Set Filters and Parameters**: Apply filters to refine the report's focus, such as by department, time frame, or employee demographic.

2.3. Scheduling and Automating Reports

Automating the generation and distribution of reports ensures that HR teams and management receive timely updates without manual intervention.

Automation Tips:

- Schedule reports to be sent at regular intervals (e.g., weekly or monthly) to relevant stakeholders.
- Configure automated alerts to notify HR leaders of significant trends or deviations.

3. Utilizing Advanced Analytics Features

3.1. Predictive Analytics for HR

ServiceNow's analytics capabilities can extend beyond descriptive statistics to predictive insights. Predictive analytics helps HR teams anticipate future workforce trends and prepare proactive strategies.

Examples of Predictive Uses:

- Forecasting employee turnover and identifying at-risk departments.
- Predicting the impact of HR policy changes on employee engagement.
- Estimating future demand for training and development programs.

3.2. Integrating External Data Sources

Enhancing ServiceNow's native analytics with data from external HR systems can provide a more comprehensive view of HR performance.

Integration Techniques:

- Connect ServiceNow with third-party HR software and databases using APIs.
- Consolidate data from payroll systems, learning management platforms, and employee engagement tools for unified analysis.

4. Best Practices for Effective HR Reporting and Analytics

4.1. Ensuring Data Accuracy and Integrity

The quality of HR analytics depends on the accuracy and integrity of the data being used. It is essential to regularly audit data sources and implement best practices for data governance.

Guidelines:

- Conduct periodic data quality checks to identify and correct inaccuracies.
- Implement user access controls to prevent unauthorized data manipulation.

4.2. Focusing on Actionable Insights

Reports and dashboards should not only display data but also provide actionable insights that HR teams can use to improve processes.

Tips for Actionable Reporting:

- Highlight key findings with annotations to guide decision-makers.

- Use trend analysis to showcase improvements or declines over time.
- Align reports with strategic HR initiatives to measure their effectiveness.

4.3. Training HR Teams on Data Interpretation

Ensuring that HR teams have the necessary skills to interpret and act on analytics is critical for effective use of ServiceNow's reporting capabilities.

Training Recommendations:

- Conduct workshops focused on data literacy and interpretation.
- Provide guides and resources for understanding various types of data visualizations.
- Encourage a culture of data-driven decision-making within the HR department.

5. Case Study: Transforming HR Operations with Advanced Analytics

Background: A global tech company was experiencing challenges with fragmented HR reporting and a lack of actionable insights across its regional offices.

Solution Implemented:

- Deployed ServiceNow's reporting and analytics tools to consolidate data from multiple HR functions.
- Created tailored dashboards for different HR teams, including recruitment, employee relations, and benefits administration.
- Integrated data from third-party systems to provide a complete view of HR operations.

Results:

- Improved data transparency and accessibility for HR leaders.
- Reduced time spent on manual data compilation and reporting by 30%.
- Enhanced strategic decision-making, leading to targeted improvements in employee engagement and retention.

6. Future Trends in HR Reporting and Analytics

6.1. Expanding Use of Artificial Intelligence (AI)

AI-driven insights are becoming increasingly common in HR analytics. ServiceNow's evolving platform will continue to integrate AI to identify deeper patterns and recommendations.

Future Capabilities to Watch:

- Enhanced predictive models for workforce planning.
- AI-generated recommendations for improving HR workflows.
- Sentiment analysis of employee feedback for real-time engagement insights.

6.2. Focus on Data-Driven Culture

The future of HR reporting and analytics will prioritize cultivating a data-driven culture where data insights are embedded into everyday decision-making.

Strategies for Building a Data-Driven Culture:

- Empower all HR professionals to understand and use data through ongoing training.
- Encourage collaboration between HR data analysts and department leaders to ensure that insights are used effectively.
- Integrate reporting tools into daily HR workflows for continuous monitoring.

Conclusion

ServiceNow's advanced HR reporting and analytics capabilities are essential for organizations seeking to optimize their HR functions and align them with business goals. By leveraging built-in and custom reporting, predictive analytics, and external data integration, HR teams can unlock new insights and drive impactful change. Adopting these practices will ensure that organizations can continue to evolve and enhance their HR strategies in an increasingly data-centric world.

Enhancing Employee Self-Service Portals

Employee self-service portals are pivotal in modern HR management, providing employees with instant access to HR services, resources, and information. Implementing and optimizing these portals within ServiceNow can significantly enhance employee experiences and reduce the workload on HR teams by promoting self-sufficiency and automation. This chapter delves into strategies and best practices for enhancing employee self-service portals in ServiceNow to maximize their impact.

1. The Importance of Employee Self-Service Portals

1.1. Empowering Employees

A well-designed self-service portal empowers employees by giving them control over various HR processes, such as requesting leave, accessing company policies, or tracking the status of submitted requests.

Key Benefits:

- Quick access to HR services, reducing dependency on HR staff.
- Improved employee satisfaction and productivity.
- Streamlined processes for routine HR tasks.

1.2. Reducing HR Workload

By enabling employees to resolve common queries and complete HR tasks independently, self-service portals can reduce the volume of direct HR interactions, allowing HR professionals to focus on strategic initiatives.

Advantages for HR:

- Minimized repetitive administrative work.
- More time to concentrate on talent management and organizational growth.

2. Building an Effective Employee Self-Service Portal in ServiceNow

2.1. User-Centric Design Principles

Designing a user-friendly portal requires an understanding of user needs and behaviors. The interface should be intuitive, ensuring employees can easily navigate the platform without extensive training.

Design Tips:

- Use a clean, organized layout with logical navigation.
- Ensure mobile responsiveness for on-the-go access.
- Highlight commonly used services and quick links.

2.2. Customizable Portal Features

ServiceNow allows for a high degree of customization to align the self-service portal with specific HR needs.

Customizable Elements:

- **Personalized Dashboards**: Allow employees to personalize their dashboard for quick access to frequently used services.
- **Knowledge Base Integration**: Integrate a comprehensive knowledge base to provide answers to common HR questions.

- **Announcements and Updates**: Use the portal to broadcast important HR updates and announcements.

2.3. Integrating Chatbots and AI Assistance

Enhancing the portal with AI-driven chatbots can offer real-time assistance and improve user interactions.

Benefits of Chatbots:

- Immediate responses to employee inquiries.
- Guided assistance for completing HR forms or processes.
- Automated ticket generation for complex issues.

3. Core Functionalities to Include

3.1. HR Service Catalog

An essential component of the portal is the HR service catalog, which lists all available services such as leave applications, benefits enrollment, and request forms.

Features to Include:

- Service descriptions and eligibility criteria.
- Step-by-step guides for completing each service.
- Automated approval workflows to expedite processes.

3.2. Case Management Integration

Integrating the portal with ServiceNow's case management system ensures that employees can track the status of their service requests.

Case Management Features:

- Real-time updates on the progress of requests.
- Notifications for completed actions or pending tasks.
- Transparent escalation paths for unresolved issues.

3.3. Self-Service Knowledge Base

Providing a robust self-service knowledge base equips employees with the information they need to resolve issues independently.

Content Suggestions:

- FAQs related to HR policies and procedures.
- Troubleshooting guides for common issues.
- Access to company policy documents and forms.

4. Optimizing the Portal for Enhanced Usability

4.1. Streamlined Navigation

Ensure that portal navigation is straightforward by categorizing services and information in a logical manner.

Tips for Streamlining:

- Group similar services under distinct categories (e.g., "Leave Management," "Benefits," "Training").
- Implement a powerful search function that suggests relevant results as users type.

4.2. Mobile-Friendly Design

A mobile-optimized portal allows employees to access HR services anytime, anywhere, which is especially beneficial for remote and field employees.

Mobile Design Best Practices:

- Use scalable and responsive design elements.
- Prioritize essential functions on the mobile interface for quick access.

4.3. Enhancing Accessibility

Ensure the portal complies with accessibility standards to support all employees, including those with disabilities.

Accessibility Features:

- Provide text-to-speech options and alternative text for images.
- Ensure compatibility with screen readers.
- Use high-contrast themes and scalable text for better readability.

5. Continuous Improvement of the Self-Service Portal

5.1. Gathering Employee Feedback

Solicit regular feedback from employees to identify areas for improvement and new features they may find helpful.

Feedback Collection Methods:

- In-portal surveys post-service completion.
- Direct feedback forms for suggestions and issues.
- Analytics on portal usage to monitor engagement and identify frequently used or underutilized features.

5.2. Leveraging Analytics for Optimization

Use ServiceNow's built-in analytics tools to track the portal's performance and identify areas for enhancement.

Analytics Insights:

- Monitor service completion times to optimize workflow processes.
- Identify popular services and ensure their visibility on the main page.
- Track the number of issues resolved through the self-service portal versus those requiring HR intervention.

5.3. Regular Updates and Iterative Improvements

As technology and organizational needs evolve, so should the self-service portal. Implement regular updates to keep the portal relevant and efficient.

Best Practices:

- Schedule periodic reviews to update content and services.
- Introduce new features based on employee feedback and changing HR practices.
- Communicate updates effectively through in-portal notifications and emails.

6. Case Study: Improving Self-Service with a Revamped Portal

Background: A mid-sized company noticed that their existing HR service delivery was inefficient, with employees often contacting HR directly for simple queries.

Solution:

- Redesigned the self-service portal with ServiceNow to include a comprehensive service catalog, integrated case tracking, and a chatbot for real-time support.
- Enhanced the portal's design for mobile and accessibility compliance.

Outcome:

- The company saw a 40% reduction in HR-related inquiries as employees were able to find answers independently.
- Increased employee satisfaction and portal engagement due to the ease of use and availability of instant support.

Conclusion

Enhancing the employee self-service portal is not just about providing access to HR services but creating a seamless, intuitive experience that empowers employees to handle their HR needs efficiently. By leveraging the customization and integration capabilities of ServiceNow, HR departments can develop robust self-service solutions that drive higher engagement, improve productivity, and support the overall digital transformation of HR services.

Best Practices for Scaling ServiceNow for Large Enterprises

Scaling ServiceNow for large enterprises requires strategic planning, robust architecture, and adherence to best practices to ensure seamless growth, consistent performance, and alignment with evolving business needs. This chapter provides a detailed overview of effective strategies and best practices for scaling ServiceNow within large organizations to support expansive HR functions and operations.

1. Understanding the Unique Challenges of Scaling

1.1. Complexity of Large Enterprises

Large enterprises often have complex structures with multiple business units, regional offices, and varied operational models. Scaling ServiceNow in such environments involves understanding and accommodating diverse requirements while maintaining a unified system.

Key Challenges:

- Balancing global and regional HR needs.
- Managing an extensive range of workflows and data sets.
- Ensuring consistent user experience across the enterprise.

1.2. Data Volume and Performance Concerns

As organizations grow, the volume of data processed by ServiceNow increases significantly, which can impact system performance if not properly managed.

Potential Issues:

- Slower load times for user interfaces.
- Increased complexity in reporting and data management.
- Potential latency in executing complex workflows.

2. Strategic Planning for Scalability

2.1. Establishing a Long-Term Vision

Developing a comprehensive roadmap for scaling ServiceNow helps ensure that all initiatives align with the enterprise's long-term HR and business strategies.

Planning Essentials:

- Define clear objectives for scaling, including key performance indicators (KPIs).
- Create phased implementation plans to roll out features progressively.
- Involve key stakeholders from different business units to gather input and align expectations.

2.2. Building a Robust Governance Model

A strong governance framework is essential to manage change and maintain the integrity of the ServiceNow platform as it scales.

Governance Focus Areas:

- Establish roles and responsibilities for platform administration.
- Develop change management policies to manage updates and new implementations.
- Ensure continuous compliance with enterprise policies and data security standards.

3. Technical Best Practices for Scaling

3.1. Optimizing Instance Architecture

Configuring the instance architecture to handle high data volumes and user interactions is crucial for scaling efficiently.

Best Practices:

- Utilize load balancing to distribute traffic and optimize response times.
- Implement database partitioning and indexing to improve data retrieval speeds.
- Regularly review system performance metrics and address bottlenecks proactively.

3.2. Implementing Modular Workflows

Design modular and reusable workflows that can be adapted for various departments and use cases without duplicating efforts.

Advantages:

- Reduces development time for new functionalities.
- Simplifies updates and maintenance.
- Ensures consistency across different business units.

3.3. Leveraging Automation and AI

Integrate automation and AI capabilities within ServiceNow to streamline processes and enhance scalability.

Key Applications:

- Use automation for routine task handling, such as data entry and request processing.
- Implement AI-driven analytics to provide insights for decision-making and process optimization.

4. Enhancing User Experience at Scale

4.1. Personalizing Employee Portals

Ensure that employee portals are adaptable and personalized to meet the needs of different user groups within the enterprise.

Customization Tips:

- Provide options for employees to customize their dashboards.
- Use user role-based content delivery to streamline relevant information.

4.2. Streamlining Access Control

As the number of users increases, managing access control becomes more complex. Develop a well-structured permissions hierarchy to ensure secure and efficient access.

Access Control Recommendations:

- Implement role-based access control (RBAC) to limit permissions based on user roles.
- Regularly audit and update access controls to reflect organizational changes.

5. Maintaining System Performance and Reliability

5.1. Conducting Regular Performance Audits

Regularly audit the system's performance to identify and resolve issues before they impact users.

Performance Auditing Tips:

- Monitor transaction response times and system uptime.
- Track the performance of integrations with third-party systems.

5.2. Scaling Infrastructure Resources

Ensure that the underlying infrastructure, including servers and storage, can support increasing demands as the enterprise scales.

Infrastructure Strategies:

- Use cloud-based scaling solutions that allow for flexible resource allocation.
- Leverage ServiceNow's high-availability features to prevent downtime.

5.3. Implementing Disaster Recovery Plans

Develop a comprehensive disaster recovery plan to protect against data loss and ensure business continuity in the event of system failures or unexpected incidents.

Core Elements of a Recovery Plan:

- Regular backups of critical data.
- Predefined protocols for recovery and data restoration.
- Simulated disaster recovery drills to test the effectiveness of the plan.

6. Best Practices for Global Deployment

6.1. Supporting Multi-Language and Multi-Currency Needs

Enterprises operating globally require localized features to support multiple languages and currencies within their ServiceNow implementation.

Localization Practices:

- Leverage ServiceNow's built-in localization tools to create multi-language interfaces.
- Integrate currency conversion functionalities for financial processes in different regions.

6.2. Aligning with Regional Compliance Regulations

Ensure that the ServiceNow implementation complies with regional and international data protection laws, such as GDPR, to avoid legal repercussions and maintain user trust.

Compliance Measures:

- Keep abreast of evolving data protection regulations in various regions.
- Collaborate with legal teams to ensure compliance with local and global standards.

7. Training and Supporting Users at Scale

7.1. Comprehensive Training Programs

Develop extensive training programs to onboard new users and upskill existing employees as new features are added.

Training Components:

- Provide role-specific training for different levels of platform interaction.
- Use a combination of in-person workshops, e-learning modules, and interactive tutorials.

7.2. Providing Ongoing Support

Establish a reliable support structure to address user questions and technical issues promptly.

Support Strategies:

- Create an internal helpdesk team dedicated to ServiceNow support.
- Implement a tiered support model to streamline issue resolution.

Conclusion

Scaling ServiceNow for large enterprises involves a combination of strategic planning, technical optimization, and user-centric approaches. By following these best practices, HR teams can ensure that their ServiceNow implementation remains robust, responsive, and capable of meeting the dynamic needs of a growing organization. Successful scaling enhances HR service delivery, supports global operations, and empowers the workforce with efficient, self-service tools.

Section 10:

Case Studies and Real-World Implementations

Success Stories of ServiceNow HR Implementations

The true testament to the power of ServiceNow in transforming HR processes lies in the success stories of organizations that have embraced its capabilities and reaped substantial benefits. This chapter delves into real-world implementations where businesses of varying sizes and industries successfully leveraged ServiceNow to optimize their HR operations.

1. Global Corporation Streamlines Onboarding Processes

Background

A multinational corporation with operations spanning multiple continents faced challenges in standardizing its onboarding processes. Each region had its own approach, leading to inefficiencies, inconsistencies, and delays in getting new employees started.

Solution Implementation

The organization implemented ServiceNow's HR Service Delivery module to create a unified onboarding workflow. This included integrating the platform with existing payroll and benefits systems, automating documentation processes, and providing a centralized portal for new hires to complete their onboarding tasks.

Results

- **Improved Onboarding Time**: Onboarding time was reduced by 30% as processes were standardized and automated.
- **Employee Experience**: New hires reported a 40% improvement in satisfaction due to the simplified and intuitive onboarding portal.
- **Efficiency Gains**: HR teams across global offices experienced significant time savings by eliminating manual administrative tasks.

Key Takeaways

- Centralizing onboarding within ServiceNow can harmonize processes across regions and enhance both HR efficiency and employee experience.
- Integrating with other systems ensures seamless data flow, reducing manual entry and potential errors.

2. Mid-Sized Company Enhances HR Service Requests

Background

A mid-sized company specializing in IT services struggled with managing HR service requests. The existing system was heavily reliant on emails and manual tracking, resulting in delayed responses and reduced employee satisfaction.

Solution Implementation

The company adopted ServiceNow's HR Case and Knowledge Management module to create a centralized system for handling service requests. Automation rules were set up to route cases to the appropriate HR teams based on categories and priorities.

Results

- **Faster Response Times**: Average response time to employee queries was reduced from three days to one.
- **Transparency**: Employees could track the status of their requests in real-time through the ServiceNow portal.
- **Knowledge Management**: A comprehensive knowledge base was built, empowering employees to find answers to common questions without direct HR intervention.

Key Takeaways

- Leveraging ServiceNow's automation capabilities for case routing can greatly enhance response times and employee satisfaction.
- Implementing a self-service knowledge base can reduce the burden on HR teams by allowing employees to find solutions independently.

3. Educational Institution Transforms Document Management

Background

A large university with thousands of faculty and staff faced difficulties in managing HR documents securely and efficiently. Paper-based documentation processes led to frequent errors, storage issues, and compliance risks.

Solution Implementation

ServiceNow's Document Management module was deployed to digitize and automate document workflows. Secure storage protocols were integrated to comply with data protection standards, and access controls were set up for specific roles and departments.

Results

- **Enhanced Security**: Document access was streamlined and secured, reducing the risk of data breaches.
- **Compliance**: The institution achieved compliance with local and international data protection regulations with automated audit trails.
- **Operational Efficiency**: HR staff reported a 50% reduction in time spent managing documents, allowing them to focus on strategic tasks.

Key Takeaways

- Digitizing document management with ServiceNow can significantly improve data security and compliance while reducing manual workload.
- Automation of workflows helps maintain accurate records and supports rapid document retrieval.

4. Healthcare Organization Optimizes Employee Case Management

Background

A large healthcare provider with thousands of employees required an efficient way to handle HR case management. The existing system was fragmented, resulting in lost information and delays in resolving cases.

Solution Implementation

The organization implemented ServiceNow's HR Case Management module to centralize case tracking, automate escalations, and improve collaboration among HR teams.

Results

- **Reduced Resolution Times**: The average case resolution time dropped by 40% due to automated prioritization and task assignments.
- **Increased Productivity**: HR teams experienced fewer interruptions and a more streamlined approach to case handling.
- **Employee Satisfaction**: Staff satisfaction surveys indicated a significant boost in the perceived efficiency and responsiveness of HR services.

Key Takeaways

- Automating case management helps ensure that issues are resolved faster, which boosts employee confidence in HR capabilities.
- Centralized case tracking allows for better data collection and reporting, aiding in continuous improvement.

5. Retail Chain Expands Self-Service Capabilities

Background

A major retail chain needed a solution that would empower its large workforce to access HR services more independently. With thousands of employees across numerous locations, HR teams were inundated with repetitive requests that could be automated.

Solution Implementation

ServiceNow's Employee Self-Service Portal was deployed to provide a user-friendly platform for employees to access HR services, submit requests, and track their status without direct HR involvement.

Results

- **Reduction in HR Workload**: The number of direct HR inquiries dropped by 60%, as employees could now resolve many of their issues via the portal.
- **Higher Engagement**: The self-service portal saw high adoption rates due to its intuitive design and comprehensive knowledge base.
- **Streamlined Operations**: HR teams were able to allocate more time to strategic initiatives instead of handling repetitive inquiries.

Key Takeaways

- Implementing a robust self-service portal enhances operational efficiency by reducing the volume of direct HR interactions.
- Intuitive design and comprehensive resources are critical for ensuring high adoption rates.

Conclusion

These success stories illustrate how ServiceNow can be adapted and scaled to meet various organizational needs, driving efficiency, employee satisfaction, and operational effectiveness. The common thread across these implementations is the focus on centralization, automation, and user-centric design, which collectively elevate the HR function to become a strategic partner within the organization.

Lessons Learned from Real-World Deployments

Implementing ServiceNow for HR is an endeavor that can greatly enhance the efficiency and effectiveness of human resources operations. However, real-world deployments often come with unique challenges and learning experiences that shape best practices and inform future projects. This chapter draws from actual implementations to outline key lessons learned, offering practical insights to help organizations optimize their ServiceNow HR implementation journey.

1. Importance of Comprehensive Planning

Lesson Learned: Start with a Clear Vision

One of the most important lessons from real-world deployments is the need for thorough and comprehensive planning. Organizations that succeeded in their implementations invested significant time in defining their project scope, understanding existing HR processes, and aligning objectives with business goals.

Key Insight: Clearly map out the entire HR process landscape and establish a vision for how ServiceNow will integrate into this ecosystem.

Lesson Learned: Involve All Stakeholders Early

Projects that brought in stakeholders from various departments early in the planning process experienced smoother rollouts and better adoption rates. Input from HR teams, IT, compliance, and even end-users ensures that the system design meets diverse needs and reduces unforeseen barriers during deployment.

Key Insight: Engage stakeholders early to capture a broad perspective and foster cross-departmental collaboration.

2. User-Centric Design is Critical

Lesson Learned: Prioritize User Experience (UX)

The success of an HR digital transformation largely hinges on user adoption. Organizations that invested in user-friendly design, intuitive interfaces, and simplified workflows saw higher levels of engagement. Real-world feedback indicated that a positive user experience accelerated the transition from legacy systems to ServiceNow.

Key Insight: Ensure the platform is intuitive for HR professionals and employees alike, with minimal learning curves.

Lesson Learned: Create Tailored Training Programs

Successful implementations included customized training programs designed to meet the specific needs of HR teams and end-users. These programs went beyond technical training and included real-world scenarios, practical exercises, and ongoing support.

Key Insight: Invest in continuous training to empower users and encourage the consistent use of new tools and features.

3. Overcoming Resistance to Change

Lesson Learned: Communication is Key

Resistance to change is common, particularly in large organizations with established processes. Successful deployments emphasized clear, ongoing communication about the benefits of the new system and how it would positively impact HR operations and the employee experience.

Key Insight: Build a robust communication plan that highlights the advantages of ServiceNow, addresses concerns, and maintains transparency throughout the implementation.

Lesson Learned: Change Management Must Be Integrated

Integrating change management strategies directly into the project plan helped organizations transition more smoothly. Strategies such as appointing change champions, holding workshops, and offering incentives for early adoption played pivotal roles in facilitating the shift.

Key Insight: Integrate change management practices to ease the transition and foster a positive perception of the change.

4. Balancing Customization with Best Practices

Lesson Learned: Avoid Over-Customization

While ServiceNow offers extensive customization capabilities, real-world implementations revealed that over-customization can lead to complexities that hinder future updates and scalability. Organizations that focused on configuring standard features to align with their processes, rather than heavily customizing the platform, experienced fewer issues during updates and expansions.

Key Insight: Strive for a balanced approach that leverages out-of-the-box features and customizations only where necessary.

Lesson Learned: Leverage Best Practices

Many organizations learned that adhering to ServiceNow's best practices not only streamlined their implementations but also maximized the platform's capabilities. Best practices provided a framework that helped avoid common pitfalls and ensured smoother operations post-implementation.

Key Insight: Utilize ServiceNow's best practice guidelines to maintain consistency and ensure a successful deployment.

5. Continuous Improvement Yields Long-Term Success

Lesson Learned: Implementation is Just the Beginning

The most successful organizations viewed their initial implementation as the starting point rather than the end goal. They committed to continuous evaluation and improvement of their HR processes, leveraging feedback from users to optimize workflows and expand the platform's capabilities.

Key Insight: Create a culture of continuous improvement by encouraging feedback and iterating on workflows and processes.

Lesson Learned: Regular Health Checks are Essential

Organizations that conducted periodic system health checks and audits were able to maintain optimal performance and security. Regularly reviewing workflows, user activity, and system updates helped identify potential issues early and kept the platform aligned with changing business needs.

Key Insight: Schedule regular system evaluations to maintain efficiency, compliance, and user satisfaction.

6. Managing Data and Compliance

Lesson Learned: Data Preparation is Key

Real-world deployments demonstrated that data migration and preparation are significant aspects of ServiceNow implementation. Organizations that took the time to clean and validate their data before migration faced fewer issues during and after deployment.

Key Insight: Invest time in thorough data preparation and validation to ensure a seamless transition.

Lesson Learned: Compliance Needs Ongoing Attention

Compliance was a recurring concern, especially for organizations operating in multiple jurisdictions. Implementations that incorporated compliance protocols from the start, such as ensuring GDPR or other data protection standards, minimized risks and maintained trust.

Key Insight: Embed compliance strategies early and maintain regular updates to adapt to new regulations.

Conclusion

The lessons learned from these real-world deployments highlight the importance of strategic planning, user engagement, balanced customization, and continuous improvement. By adopting these practices, organizations can navigate the complexities of implementing ServiceNow for HR and harness its full potential for digital transformation.

Common Pitfalls and How to Avoid Them

The journey of implementing ServiceNow for HR can bring significant benefits but is not without its challenges. By understanding the common pitfalls experienced by organizations in real-world deployments, HR leaders and project teams can proactively avoid these challenges and ensure a smoother implementation process. This chapter highlights these common pitfalls and provides strategies to mitigate them for a successful ServiceNow rollout.

1. Inadequate Planning and Scope Creep

Pitfall: Insufficient Initial Planning

A recurring issue in many implementations is the failure to plan comprehensively from the outset. When organizations do not allocate enough time and resources to define project goals, timelines, and budgets, the project can easily run into delays and cost overruns.

How to Avoid:

- Develop a detailed project plan that includes clear milestones, deliverables, and risk assessments.
- Ensure alignment between project goals and the organization's broader HR strategy.
- Regularly review the project scope to ensure that it remains consistent and manageable.

Pitfall: Scope Creep

Scope creep occurs when additional requirements or features are added to the project without proper evaluation, leading to delays and increased costs.

How to Avoid:

- Establish a change management process for evaluating and approving changes to the project scope.
- Prioritize features and requirements that align with key project objectives.

2. Insufficient Stakeholder Involvement

Pitfall: Lack of Stakeholder Engagement

Implementations that do not involve stakeholders from relevant departments often miss crucial insights that can affect the project's success. HR, IT, compliance teams, and end-users all play a critical role in shaping the final product.

How to Avoid:

- Involve stakeholders early and continuously throughout the project lifecycle.
- Conduct regular stakeholder meetings to gather feedback and align expectations.

Pitfall: Poor Communication

Failure to maintain open lines of communication can lead to misunderstandings, resistance to change, and missed requirements.

How to Avoid:

- Create a communication plan that outlines how updates will be shared with stakeholders and project teams.
- Use tools such as dashboards and status reports to keep all relevant parties informed.

3. Underestimating Data Migration Complexity

Pitfall: Inadequate Data Preparation

Data migration is one of the most complex aspects of ServiceNow implementation. Underestimating the time and resources required to clean, validate, and transfer data can lead to inaccuracies and delays.

How to Avoid:

- Conduct a thorough data audit to identify inconsistencies or gaps in data before migration.
- Use data migration tools and scripts designed to streamline the process.
- Plan for data testing phases to verify data integrity post-migration.

4. Customization Overload

Pitfall: Excessive Customization

While customization can enhance ServiceNow's fit for an organization, going beyond necessary customizations can make the system difficult to maintain and update. This can lead to increased costs and future limitations when integrating new features or upgrades.

How to Avoid:

- Follow ServiceNow's best practice guidelines for customization.
- Evaluate whether a specific customization is essential or if existing out-of-the-box features can meet the need.
- Document all customizations for future reference and support.

5. Inadequate User Training and Change Management

Pitfall: Lack of Comprehensive Training

Without proper training, users are less likely to fully utilize ServiceNow's capabilities, leading to low adoption rates and inefficiencies.

How to Avoid:

- Develop a training program that includes practical, hands-on learning experiences tailored to different user roles.
- Offer continuous learning opportunities such as refresher courses, workshops, and online tutorials.

Pitfall: Ignoring Change Management

Implementations that do not account for change management often face resistance from users accustomed to legacy systems.

How to Avoid:

- Implement a robust change management strategy that includes workshops, pilot programs, and open forums for feedback.
- Appoint change champions within each department to advocate for the new system and provide on-the-ground support.

6. Neglecting Post-Implementation Support

Pitfall: Limited Post-Deployment Support

Many organizations view the go-live date as the end of the project, leading to limited resources for support and troubleshooting post-implementation.

How to Avoid:

- Plan for ongoing support and maintenance as part of the initial project budget.
- Assign a dedicated support team to handle any issues that arise and to assist with user questions.
- Establish a feedback loop to capture user experiences and continuously improve the system.

Pitfall: Ignoring Performance Monitoring

A lack of performance monitoring can result in a decline in system efficiency and user satisfaction.

How to Avoid:

- Implement regular system health checks and performance metrics to identify issues early.
- Use dashboards and reporting tools within ServiceNow to monitor usage and process efficiency.

7. Compliance and Security Oversights

Pitfall: Overlooking Compliance Requirements

Failing to incorporate compliance standards from the beginning can expose the organization to legal and reputational risks.

How to Avoid:

- Include compliance officers in the implementation team to ensure that data protection and security protocols are met.
- Regularly review regulatory changes and update ServiceNow configurations to maintain compliance.

Pitfall: Security Gaps

Security oversights, such as weak user permissions and inadequate role management, can compromise sensitive HR data.

How to Avoid:

- Implement robust user access controls and review them regularly.
- Conduct security audits to identify and mitigate vulnerabilities.

Conclusion

Recognizing and addressing these common pitfalls can greatly improve the success of your ServiceNow HR implementation. By investing in proper planning, involving key stakeholders, managing data effectively, and maintaining strong post-implementation practices, organizations can avoid costly mistakes and realize the full potential of their ServiceNow platform.

Industry-Specific Use Cases and Solutions

The adaptability of ServiceNow allows HR teams across various industries to tailor the platform to meet unique challenges and leverage its capabilities to streamline their workflows. This chapter explores industry-specific use cases and solutions to illustrate how ServiceNow has been implemented successfully in diverse sectors, highlighting tailored approaches, best practices, and results.

1. Healthcare: Streamlining Employee Credentialing and Compliance

Use Case Overview

In the healthcare industry, ensuring that employee credentials are valid and up-to-date is crucial for patient safety and compliance with regulations. Manual tracking of credentials can be time-consuming and prone to errors, putting healthcare facilities at risk.

Solution Implementation

ServiceNow was configured to create automated workflows that track credential expiration dates, notify employees and HR administrators of upcoming renewals, and maintain an audit trail for compliance checks. Integrating ServiceNow with credentialing verification systems ensured real-time updates and streamlined verification processes.

Results

- Improved efficiency in managing employee credentials.
- Reduced instances of non-compliance through automated notifications.
- Enhanced transparency and reporting capabilities.

Best Practices

- Configure dashboards to monitor credential status across the organization.
- Use ServiceNow's document management features for storing and securing credential-related documents.

2. Financial Services: Enhancing Security and Data Privacy

Use Case Overview

Financial institutions prioritize the protection of sensitive employee and client data. HR processes in this sector must align with stringent security protocols and data privacy regulations.

Solution Implementation

ServiceNow's HR module was customized to include advanced user permissions, ensuring that sensitive data could only be accessed by authorized personnel. Multi-factor authentication (MFA) and encrypted data storage were implemented to enhance security. Additionally, automated compliance checks were set up to ensure adherence to financial regulations.

Results

- Strengthened data protection with advanced security protocols.
- Streamlined audits and compliance reporting.
- Reduced the risk of data breaches and unauthorized access.

Best Practices

- Integrate ServiceNow with security information and event management (SIEM) tools for real-time threat detection.
- Regularly update and review user roles and permissions.

3. Manufacturing: Simplifying Employee Onboarding Processes

Use Case Overview

In the manufacturing industry, high turnover rates and frequent onboarding of new employees present challenges in maintaining consistent and efficient HR practices.

Solution Implementation

ServiceNow's onboarding module was tailored to create an automated onboarding process that included pre-configured checklists, integration with payroll and benefits platforms, and seamless coordination between HR and other departments such as IT and facilities. This ensured that new employees were equipped and ready to start work promptly.

Results

- Reduced onboarding time by 40%.
- Enhanced new hire experience through structured and automated workflows.
- Decreased manual workload for HR staff, allowing them to focus on strategic initiatives.

Best Practices

- Use ServiceNow's task assignments to ensure cross-departmental coordination.
- Customize onboarding templates to fit various job roles.

4. Retail: Managing Seasonal Workforce Fluctuations

Use Case Overview

Retail companies face the challenge of ramping up their workforce during peak seasons. Managing a large influx of temporary employees requires efficient scheduling, contract management, and payroll adjustments.

Solution Implementation

ServiceNow was configured to handle high-volume onboarding and contract management workflows. Automated scheduling tools integrated into ServiceNow allowed HR teams to manage shifts efficiently, while real-time reporting helped track payroll adjustments for seasonal workers.

Results

- Streamlined hiring and onboarding processes for temporary staff.
- Increased accuracy in shift scheduling and payroll management.
- Enhanced workforce planning through real-time data analytics.

Best Practices

- Develop reusable templates for seasonal hiring.
- Implement mobile access features to facilitate communication and scheduling for temporary employees.

5. Technology: Integrating HR with IT for Seamless Operations

Use Case Overview

In the tech industry, seamless integration between HR and IT departments is vital for efficient onboarding, resource allocation, and ongoing support for employees.

Solution Implementation

ServiceNow was leveraged to connect HR processes with IT operations management. Automated workflows were created for provisioning and de-provisioning access to software and equipment. This integration enabled HR teams to coordinate with IT effortlessly when setting up new hires or managing offboarding tasks.

Results

- Improved onboarding efficiency by automating equipment and software setup.
- Enhanced collaboration between HR and IT departments.
- Minimized delays in providing new employees with necessary resources.

Best Practices

- Integrate ServiceNow with asset management systems to track equipment usage.
- Use workflow automation to reduce the need for manual coordination between HR and IT.

6. Education: Simplifying Faculty and Staff Management

Use Case Overview

Educational institutions often face the complex task of managing faculty, administrative staff, and part-time employees with diverse roles and contract terms.

Solution Implementation

ServiceNow's HR capabilities were customized to create workflows that manage faculty contracts, tenure tracking, and performance appraisals. Additionally, automated processes were established for handling leave requests, professional development scheduling, and contract renewals.

Results

- Streamlined contract management processes, improving HR efficiency.
- Enhanced faculty experience with transparent and efficient HR workflows.
- Reduced administrative burden through automation of repetitive tasks.

Best Practices

- Utilize ServiceNow's reporting tools for tracking tenure and contract timelines.
- Implement role-specific workflows to accommodate different employment types.

Conclusion

Industry-specific adaptations of ServiceNow's HR platform demonstrate its versatility and effectiveness in addressing unique challenges across sectors. Whether it's ensuring compliance in healthcare, managing seasonal staff in retail, or integrating HR and IT in tech, ServiceNow's configurable nature enables organizations to implement targeted solutions that improve processes and outcomes. By learning from these use cases, organizations can tailor their own implementations to maximize efficiency, compliance, and user satisfaction.

Future Trends in HR Technology and ServiceNow

As organizations continue to evolve and adapt to new workplace dynamics, HR technology plays a pivotal role in driving growth and maintaining competitive advantages. ServiceNow, as a leading digital workflow platform, is at the forefront of these changes, setting the stage for how HR processes will continue to transform. This chapter explores the future trends in HR technology, highlighting how ServiceNow is positioned to meet the demands of the future and enhance HR operations.

1. The Integration of AI and Machine Learning

The Trend

Artificial Intelligence (AI) and machine learning are shaping the future of HR by automating tasks, analyzing data at scale, and providing predictive insights. These technologies allow HR departments to focus more on strategic planning and less on manual, repetitive tasks.

How ServiceNow Adapts

ServiceNow's HR platform is expanding its capabilities by integrating advanced AI-powered features. These enhancements include chatbots for employee self-service, intelligent routing of HR cases based on past behavior, and automated document generation. Machine learning models are also being incorporated to predict HR trends, such as attrition rates and training needs, giving HR leaders data-backed insights for proactive decision-making.

Benefits

- **Improved Efficiency**: AI-powered automation streamlines administrative tasks, reducing manual workload.
- **Enhanced User Experience**: Chatbots and intelligent self-service portals improve response times and employee satisfaction.
- **Data-Driven Insights**: Machine learning provides predictive analytics for better workforce planning and strategy formulation.

2. Employee Experience as a Central Focus

The Trend

Employee experience (EX) has become a key priority for HR departments, as a positive EX directly correlates with productivity, retention, and overall organizational success. Modern HR platforms are focusing on making processes more intuitive and personalized for employees.

How ServiceNow Adapts

ServiceNow has introduced enhancements that prioritize the employee experience. Customizable HR portals, personalized dashboards, and integrated mobile solutions are becoming standard features. The platform is also focusing on providing employees with more seamless access to HR services, enabling them to resolve issues, request support, and receive communications all in one unified space.

Benefits

- **Higher Engagement Levels**: Streamlined and user-friendly interfaces keep employees engaged and satisfied with HR services.
- **Improved Retention**: Enhanced EX contributes to greater job satisfaction and lowers turnover rates.
- **Flexible Access**: Mobile-first features ensure employees can access HR services from anywhere, supporting remote and hybrid work environments.

3. The Rise of Data Privacy and Compliance Solutions

The Trend

With data breaches and regulatory pressures on the rise, ensuring data privacy and compliance has become a non-negotiable aspect of HR technology. Organizations must adhere to evolving privacy laws, such as GDPR and CCPA, to protect employee information.

How ServiceNow Adapts

ServiceNow is continuously updating its data security and compliance modules to align with the latest regulations. The platform offers tools for automatic data masking, secure document management, and robust audit trails. New compliance features help HR teams stay compliant with local, regional, and international laws without compromising efficiency.

Benefits

- **Enhanced Security**: Advanced security measures protect sensitive employee data.
- **Simplified Auditing**: Automated compliance tools streamline internal and external audits.
- **Regulatory Adherence**: Continuous updates ensure alignment with the latest data protection regulations.

4. Expanding Capabilities with Low-Code/No-Code Solutions

The Trend

Low-code and no-code platforms are empowering HR teams to build custom applications and workflows without the need for extensive coding knowledge. This trend democratizes technology and enables faster, more tailored solutions.

How ServiceNow Adapts

ServiceNow's Now Platform provides low-code/no-code capabilities through its App Engine, allowing HR professionals to create custom workflows, applications, and integrations. This enables organizations to rapidly adapt to changing needs, such as new HR policies, employee onboarding processes, and remote work protocols.

Benefits

- **Rapid Deployment**: Custom solutions can be built and implemented quickly.
- **Reduced IT Dependence**: HR teams gain more control over their processes without heavy reliance on IT support.
- **Personalized Solutions**: Tailored applications meet specific organizational needs.

5. Enhanced Analytics and Reporting

The Trend

Advanced analytics and business intelligence are becoming essential for HR departments to make informed, data-driven decisions. Future trends indicate a greater reliance on real-time data for assessing HR performance and predicting trends.

How ServiceNow Adapts

ServiceNow has introduced advanced reporting and analytics tools that integrate seamlessly with existing HR workflows. These tools offer real-time dashboards, predictive analytics, and enhanced visualization capabilities that make it easier to understand complex data sets. HR teams can leverage these tools to monitor key metrics such as employee satisfaction, workflow efficiency, and process bottlenecks.

Benefits

- **Better Decision-Making**: Real-time data supports quicker and more informed decisions.
- **Proactive HR Management**: Predictive insights allow HR teams to address potential issues before they escalate.
- **Enhanced Transparency**: Visual reporting provides clear and actionable insights for stakeholders.

6. Integration with Emerging Technologies

The Trend

Emerging technologies such as blockchain, augmented reality (AR), and the Internet of Things (IoT) are beginning to find applications in HR processes, from verifying credentials to enhancing training programs.

How ServiceNow Adapts

ServiceNow is exploring integrations with emerging technologies to expand its capabilities. Blockchain integration, for example, can be used for secure credential verification, while AR tools can be leveraged for immersive employee training experiences. IoT-enabled devices may support workforce management by tracking real-time data related to employee productivity and wellness.

Benefits

- **Enhanced Verification Processes**: Blockchain technology ensures the secure and tamper-proof verification of credentials.
- **Interactive Training**: AR-based training programs provide immersive learning experiences.
- **Holistic Employee Monitoring**: IoT integrations offer insights into employee wellness and productivity.

Conclusion

The future of HR technology is marked by innovation, agility, and a commitment to enhancing both operational efficiency and employee experience. ServiceNow continues to position itself as a leader in this evolving landscape by incorporating cutting-edge solutions such as AI, data privacy features, low-code tools, and emerging technologies. By staying ahead of these trends, HR leaders can harness the full potential of ServiceNow to build resilient, future-ready HR processes that adapt to the needs of a dynamic workforce.

Section 11:
Compliance and Security Considerations

Ensuring GDPR and Data Protection Compliance

In today's digital landscape, compliance with data protection laws such as the General Data Protection Regulation (GDPR) is more than a best practice—it is a legal necessity. HR departments must prioritize data privacy and protection not only to avoid legal consequences but also to build trust with their employees. ServiceNow, with its robust data management features, offers comprehensive tools and practices to ensure organizations remain compliant with GDPR and other data protection standards.

1. Understanding GDPR and Its Implications for HR

Key Points of GDPR

The GDPR, enforced by the European Union, is one of the most stringent data protection regulations in the world. Its main principles include:

- **Transparency**: Informing individuals how their data is collected, processed, and used.
- **Accountability**: Ensuring that organizations are responsible for adhering to GDPR standards.
- **Data Minimization**: Collecting only necessary data and processing it in a way that aligns with the intended purpose.
- **Right to Access and Erasure**: Empowering individuals with rights such as accessing their data and requesting its deletion.

Implications for HR

HR departments handle a vast amount of personal employee data, from contact details to sensitive records like medical and performance data. Compliance with GDPR means ensuring that:

- Employees are informed about how their data is processed.
- HR systems provide mechanisms for data access, correction, and deletion requests.
- Adequate security measures are in place to protect data against breaches.

2. Leveraging ServiceNow for GDPR Compliance

Data Privacy by Design

ServiceNow's platform is built with privacy and security as foundational elements. This "privacy by design" approach supports HR departments in implementing processes that inherently align with GDPR standards.

Key Features in ServiceNow for Compliance

- **Data Encryption**: ServiceNow provides end-to-end data encryption, ensuring that sensitive information remains secure during transit and storage.
- **Access Control and Role-Based Permissions**: HR teams can control who accesses specific data, ensuring that only authorized personnel can view or modify sensitive information.
- **Audit Trails**: The platform maintains comprehensive logs of data access and modifications, providing accountability and transparency required for GDPR compliance.

- **Automated Data Management**: ServiceNow can automate processes such as data anonymization and deletion, facilitating adherence to the "right to be forgotten" principle.

Implementing GDPR-Focused Workflows

Custom workflows can be configured in ServiceNow to manage GDPR requests. For example:

- **Data Access Requests**: Automated workflows can be designed to handle employee requests for accessing their personal data, ensuring timely responses and documentation.
- **Data Deletion and Anonymization**: HR can create workflows to comply with data erasure requests, removing or anonymizing data in line with GDPR requirements.

3. Data Protection Best Practices

Comprehensive Data Mapping

Before implementing GDPR-compliant processes, HR must understand where all employee data is stored and processed. This involves:

- **Cataloging Data Sources**: Identifying all systems, databases, and repositories where employee data is stored.
- **Understanding Data Flow**: Documenting how data moves within and outside the organization.

Implementing Data Protection Impact Assessments (DPIAs)

DPIAs are essential for assessing the risks associated with processing personal data. ServiceNow's reporting and analytics capabilities can help HR conduct these assessments effectively by:

- Providing visual dashboards to monitor data handling.
- Highlighting potential risks and suggesting mitigation measures.

Training and Awareness

Ensuring compliance is not solely the responsibility of the HR department; it requires organization-wide awareness. ServiceNow supports training initiatives by:

- Facilitating the creation and distribution of compliance training materials.
- Tracking completion rates and participation to ensure all employees understand their role in data protection.

4. Addressing Data Breaches

Proactive Measures

ServiceNow's platform offers tools for proactive data breach prevention, such as:

- **Real-Time Monitoring**: Detecting and flagging potential data vulnerabilities.
- **Automated Alerts**: Notifying HR and compliance teams if a data breach is suspected.

Response Plan

GDPR mandates that data breaches be reported within 72 hours of discovery. ServiceNow helps streamline this process by:

- Enabling automated incident management workflows.
- Generating detailed incident reports for submission to regulatory authorities.

5. Compliance Beyond GDPR

While GDPR is specific to the EU, many countries have enacted or are enacting similar data protection regulations. ServiceNow's adaptable platform can help HR teams manage compliance with global standards, such as:

- **CCPA (California Consumer Privacy Act)**: Similar rights to GDPR, focusing on consumer data protection.
- **LGPD (Lei Geral de Proteção de Dados)**: Brazil's data protection law with similar principles to GDPR.

ServiceNow's scalable architecture allows HR teams to stay compliant as regulations evolve globally, ensuring data protection best practices are consistently maintained.

Conclusion

Ensuring GDPR and data protection compliance is crucial for HR departments managing sensitive employee data. ServiceNow's platform, with its focus on security, transparency, and automation, provides a powerful toolset for HR leaders to navigate the complexities of GDPR and other data regulations. By leveraging these capabilities, organizations can maintain legal compliance, foster trust, and protect their most valuable asset: their employees.

HR Data Privacy Best Practices

In an era defined by the rapid digitization of HR functions, ensuring the privacy and protection of employee data is paramount. HR teams are custodians of highly sensitive information, and protecting this data requires robust strategies and compliance with both internal and external regulations. This chapter explores best practices for managing data privacy within HR departments, leveraging ServiceNow's advanced capabilities to uphold high standards of security and trust.

1. Understanding the Importance of HR Data Privacy

Why HR Data Privacy Matters

Employee data encompasses a wide range of personal and professional information, from contact details and payroll data to performance evaluations and health records. Unauthorized access or breaches can have severe consequences, including:

- **Legal and Regulatory Penalties**: Non-compliance with privacy laws such as GDPR, CCPA, and other data protection regulations can lead to significant fines.
- **Reputation Damage**: Data breaches erode trust, damaging the organization's credibility with both employees and stakeholders.
- **Employee Trust**: A strong privacy policy reassures employees that their data is handled with care, fostering trust and confidence in HR processes.

2. Establishing Comprehensive Data Privacy Policies

Key Components of a Privacy Policy

A clear and comprehensive data privacy policy is the foundation for protecting employee data. Such a policy should include:

- **Purpose of Data Collection**: Clearly outline why employee data is collected and how it will be used.
- **Data Access Controls**: Specify which individuals or teams have access to particular types of data and under what conditions.
- **Data Retention Guidelines**: Define how long data will be stored and the processes for its safe disposal.
- **Employee Rights**: Ensure employees are aware of their rights, such as accessing, correcting, or requesting the deletion of their data.

Communicating Privacy Policies

It is essential for HR teams to ensure that all employees are informed about the organization's data privacy policies. This can be achieved through:

- **Workshops and Training Sessions**: Regular training for employees and HR staff on privacy protocols.
- **Accessible Documentation**: Publishing policies on an internal portal that employees can easily access.

3. Leveraging ServiceNow for Data Privacy Management

Built-In Privacy Features

ServiceNow offers a robust set of features designed to uphold data privacy standards, including:

- **Role-Based Access Control (RBAC)**: Limit access to sensitive data based on user roles, ensuring only authorized personnel can view or modify specific information.
- **Audit Logs and Activity Tracking**: Maintain detailed logs of data access and modifications to promote accountability and transparency.
- **Data Encryption**: Protect data in transit and at rest with comprehensive encryption protocols to minimize the risk of breaches.

Automation of Privacy Processes

ServiceNow's automation capabilities can streamline various data privacy tasks, such as:

- **Data Deletion Requests**: Automate the workflow for handling data deletion requests, ensuring timely compliance with regulations like GDPR.
- **Privacy Assessments**: Use automated workflows to conduct regular privacy impact assessments (PIAs) to identify and mitigate data privacy risks.

4. Implementing Best Practices for Data Handling

Data Minimization

Only collect and retain data that is essential for HR functions. This reduces the risk of data exposure and ensures compliance with the principle of data minimization outlined in many data protection laws.

Regular Privacy Audits

Conduct regular audits to ensure that data handling practices align with organizational policies and legal requirements. ServiceNow's analytics and reporting tools can provide insights into data usage and potential areas for improvement.

Secure Data Sharing

When data sharing between departments or with third-party service providers is necessary, implement strict protocols:

- **Use Secure Transfer Methods**: Ensure data is shared using secure, encrypted channels.
- **Third-Party Compliance Checks**: Verify that any third parties involved in data processing meet the organization's privacy standards and comply with applicable laws.

5. Educating and Training HR Staff

Continuous Training Programs

HR teams should undergo continuous training to stay informed about the latest data privacy trends, regulations, and technologies. ServiceNow can facilitate this by providing tools for creating and tracking training programs.

Creating a Culture of Data Privacy

Foster a culture where data privacy is a shared responsibility. Encourage HR staff to be vigilant and proactive in protecting employee data and reporting potential privacy concerns.

6. Responding to Data Breaches

Incident Response Plan

Despite the best precautions, data breaches can occur. Having a well-defined response plan is critical for minimizing damage and ensuring compliance with reporting requirements:

- **Immediate Notification**: Inform key stakeholders and affected employees promptly.
- **Investigation and Containment**: Use ServiceNow's incident management tools to investigate the breach, identify the source, and contain it.
- **Regulatory Reporting**: Ensure compliance with any mandatory breach reporting regulations, such as GDPR's 72-hour notification requirement.

Post-Breach Analysis

Conduct a thorough analysis after a breach to identify lessons learned and implement measures to prevent future incidents. ServiceNow's post-incident review tools can support this process by compiling comprehensive reports.

7. Ensuring Ongoing Compliance

Keeping Up with Evolving Regulations

Data protection laws are continually evolving. HR departments must stay updated on new regulations and adapt their privacy practices accordingly. ServiceNow's flexible platform allows for easy modifications to workflows and policies to accommodate new compliance requirements.

Periodic Policy Reviews

Regularly review and update data privacy policies to reflect changes in laws, technologies, and organizational needs. ServiceNow can facilitate the version control and distribution of updated policies across the HR department.

Conclusion

Ensuring data privacy within HR is an ongoing commitment that involves robust policies, secure technology solutions, and continuous education. ServiceNow's comprehensive platform supports HR teams in implementing best practices for data privacy, empowering them to protect employee information and maintain compliance with global data protection standards. By adopting these practices, organizations can build a culture of trust, demonstrating their commitment to protecting the privacy of their workforce.

Security Protocols for HR Data on ServiceNow

Ensuring data security is a critical concern for any organization, particularly when dealing with sensitive HR data. HR departments handle extensive personal and professional information, including employee records, payroll, health information, and performance reviews. ServiceNow, as a comprehensive platform for managing HR workflows, incorporates robust security protocols designed to safeguard data and maintain compliance with global security standards. This chapter outlines the key security protocols that HR teams can implement on ServiceNow to protect sensitive HR data.

1. Understanding the Importance of Data Security for HR

Key Concerns for HR Data Security

HR data security involves protecting data from unauthorized access, maintaining data integrity, and ensuring its availability when needed. Key concerns include:

- **Confidentiality**: Ensuring that only authorized personnel have access to sensitive HR data.
- **Integrity**: Protecting data from unauthorized modification to maintain its accuracy and trustworthiness.
- **Availability**: Guaranteeing that data is accessible when needed by authorized users without unnecessary delays.

2. ServiceNow's Security Framework

Core Security Features

ServiceNow provides a variety of built-in security features that support the secure handling of HR data, including:

- **Role-Based Access Control (RBAC)**: ServiceNow's RBAC ensures that only individuals with specific roles can access or modify HR data. HR administrators can define roles and permissions based on job functions to limit data exposure.
- **Data Encryption**: Both in transit and at rest, ServiceNow ensures that data is encrypted to prevent unauthorized access or interception.
- **Multi-Factor Authentication (MFA)**: MFA adds an additional layer of security by requiring more than one method of verification to access sensitive HR data.

Data Segmentation and Separation

HR data should be segmented and separated from other business data to reduce risk exposure. ServiceNow allows for the use of data segmentation to create isolated data environments, ensuring that sensitive HR information remains separate from other organizational data.

3. Implementing Advanced Security Protocols

Encryption Protocols

ServiceNow supports encryption protocols such as Advanced Encryption Standard (AES) to secure HR data. Organizations should:

- **Use End-to-End Encryption**: Apply end-to-end encryption for data sent between the ServiceNow platform and user devices.
- **Encrypt Sensitive Fields**: Use ServiceNow's data encryption capabilities to protect highly sensitive fields within HR records, such as social security numbers and medical data.

Access Control Mechanisms

Develop strict access control mechanisms using ServiceNow's robust security model:

- **Granular Access Permissions**: Configure access controls at various levels, including field, record, and table-level permissions, to prevent unauthorized access.
- **Least Privilege Principle**: Implement the principle of least privilege to limit user access rights to only those necessary for their roles.
- **Audit and Monitoring of Access Logs**: Regularly audit access logs to identify any suspicious activity or unauthorized access attempts.

Multi-Layered Authentication

Strengthen security with multi-layered authentication strategies:

- **Enable Multi-Factor Authentication (MFA)**: Ensure MFA is activated for all HR personnel accessing sensitive data.
- **Single Sign-On (SSO) Integration**: Integrate SSO to simplify access while maintaining a high level of security across platforms.

4. Regular Security Assessments and Compliance Checks

Conducting Security Audits

Regular security audits are vital for ensuring the HR data on ServiceNow remains secure. This involves:

- **Vulnerability Assessments**: Schedule and conduct vulnerability assessments to identify and mitigate potential risks.
- **Penetration Testing**: Implement penetration testing to simulate cyber-attacks and test the platform's defenses.
- **Compliance Reviews**: Regularly review security protocols to ensure they align with industry standards and regulatory requirements such as GDPR and CCPA.

Continuous Monitoring

Use ServiceNow's built-in monitoring tools to track user activity, data access patterns, and potential security incidents:

- **Real-Time Alerts**: Configure alerts for unusual access attempts or unauthorized data modifications.
- **Anomaly Detection**: Leverage ServiceNow's AI capabilities to detect anomalies in data usage that could indicate security threats.

5. Educating HR Teams on Security Best Practices

Security Awareness Training

A well-trained HR team is essential for maintaining data security. Training should focus on:

- **Recognizing Phishing Attempts**: Teach HR employees how to identify and report phishing and other social engineering attacks.
- **Secure Password Practices**: Encourage the use of strong, unique passwords and the use of password managers if necessary.
- **Data Handling Protocols**: Reinforce the importance of handling HR data in a secure manner, including appropriate use of the ServiceNow platform.

Incident Response Training

Ensure HR teams are prepared to respond quickly to data breaches or security incidents by:

- **Defining Incident Protocols**: Establish a clear incident response plan with specific steps for identifying, reporting, and mitigating data breaches.
- **Simulating Security Drills**: Regularly conduct security drills to practice the incident response plan and ensure that HR teams are confident in their ability to act swiftly.

6. Enhancing Security with Advanced Technologies

Integrating Artificial Intelligence (AI)

Utilize ServiceNow's AI-driven security features to enhance data protection:

- **AI-Powered Monitoring**: Use AI algorithms to monitor data access and detect potential security breaches based on behavioral patterns.
- **Automated Threat Response**: Implement automated threat response protocols to rapidly address security incidents and reduce manual intervention.

Leveraging Blockchain for Data Integrity

Explore the use of blockchain technology to ensure data integrity:

- **Immutable Records**: Blockchain can provide a tamper-proof record of data transactions, adding an additional layer of trust and security for sensitive HR information.

Conclusion

Securing HR data on the ServiceNow platform requires a comprehensive approach that incorporates advanced security features, regular audits, and continuous training. By implementing robust security protocols and leveraging ServiceNow's powerful security tools, organizations can ensure that sensitive HR data remains protected and compliant with global standards. This proactive approach not only minimizes risk but also builds trust among employees and stakeholders, reinforcing the organization's commitment to data privacy and security.

Auditing and Monitoring for Compliance

Ensuring compliance with regulatory standards and maintaining data integrity are essential components of managing HR operations effectively. Implementing a robust auditing and monitoring framework within ServiceNow helps HR teams adhere to global regulations, reduce risks, and sustain trust with employees. This chapter outlines best practices for auditing and monitoring HR data and workflows to ensure compliance on the ServiceNow platform.

1. The Importance of Auditing and Monitoring in HR

Why Compliance Matters

HR teams are custodians of sensitive employee information, and failure to meet regulatory requirements can result in severe penalties, reputational damage, and erosion of trust. Key regulations that impact HR data management include:

- **General Data Protection Regulation (GDPR)**: Ensures data privacy and protection for individuals in the European Union.
- **California Consumer Privacy Act (CCPA)**: Provides data privacy rights to California residents.
- **Health Insurance Portability and Accountability Act (HIPAA)**: Protects health information in the U.S.
- **Other regional and industry-specific regulations**: Various global standards specific to different regions and industries.

Benefits of Auditing and Monitoring

- **Ensures Compliance**: Helps maintain adherence to regulations by tracking data access and processing.
- **Improves Data Integrity**: Detects unauthorized changes and ensures data accuracy.
- **Enhances Security**: Identifies suspicious activity that could indicate potential data breaches.
- **Builds Trust**: Demonstrates the organization's commitment to data protection and compliance.

2. ServiceNow's Compliance Features for Auditing and Monitoring

Built-in Audit Trails

ServiceNow provides built-in audit trails that allow HR teams to track changes to records, access logs, and user activities. These logs provide a comprehensive history of:

- **Who accessed the data**: User identification and role.
- **When it was accessed**: Date and time stamps for auditing purposes.
- **What changes were made**: Detailed records of modifications or actions performed.

Compliance Dashboards

ServiceNow includes customizable compliance dashboards to monitor data usage, access patterns, and potential compliance breaches. These dashboards provide real-time insights into:

- **Audit logs and reports**: Visual representations of recent activities.
- **Compliance metrics**: Key performance indicators (KPIs) related to adherence to specific regulatory standards.
- **Alerts for non-compliance**: Notifications for activities that deviate from set compliance protocols.

3. Implementing a Comprehensive Auditing Strategy

Establishing Clear Policies

Before leveraging ServiceNow's auditing features, it is important to define clear policies for data access, modification, and retention:

- **Access Control Policies**: Define roles and permissions to ensure that only authorized personnel have access to sensitive HR data.
- **Data Retention Policies**: Establish guidelines for how long data should be kept and when it should be deleted or archived.
- **Audit Frequency**: Set the frequency of audits based on the sensitivity of the data and regulatory requirements.

Configuring Audit Logs

ServiceNow allows for the configuration of audit logs tailored to specific compliance needs:

- **Field-level Auditing**: Enable auditing for key data fields that require heightened oversight, such as social security numbers, payroll details, and health records.
- **User Activity Tracking**: Set up logs to capture user actions, including data entry, modifications, and deletions.
- **Report Generation**: Create custom audit reports that can be shared with compliance officers and stakeholders.

Automation of Monitoring Processes

Automating compliance checks and alerts ensures continuous adherence to policies:

- **Automated Alerts**: Set up automatic notifications for any suspicious activity or deviations from normal data access patterns.
- **Scheduled Reports**: Schedule regular reports that provide an overview of audit logs and compliance status.

4. Best Practices for Effective Monitoring

Proactive Compliance Reviews

Regular compliance reviews help organizations identify gaps and implement corrective measures:

- **Monthly Compliance Meetings**: Conduct monthly or quarterly meetings to review compliance reports and address any issues.
- **Internal Compliance Audits**: Schedule periodic internal audits to assess adherence to policies before external audits are conducted.

Real-Time Monitoring Tools

Leverage ServiceNow's real-time monitoring tools for ongoing oversight:

- **Continuous Data Analysis**: Utilize continuous data analysis to detect anomalies and trends that could signal compliance issues.
- **Integrated Security Protocols**: Ensure that real-time monitoring tools are integrated with security protocols to provide immediate response options for potential breaches.

Employee Training and Awareness

Ensure that HR staff and relevant personnel are aware of their roles in maintaining compliance:

- **Training Programs**: Implement regular training sessions focused on data handling best practices and compliance protocols.
- **Awareness Campaigns**: Create awareness campaigns that remind employees of the importance of compliance and security in handling HR data.

5. Addressing Compliance Challenges

Managing Cross-Border Data Transfers

For organizations that operate globally, cross-border data transfers pose additional compliance challenges:

- **Data Localization Policies**: Familiarize the HR team with data localization requirements in different regions.
- **Data Protection Agreements**: Ensure that cross-border data transfers are governed by agreements that comply with international data protection laws.

Responding to Compliance Breaches

Develop a clear protocol for handling compliance breaches:

- **Immediate Action Plan**: Establish a response plan that includes immediate data isolation, investigation, and remediation.
- **Notification Protocols**: Create a process for notifying affected individuals and regulatory authorities, as required by law.

6. Leveraging ServiceNow's Advanced Capabilities

Integration with Third-Party Compliance Tools

ServiceNow can be integrated with other third-party tools to enhance compliance monitoring:

- **Compliance Management Software**: Integrate specialized compliance management software to expand auditing and reporting capabilities.
- **Security Information and Event Management (SIEM)**: Utilize SIEM tools to centralize and analyze security data from multiple sources.

Utilizing AI for Predictive Analysis

Incorporate artificial intelligence to predict and prevent potential compliance issues:

- **AI-Driven Insights**: Use AI to analyze historical data and detect patterns that could lead to compliance breaches.
- **Automated Recommendations**: Receive AI-powered suggestions for policy adjustments based on observed data trends.

Conclusion

Effective auditing and monitoring for compliance are essential for any HR department handling sensitive data. By leveraging ServiceNow's powerful auditing features, compliance dashboards, and automation capabilities, organizations can ensure that their HR data remains secure, compliant, and trustworthy. Regular audits, continuous monitoring, and proactive compliance measures not only safeguard data but also reinforce an organization's commitment to ethical and legal data practices.

Section 12:
Continuous Improvement and Future Prospects

Leveraging Feedback for HR Workflow Enhancements

Continuous improvement is vital for sustaining the effectiveness and relevance of HR workflows in an organization. One of the most effective strategies for fostering improvement is leveraging feedback from various sources. This chapter delves into the importance of feedback in enhancing HR processes on the ServiceNow platform, strategies for gathering and analyzing feedback, and implementing the insights to optimize workflows.

1. The Role of Feedback in HR Workflow Improvement

Feedback serves as a critical tool for understanding how well current HR processes meet the needs of the organization and employees. It helps HR leaders identify strengths, weaknesses, and opportunities for improvement. Some of the key benefits of leveraging feedback include:

- **Enhanced User Experience**: Direct input from users provides insights into pain points and areas for user experience improvement.
- **Increased Efficiency**: Continuous feedback helps refine processes to eliminate redundancies and streamline tasks.
- **Proactive Problem Solving**: Early identification of potential issues before they escalate into significant problems.
- **Informed Decision-Making**: Empowers HR leaders to make data-driven decisions for workflow adjustments and future enhancements.

2. Strategies for Collecting Feedback

To effectively use feedback for workflow improvements, it is essential to gather it systematically. Below are several strategies for collecting meaningful feedback:

a. Direct Employee Surveys

Develop surveys targeted at employees who interact with HR workflows. These surveys should be:

- **Clear and Concise**: Questions should be straightforward to ensure high response rates.
- **Anonymous**: Providing anonymity encourages honest feedback.
- **Targeted**: Questions should focus on specific HR processes to capture detailed insights.

b. Feedback Portals on ServiceNow

Implement feedback mechanisms directly within the ServiceNow platform. For example:

- **Feedback Widgets**: Embed widgets in the HR service portal where users can submit their opinions and suggestions.
- **Post-Interaction Surveys**: Trigger surveys automatically after employees complete an interaction, such as submitting a request or accessing knowledge articles.

c. Focus Groups

Conduct focus groups with a cross-section of employees from various departments to gather qualitative feedback. These groups provide deeper insights into employee experiences and challenges.

d. Performance Metrics and Analytics

Leverage ServiceNow's reporting and analytics capabilities to collect indirect feedback through data analysis:

- **Usage Reports**: Analyze which features are being used most frequently.
- **Completion Rates**: Monitor task and workflow completion rates to identify bottlenecks.
- **Error Reports**: Assess the number of errors or issues reported during the use of HR workflows.

3. Analyzing Feedback for Actionable Insights

Collecting feedback is only the first step. Analyzing the data to derive actionable insights is crucial for meaningful improvements. Here's how to approach feedback analysis:

a. Categorize Feedback

Organize feedback into categories such as usability, functionality, performance, and user satisfaction. This helps prioritize areas that need immediate attention.

b. Identify Trends and Patterns

Look for recurring themes or issues raised by multiple users. If several employees report similar challenges, it signals an area that requires attention.

c. Prioritize Based on Impact

Not all feedback will carry equal weight. Prioritize feedback that has the potential to make the most significant impact on user experience and workflow efficiency.

d. Use AI Tools for Analysis

Leverage ServiceNow's AI-driven analytics to automatically sift through large volumes of feedback and highlight critical areas for improvement.

4. Implementing Workflow Enhancements Based on Feedback

Once feedback has been collected and analyzed, the next step is to implement changes that address identified issues. Here's how to effectively integrate improvements:

a. Develop a Clear Action Plan

Outline the specific improvements to be made and set timelines for implementation. Assign responsibilities to relevant team members for each task.

b. Communicate Changes

Ensure that any changes made to HR workflows are communicated clearly to all relevant stakeholders:

- **Internal Memos**: Use internal communications to inform employees of updates.
- **Training Sessions**: Provide training or informational sessions to familiarize HR teams with the changes.
- **Guidelines and Documentation**: Update workflow documentation to reflect new procedures and best practices.

c. Pilot Changes

Before fully rolling out new workflow enhancements, consider conducting a pilot program:

- **Select a Test Group**: Implement changes with a small group of employees to test the effectiveness.
- **Collect Immediate Feedback**: Gather input from the test group to identify any issues that need addressing before a full-scale rollout.

d. Monitor and Adjust

Post-implementation, continue monitoring the performance of the enhanced workflow. Use ServiceNow's monitoring tools to track:

- **User Engagement**: Measure if user satisfaction has improved.
- **Efficiency Metrics**: Evaluate whether workflows are being completed faster or with fewer errors.
- **Compliance Adherence**: Ensure that the changes align with regulatory requirements.

5. Best Practices for Sustaining Workflow Enhancements

a. Establish an Ongoing Feedback Loop

Create a continuous feedback loop where employees regularly provide input. This ensures that HR workflows remain agile and adaptable to changing needs.

b. Encourage a Feedback Culture

Promote a culture where employees feel empowered to share their thoughts. Recognize and reward employees who contribute valuable feedback.

c. Integrate Feedback into Regular Reviews

Make feedback analysis and workflow enhancement a part of regular HR process reviews. Schedule quarterly or bi-annual meetings to assess the effectiveness of implemented changes.

d. Leverage Technology for Continuous Monitoring

Use ServiceNow's advanced tools such as machine learning and predictive analytics to monitor workflows and suggest proactive adjustments.

Conclusion

Leveraging feedback for HR workflow enhancements is essential for creating a dynamic, responsive, and efficient HR environment. By systematically collecting, analyzing, and acting on feedback, organizations can optimize their HR processes to better serve their employees and align with strategic objectives. ServiceNow's powerful capabilities provide the tools necessary to make these enhancements seamless and impactful, fostering an HR department that is continually evolving to meet the needs of the modern workforce.

Innovations in ServiceNow HR Services

Innovation in HR technology is a driving force behind more efficient, streamlined, and user-centric HR processes. ServiceNow, as a leader in digital workflow solutions, continues to evolve its HR services by incorporating cutting-edge technology and responding to the ever-changing demands of modern organizations. This chapter explores recent and emerging innovations in ServiceNow HR services, their potential impacts, and how HR teams can leverage these advancements for continuous improvement.

1. Integration of Artificial Intelligence (AI) and Machine Learning (ML)

One of the most significant innovations in ServiceNow's HR services is the integration of AI and ML. These technologies empower HR teams to automate processes, analyze data efficiently, and enhance user interactions. Key benefits of incorporating AI and ML in HR services include:

- **Automated Task Management**: AI-driven automation helps handle repetitive HR tasks such as leave requests, approvals, and document management, allowing HR professionals to focus on strategic activities.
- **Predictive Analytics**: ML algorithms can forecast workforce trends, identify potential employee churn, and predict the need for recruitment or resource allocation.
- **Enhanced User Experience**: AI-powered chatbots and virtual agents offer instant support to employees by answering FAQs, guiding them through HR processes, and resolving common queries.

Example Use Case: Virtual HR Assistant

A virtual HR assistant built on ServiceNow's platform can assist employees with routine tasks like submitting expense reports, updating personal information, and accessing HR policies—all through conversational AI. This innovation reduces the workload on HR staff and improves response times.

2. Enhanced Employee Experience through Personalization

ServiceNow's focus on user-centric design has led to enhancements in personalizing the employee experience. Modern HR services on the platform can tailor interactions based on employee roles, previous interactions, and preferences. This personalization manifests in:

- **Targeted Content Delivery**: Employees receive personalized notifications and updates relevant to their specific roles and departments.
- **Customizable Portals**: HR service portals can be configured to display content and services that align with individual employee needs.
- **Learning and Development Recommendations**: ServiceNow's system can suggest training programs or resources that match an employee's career goals and job requirements.

Example Use Case: Onboarding Experience

New hires benefit from a personalized onboarding portal that guides them through orientation, introduces team members, and provides role-specific resources. This tailored approach accelerates their integration into the company and enhances engagement from the start.

3. Integration with Collaborative Tools

The ability to integrate with third-party tools and communication platforms is another area where ServiceNow has introduced innovations. This seamless integration supports collaboration across HR teams and enhances workflow continuity. Examples include:

- **Microsoft Teams and Slack Integration**: Employees can interact with HR services, submit requests, and receive updates directly within their preferred communication platforms.
- **Unified Workspaces**: Integrations provide a single platform where HR professionals can manage tasks, communicate with colleagues, and access HR data without switching between multiple applications.

4. Low-Code/No-Code Development for HR Customization

ServiceNow has made significant strides in enabling HR teams to customize workflows and applications through low-code/no-code development tools such as the Flow Designer and App Engine. These innovations empower HR teams to:

- **Quickly Adapt to Change**: Create and modify workflows to address evolving business needs without heavy reliance on IT departments.
- **Enhance Efficiency**: Streamline processes by automating tasks that previously required manual intervention.
- **Improve Agility**: Implement new HR solutions faster, enabling quicker responses to organizational changes or regulatory requirements.

Example Use Case: Custom Leave Approval Workflow

HR teams can use low-code tools to design a custom leave approval workflow that includes multi-tiered approvals, automatic notifications, and data validation—all without extensive coding expertise.

5. Mobile-First Approach

ServiceNow's emphasis on mobile optimization has redefined how HR services are accessed by employees. The mobile-first approach ensures that employees can interact with HR workflows anytime and anywhere, contributing to greater accessibility and engagement. Innovations in this space include:

- **Mobile Apps**: ServiceNow's mobile apps offer employees an intuitive way to submit requests, view HR policies, and track the status of ongoing processes.
- **Push Notifications**: Immediate alerts for approvals, document submissions, and policy updates keep employees informed and engaged.

6. Advanced Data Security and Compliance Features

Given the sensitivity of HR data, ServiceNow has innovated its security protocols to ensure data privacy and regulatory compliance. Advanced security measures include:

- **End-to-End Encryption**: Protects data during transfer and storage.
- **Compliance Management**: Built-in features to assist HR teams in adhering to GDPR, CCPA, and other relevant regulations.
- **Role-Based Access Control**: Limits data access to authorized personnel, ensuring data security and reducing the risk of breaches.

Example Use Case: Compliance Dashboard

ServiceNow's compliance dashboards help HR leaders monitor adherence to data protection regulations, conduct audits, and prepare for external assessments seamlessly.

7. Future-Proofing with Continuous Upgrades

ServiceNow's commitment to innovation extends to regular platform updates that include new features, performance enhancements, and security upgrades. HR teams can future-proof their operations by:

- **Embracing Continuous Updates**: Leveraging new functionalities as they are released without major disruptions.
- **Training for New Capabilities**: Ensuring HR staff are equipped with the knowledge and training to make the most of the latest innovations.

Conclusion

Innovations in ServiceNow HR services are revolutionizing the way HR teams manage and enhance workflows. By incorporating AI and ML, emphasizing personalization, integrating with collaborative tools, embracing low-code customization, focusing on mobile accessibility, strengthening security, and adopting continuous updates, HR departments can stay ahead of the curve and meet the demands of the modern workforce. These innovations not only improve the efficiency and effectiveness of HR processes but also foster a more engaging and secure environment for employees.

Planning for Future Upgrades and Expansions

As organizations continue to evolve, so too do their HR needs. Effective planning for future upgrades and expansions in ServiceNow's HR services is essential to maintaining a scalable, resilient, and adaptable HR system. This chapter outlines strategic approaches and practical tips for preparing your HR platform for future growth and continuous enhancement.

1. Understanding the Importance of Future-Proofing

Future-proofing your ServiceNow implementation ensures that your HR system remains efficient, relevant, and capable of meeting new challenges as they arise. With the rapid pace of technological advancements and changes in workforce expectations, planning for updates and expansions helps HR teams stay ahead of the curve and adapt smoothly to new demands.

Key Benefits of Future Planning:

- **Enhanced Scalability**: Preparing for future growth ensures that your system can support an increasing number of users and more complex processes.
- **Cost Efficiency**: Proactive planning reduces the likelihood of costly overhauls or emergency fixes.
- **Sustained Performance**: Regular updates and expansions maintain system performance and security.

2. Establishing a Strategic Roadmap

A strategic roadmap provides a structured plan for how your organization will approach future upgrades and expansions. This roadmap should include:

- **Assessment of Current Capabilities**: Identify existing strengths and limitations within your ServiceNow HR implementation.
- **Goals for Expansion**: Define clear objectives, such as adding new HR modules, integrating advanced analytics tools, or scaling services to accommodate a larger workforce.
- **Timeline for Upgrades**: Establish realistic timelines for implementing updates, taking into account testing, training, and deployment phases.

Example: Planning to Incorporate AI-Driven Insights

If your HR department plans to integrate AI-driven insights, the roadmap should outline the required infrastructure, training for HR staff, and a phased rollout strategy.

3. Prioritizing Upgrades for Optimal Impact

When planning future upgrades, prioritize those that will deliver the most significant value to the organization. Consider the following criteria:

- **Urgency of Needs**: Address any current system inefficiencies or pressing requirements.
- **Potential for Impact**: Focus on upgrades that enhance productivity, user experience, or compliance capabilities.
- **Feasibility and Resources**: Evaluate the availability of budget and resources needed to implement each upgrade.

Top Priority Upgrades:

- **Enhanced User Interface (UI) Updates**: Streamlined and intuitive UI changes can greatly improve user experience and adoption rates.
- **Mobile Capabilities**: Expanding mobile access for HR services supports a more flexible and responsive workforce.

4. Ensuring Compatibility and System Readiness

Compatibility checks are vital when planning major updates or expansions to prevent disruptions. Before launching any upgrade:

- **Assess Integration Points**: Ensure that new features or expansions are compatible with existing integrations, such as third-party HR applications or collaborative tools.
- **Validate System Requirements**: Confirm that your current hardware, software, and network infrastructure can support the proposed updates.
- **Test in a Sandbox Environment**: Use a test environment to simulate how new features or updates will perform in your production system.

Example: Upgrading Knowledge Management Modules

When upgrading knowledge management modules, run compatibility tests to ensure that existing data structures, workflows, and user roles are not disrupted.

5. Training and Support for Upgrades

An upgrade is only successful if the HR team and other stakeholders are prepared to use it effectively. Key strategies for ensuring readiness include:

- **Training Programs**: Offer comprehensive training sessions for HR personnel on new functionalities, tools, or expanded features.
- **Documentation Updates**: Refresh user guides, training manuals, and support documentation to reflect the latest changes.
- **Feedback Mechanisms**: Implement feedback loops post-upgrade to capture user experiences and address any issues quickly.

6. Managing Incremental vs. Major Upgrades

Organizations must decide whether to pursue incremental updates or larger, less frequent upgrades. Both approaches have their benefits:

- **Incremental Upgrades**: Allow for more manageable, gradual changes that minimize disruptions and require less intensive training.
- **Major Upgrades**: Provide substantial new features or overhaul existing processes but may involve more downtime and extensive training.

Choosing the Right Approach:

Evaluate your organization's capacity for change and available resources. Incremental updates might be preferable for continuous improvement, whereas major upgrades may be needed for significant overhauls.

7. Expanding ServiceNow Capabilities

Beyond upgrades, consider expanding your ServiceNow HR services by incorporating additional modules and features:

- **Global Scalability**: Enable HR processes to support international operations, including localized workflows for different regions.
- **Advanced Reporting Tools**: Integrate reporting tools that offer deeper data insights and advanced analytics capabilities.
- **Self-Service Enhancements**: Expand self-service portals to include more comprehensive options for employees, such as automated responses for common HR inquiries.

8. Preparing for Future Technology Trends

Stay informed about emerging trends in HR technology and ensure your planning incorporates them. Examples of impactful future trends include:

- **AI-Driven HR Analytics**: Machine learning tools that can analyze patterns and predict HR outcomes.
- **Blockchain for Data Security**: Enhancing data security and transparency in HR records.
- **Virtual Reality (VR) for Training**: Implementing VR technology for immersive training experiences.

Staying Ahead:

Regularly review industry publications, attend HR technology conferences, and consult with ServiceNow experts to keep your system aligned with future technological advancements.

Conclusion

Effective planning for future upgrades and expansions is essential for maximizing the long-term benefits of your ServiceNow HR implementation. By building a strategic roadmap, prioritizing impactful changes, ensuring compatibility, and preparing your team for new capabilities, your organization can continue to leverage ServiceNow as a powerful tool for HR digital transformation. This forward-thinking approach ensures your HR department remains agile, competitive, and capable of adapting to future needs with confidence.

Embracing New ServiceNow Features for HR

As technology evolves, ServiceNow continues to enhance its platform by introducing new features designed to improve user experience, increase efficiency, and adapt to changing business needs. To maintain an effective and modern HR department, organizations must proactively embrace these new features and integrate them seamlessly into existing workflows. This chapter will explore strategies for staying updated with the latest ServiceNow advancements and effectively implementing new features to maximize their potential benefits.

1. The Importance of Keeping Up with ServiceNow Updates

ServiceNow's commitment to innovation means regular updates and new features are introduced to optimize platform performance and user capabilities. Adopting these features promptly can significantly enhance HR operations by:

- **Streamlining Processes**: New tools can automate and simplify complex HR workflows.
- **Enhancing User Experience**: Updated interfaces and functionalities can improve the ease of use for HR teams and employees.
- **Boosting Productivity**: Advanced features often provide shortcuts and automation that save time and resources.
- **Ensuring Compliance**: New features often include updates to ensure adherence to the latest compliance and security standards.

2. Monitoring and Understanding New Releases

To stay ahead, HR leaders and ServiceNow administrators should establish a process for keeping track of new releases. Consider the following steps:

- **Subscribe to ServiceNow Updates**: Sign up for newsletters and alerts from ServiceNow to receive information on upcoming releases and new features.
- **Review Release Notes**: Each ServiceNow release is accompanied by detailed documentation outlining new features, enhancements, and deprecated elements. Reviewing these notes is essential to understand which updates are most relevant to your HR processes.
- **Engage in ServiceNow Communities**: Participate in forums, webinars, and community groups to learn from other organizations' experiences with new features and get insights on best practices.

3. Evaluating New Features for Relevance

Not every new feature may be applicable to your HR department's current needs. It's essential to evaluate each update and prioritize implementation based on potential impact. Use the following criteria:

- **Alignment with Business Goals**: Determine whether a new feature supports your HR department's strategic objectives.
- **Ease of Integration**: Assess how seamlessly the feature can be integrated into existing workflows and systems.
- **Training Requirements**: Identify whether significant training is needed for the HR team or employees to use the new feature effectively.

Example Evaluation Matrix:

Feature Name	Business Impact	Ease of Integration	Training Requirement	Priority Level
Automated Case Routing	High	Moderate	Low	High

Enhanced Analytics Dashboard	Medium	High	Medium	Medium
New Mobile Interface Updates	Low	High	Low	Low

4. Planning and Executing the Rollout of New Features

Successful implementation of new ServiceNow features requires careful planning. Follow these steps for a smooth rollout:

1. **Develop an Implementation Plan**:
   - **Set Clear Objectives**: Define what you aim to achieve by adopting the new feature (e.g., reducing processing time for HR cases).
   - **Allocate Resources**: Ensure you have the necessary budget, staff, and technical support for the rollout.
2. **Test in a Sandbox Environment**:
   - Conduct thorough testing in a non-production environment to identify potential issues and make necessary adjustments.
3. **Train and Prepare HR Teams**:
   - Provide comprehensive training sessions and resources tailored to the needs of different user groups within the HR department.
4. **Communicate with Stakeholders**:
   - Notify key stakeholders, including IT, HR leadership, and end-users, about the new feature, its benefits, and the expected timeline for implementation.
5. **Launch in Phases**:
   - Consider a phased rollout to manage risk and gather user feedback for further refinement before full-scale implementation.

5. Leveraging Feedback Post-Implementation

Gathering and acting on feedback after rolling out new features is crucial to ensure they meet user expectations and enhance HR processes effectively. Implement the following practices:

- **Collect User Feedback**: Use surveys, focus groups, and direct feedback channels to collect input from HR staff and employees.
- **Analyze Performance Metrics**: Assess whether the new feature meets the objectives set during the planning phase by tracking key performance indicators (KPIs).
- **Iterate and Improve**: Make iterative changes based on feedback and performance analysis to optimize the feature's usage.

Example of a Feedback Loop:

1. **Initial Launch**: Roll out the feature and monitor usage.
2. **Collect Feedback**: Gather input from HR teams through surveys and direct communication.
3. **Review Metrics**: Analyze data such as processing times and error rates.
4. **Implement Improvements**: Adjust configurations or provide additional training as needed.
5. **Ongoing Monitoring**: Continue to review and enhance the feature's usage over time.

6. Staying Ahead with Future Innovations

To continuously benefit from ServiceNow's advancements, maintain a proactive approach by:

- **Attending ServiceNow Conferences**: Events like Knowledge (ServiceNow's annual conference) offer insights into new releases and best practices.
- **Partnering with ServiceNow Experts**: Collaborate with consultants or ServiceNow experts to get tailored advice and support for feature implementation.
- **Building an Agile Mindset**: Cultivate an organizational culture that embraces change and innovation. Encourage HR teams to be open to learning and adapting as new capabilities are introduced.

Conclusion

Embracing new ServiceNow features for HR is essential for keeping your organization at the forefront of digital transformation. By staying informed, planning strategically, and leveraging feedback for continuous improvement, your HR department can harness the power of new tools and functionalities to drive efficiency, productivity, and user satisfaction. Regularly integrating new features ensures that your HR operations remain agile and capable of supporting your workforce's evolving needs.

Maintaining Competitive Edge with HR Digital Workflows

In an era where digital transformation is reshaping how businesses operate, maintaining a competitive edge requires HR departments to consistently leverage technology, such as ServiceNow, to optimize workflows and meet evolving business needs. This chapter explores how HR departments can continue to innovate and refine their processes to remain ahead of the competition, focusing on best practices and forward-thinking strategies for long-term success.

1. The Importance of a Competitive Edge in HR Operations

The modern workforce demands efficiency, flexibility, and a seamless experience, both for employees and HR professionals. Maintaining a competitive edge in HR digital workflows allows organizations to:

- **Attract and Retain Top Talent**: Streamlined and user-friendly HR processes contribute to a positive employee experience.
- **Enhance Productivity**: Efficient workflows reduce time spent on administrative tasks, allowing HR teams to focus on strategic initiatives.
- **Adapt to Changing Business Needs**: Agile workflows enable the organization to respond swiftly to new challenges and opportunities.
- **Strengthen Brand Reputation**: Organizations known for their advanced HR capabilities are perceived as leaders in innovation and employee engagement.

2. Strategies for Sustaining a Competitive Edge

a. Continuous Process Optimization

To maintain an advantage, HR leaders should continuously review and refine existing workflows. Key actions include: .

- **Routine Workflow Assessments**: Conduct regular audits to identify bottlenecks and areas for improvement.
- **Implementing Best Practices**: Adopt industry best practices for process optimization, such as automation of repetitive tasks and the use of decision trees for faster case resolution.
- **Feedback Integration**: Use employee feedback to adjust workflows for better usability and efficiency.

b. Leveraging Data Analytics

Data is an invaluable asset for understanding HR performance and making informed decisions. Utilize ServiceNow's analytics tools to:

- **Track Key Performance Indicators (KPIs)**: Monitor metrics such as case resolution time, employee satisfaction scores, and request completion rates.
- **Predict Trends**: Analyze historical data to predict future HR needs and potential challenges.
- **Enhance Reporting**: Create customized reports that offer deep insights into workflow performance and employee interactions.

c. Prioritizing Employee Experience

A seamless employee experience is crucial for maintaining engagement and satisfaction. Steps to prioritize this include:

- **User-Centric Design**: Ensure that workflows are intuitive and accessible, focusing on the end-user experience.

- **Self-Service Enhancements**: Regularly update and improve self-service options to empower employees to resolve their HR needs independently.
- **Training and Support**: Offer ongoing training for employees to effectively utilize digital HR tools and processes.

3. Embracing Emerging Technologies

Adopting the latest technological innovations helps HR departments maintain a forward-looking approach. Key areas to focus on include:

a. Artificial Intelligence and Machine Learning

Incorporate AI and machine learning into HR workflows for improved efficiency and decision-making. This can include:

- **Chatbots for Employee Support**: Use AI-driven chatbots to provide 24/7 support and answer common HR-related queries.
- **Predictive Analytics**: Employ machine learning algorithms to predict employee turnover and identify factors contributing to job satisfaction.
- **Automated Data Processing**: Leverage AI to automate data entry and analysis for quicker insights.

b. Advanced Mobile Capabilities

Ensure that HR workflows are optimized for mobile access to cater to an increasingly mobile workforce. This can include:

- **Mobile-First Design**: Develop HR processes with a mobile-friendly interface to facilitate ease of use on smartphones and tablets.
- **Push Notifications and Alerts**: Utilize mobile notifications to keep employees informed about important HR updates and reminders.
- **Remote Access**: Enable secure remote access to HR tools for employees working from various locations.

4. Fostering a Culture of Innovation

To keep HR workflows competitive, cultivate a workplace culture that embraces innovation. Strategies to achieve this include:

- **Encouraging Idea Sharing**: Create platforms where HR staff and employees can suggest improvements and innovative ideas for workflow enhancement.
- **Collaborative Teams**: Form cross-functional teams that include IT, HR, and other departments to collaborate on workflow advancements.
- **Recognition and Incentives**: Recognize and reward employees who contribute to innovative solutions that improve HR processes.

5. Preparing for Future Developments

The digital landscape is constantly changing, and HR leaders must be prepared for future developments. To stay proactive:

- **Stay Informed**: Regularly attend HR and tech conferences, webinars, and training programs to learn about the latest trends and updates in HR technology.
- **Pilot New Features**: When ServiceNow releases new updates, consider piloting these features to assess their impact on current workflows before full implementation.

- **Invest in Continuous Learning**: Encourage HR teams to participate in ongoing training and certification programs to keep their skills sharp and aligned with technological advancements.

Conclusion

Maintaining a competitive edge in HR digital workflows with ServiceNow requires a proactive, data-driven, and employee-focused approach. By continuously optimizing processes, leveraging new technologies, and fostering a culture of innovation, HR departments can ensure their operations remain efficient, adaptive, and aligned with the evolving needs of the workforce. This ongoing commitment to excellence helps organizations not only stay competitive but also position themselves as leaders in HR management and employee satisfaction.

Appendices

Appendix A: Glossary of ServiceNow HR Terms

This glossary provides definitions of key terms and concepts used throughout the book.

A

- **API (Application Programming Interface)**: A set of functions and protocols that allows applications to communicate and share data.
- **Automation**: The use of technology to perform tasks without human intervention, streamlining processes and improving efficiency.

B

- **Business Rule**: A server-side script in ServiceNow that automatically runs when certain conditions are met, used to enforce policies and automate workflows.

C

- **Case Management**: The process of handling HR cases or inquiries efficiently, tracking their progress, and resolving them using predefined workflows.
- **Change Management**: A structured approach to transitioning individuals, teams, and organizations from a current state to a desired future state, ensuring seamless integration of new processes or technologies.
- **Configuration Management Database (CMDB)**: A repository that acts as a data warehouse for IT installations and includes details about the configuration of various systems and services.

D

- **Dashboard**: A visual representation of data that provides quick access to key performance indicators (KPIs) and other critical metrics.
- **Digital Workflow**: A series of automated actions that move data or tasks between people, systems, or processes to achieve a business outcome.

E

- **Employee Self-Service (ESS) Portal**: A digital platform where employees can access HR resources, request services, and manage their HR needs independently.
- **Escalation**: A process where a case or task is automatically routed to a higher authority or different user when predefined criteria are not met within a specified timeframe.

F

- **Flow Designer**: A tool within ServiceNow that allows users to build automated processes without the need for complex coding.
- **Form View**: The layout used to display a single record from a table, such as an HR case or request.

G

- **GDPR (General Data Protection Regulation)**: A regulatory framework that sets guidelines for the collection and processing of personal information of individuals within the European Union (EU).

- **Governance**: The framework of rules and practices by which an organization ensures accountability, fairness, and transparency in its relationships and workflows.

H

- **HR Service Delivery (HRSD)**: A ServiceNow module that streamlines and automates HR workflows, improving service delivery and employee experience.

I

- **Incident Management**: The process of identifying, analyzing, and resolving incidents to restore normal service operations as quickly as possible.
- **Integration**: The process of connecting different systems and applications to enable them to work together seamlessly and share data.

J

- **Job Role**: A defined set of permissions and capabilities assigned to users to control access to various functions within the ServiceNow platform.

K

- **Knowledge Base (KB)**: A repository of articles, FAQs, and documentation designed to provide users with information and self-service resources.

L

- **Localization**: The process of adapting content and processes to suit different languages and regional needs within the platform.

M

- **Multi-Currency Support**: The ability to handle transactions and data in different currencies within a global organization.
- **Multi-Language Support**: The capacity for the ServiceNow platform to operate in various languages to accommodate diverse employee bases.

N

- **Notification**: An automated alert sent to users when specific events or changes occur within the system.

O

- **Onboarding**: The process of integrating a new employee into the organization, including tasks like documentation, training, and orientation.

P

- **Portal**: A customized interface that allows users to access services and resources specific to their needs, such as the HR Service Portal.
- **Process Optimization**: The practice of improving and refining workflows to enhance efficiency and effectiveness.

Q

- **Query**: A request for information from a database, often used to retrieve specific data within ServiceNow.

R

- **Record**: A single entry in a ServiceNow table that stores related information, such as a service request or HR case.
- **Reporting**: The process of compiling data and presenting it in a format that is easy to interpret, helping HR teams track performance and make informed decisions.

S

- **Scripted Workflow**: A workflow in ServiceNow that uses custom scripts to automate complex processes.
- **Service Catalog**: A collection of services and offerings that users can request via the HR Service Portal.
- **Service Level Agreement (SLA)**: A defined set of service delivery expectations agreed upon between the service provider and the customer.

T

- **Ticketing System**: A system used to create, manage, and resolve service requests or issues reported by employees.
- **Transformation Map**: A visual tool used to outline the path for transitioning from current processes to new, optimized workflows.

U

- **User Roles**: Sets of permissions within ServiceNow that dictate what users can see and do on the platform.
- **User Experience (UX)**: The overall experience of a person using a product or service, particularly in terms of how easy or pleasing it is to use.

V

- **Virtual Agent**: An AI-powered chatbot in ServiceNow that provides automated assistance and responses to common HR queries.
- **Visibility Settings**: Controls that determine what information users can view or access within the ServiceNow platform.

W

- **Workflow Automation**: The use of technology to create, streamline, and execute sequences of tasks without human intervention.
- **Workforce Analytics**: The practice of analyzing workforce data to optimize HR strategies and improve decision-making.

Y

- **Yield Analysis**: A method of evaluating the effectiveness of a workflow or process in achieving desired outcomes.

Z

- **Zero Touch HR**: An automated approach in HR services that reduces or eliminates the need for manual intervention, enhancing efficiency.

Appendix B: Useful Resources and Tools for HR Professionals

This appendix offers a curated list of resources and tools to enhance HR professionals' capabilities in managing and optimizing ServiceNow implementations and general HR workflows. These resources cover various aspects, from official documentation and training to insightful blogs and tools for ongoing professional growth.

1. Official ServiceNow Resources

- **ServiceNow Documentation Center**: A comprehensive repository of documentation covering all aspects of ServiceNow, including HR Service Delivery (HRSD) module details. [Visit: docs.servicenow.com] (https://docs.servicenow.com)
- **ServiceNow Community**: Engage with other ServiceNow users, share experiences, ask questions, and access a range of discussions and resources. [Visit: community.servicenow.com] (https://community.servicenow.com)
- **ServiceNow Developer Portal**: A resourceful site for developers and technical HR teams working with ServiceNow, featuring free development instances and learning tools. [Visit: developer.servicenow.com] (https://developer.servicenow.com)

2. Training and Certification

- **ServiceNow HR Service Delivery Training**: ServiceNow offers targeted training sessions that focus on HR Service Delivery, enabling HR professionals to leverage the platform effectively.
- **Coursera and LinkedIn Learning**: Platforms that provide courses related to HR technology, digital transformation, and ServiceNow functionalities.
- **ServiceNow Certified Implementation Specialist (HR)**: A specialized certification that validates expertise in implementing and managing HR services using ServiceNow.

3. Professional HR Associations

- **Society for Human Resource Management (SHRM)**: Offers training, certifications, and a wealth of resources tailored for HR professionals.
- **Human Capital Institute (HCI)**: Provides insights, webinars, and training focused on HR innovation and technology adoption.
- **International Association for Human Resource Information Management (IHRIM)**: Focuses on the intersection of HR and technology, including resources related to HRIS and ServiceNow.

4. Technology and Integration Tools

- **Zapier**: A tool that facilitates integration between ServiceNow and other third-party applications, automating workflows and enhancing productivity.
- **Jira**: For teams that collaborate with IT and developers, Jira can be integrated with ServiceNow for smoother task and issue management.
- **Slack and Microsoft Teams**: Enhance communication by integrating ServiceNow notifications and updates with team collaboration platforms.

5. Industry Blogs and Thought Leadership

- **HR Technologist**: Covers trends and technologies that are transforming HR, with insights into platforms like ServiceNow.
- **Josh Bersin's Blog**: Provides thought leadership on HR technology and trends that impact digital HR transformations.

- **HR Dive**: Offers the latest news, expert insights, and resources for HR professionals navigating the evolving digital landscape.

6. Productivity and Workflow Enhancement Tools

- **Flow Designer in ServiceNow**: A built-in tool that allows HR teams to create automated workflows with minimal coding.
- **Power BI**: A powerful business analytics tool that integrates with ServiceNow for detailed data visualization and reporting.
- **Trello**: For teams seeking simple project management solutions that can be connected to ServiceNow for streamlined task tracking.

7. Additional Resources

- **Books on HR Technology**: Explore books like *"HR Technology for Dummies"* and *"Digital HR Strategy: Achieving Sustainable Transformation"* for deeper knowledge on how to integrate and maximize digital tools within HR.
- **Webinars and Podcasts**:
  - **ServiceNow's Official Webinars**: Covering new features, best practices, and case studies.
  - **HR Leaders Podcast**: Discusses challenges and opportunities in HR technology, featuring industry experts.
- **Online Forums**:
  - **Reddit's HR and ServiceNow Subreddits**: Platforms where HR and ServiceNow enthusiasts share their insights, troubleshoot issues, and stay updated on industry news.

8. Emerging Tools and Innovations

- **AI and Machine Learning Solutions**: Tools like ChatGPT can be used alongside ServiceNow's AI capabilities to enhance HR service delivery and employee interaction.
- **HR Analytics Platforms**: Services such as PeopleSoft and Workday can complement ServiceNow for broader HR analytics and performance metrics.
- **Mobile-Friendly HR Tools**: Solutions that integrate mobile access with ServiceNow to provide a seamless HR experience for on-the-go employees.

Appendix C: Training and Certification Programs for ServiceNow HR

This appendix serves as a comprehensive guide for HR professionals and implementation specialists who wish to enhance their expertise with ServiceNow's HR Service Delivery (HRSD) through structured training and certification programs. These resources help individuals and teams gain the necessary knowledge, skills, and credentials to effectively implement and manage ServiceNow for HR.

1. ServiceNow Training Programs

- **HR Service Delivery Fundamentals**: This foundational course is designed for HR professionals and ServiceNow administrators who need to understand the core capabilities of HRSD. It covers topics like workflow management, case management, and employee service centers.
- **Advanced HRSD Workshops**: For those who already have basic knowledge, advanced workshops offer deeper insights into customizing HR processes, utilizing advanced scripting, and automating complex workflows.
- **ServiceNow Knowledge Center**: The Knowledge Center provides an extensive library of self-paced learning modules, guides, and tutorials on various ServiceNow capabilities, including HR applications.

2. ServiceNow Certifications

- **Certified Implementation Specialist – HR Service Delivery (CIS-HR)**: This certification validates the expertise required to successfully implement ServiceNow HRSD solutions. It covers HR application configuration, integration, and best practices for ensuring efficient HR operations.
- **Certified System Administrator (CSA)**: Although more general, this certification is essential for HR professionals who need to understand the broader ServiceNow platform. It lays the groundwork for more specialized training in HRSD.
- **Certified Application Developer (CAD)**: Ideal for HR IT teams or HR professionals who wish to develop custom applications within ServiceNow. It focuses on building and deploying applications on the Now Platform.

3. Third-Party Training Platforms

- **LinkedIn Learning**: Offers courses that cover ServiceNow basics, HR digital transformation strategies, and insights into best practices for using the platform in an HR context.
- **Coursera**: Provides courses focused on the implementation of digital workflows, HR technology transformation, and ServiceNow-specific training.
- **Udemy**: Features a range of courses from beginner to advanced levels that include hands-on projects for applying ServiceNow capabilities to real-world HR scenarios.

4. Workshops and Boot Camps

- **ServiceNow Live Boot Camps**: Intensive training sessions that provide hands-on experience with ServiceNow's HR modules, often led by certified trainers.
- **Custom Corporate Workshops**: Many training providers offer tailored workshops for companies looking to train HR teams or IT staff on ServiceNow implementation specific to their needs.

5. Webinars and Virtual Training Events

- **ServiceNow Webinars**: Regularly hosted webinars provide updates on new HRSD features, best practices for configuration, and case studies from successful implementations.

- **Industry Conferences and Virtual Events**: Events like the annual ServiceNow Knowledge conference feature specialized HR tracks and workshops focused on HR digital transformation and workflow optimization.

6. Certification Preparation Resources

- **Official Study Guides and Practice Exams**: ServiceNow offers study materials and practice tests to help candidates prepare for certification exams, including the CIS-HR.
- **Community Support**: The ServiceNow Community Forum is a valuable resource for sharing insights, tips, and solutions related to HRSD training and certification preparation.
- **Mentorship Programs**: Some organizations provide mentorship programs where certified professionals guide newcomers through their learning and certification journey.

7. Continuous Learning Opportunities

- **HR Technology Blogs and Journals**: Reading materials such as the *HR Tech Outlook* and *HR Technologist* provide ongoing learning and keep HR professionals informed about the latest trends in HR technology, including new developments in ServiceNow.
- **Online Forums and Groups**: Platforms like Reddit's ServiceNow and HR-focused subreddits offer advice, tips, and peer support for professionals at all levels.
- **Podcasts**: Tune into HR tech-focused podcasts that often cover innovations in HR service delivery and discuss how tools like ServiceNow are transforming HR functions.

8. Tips for Maximizing Training Outcomes

- **Hands-On Practice**: Enroll in training that provides practical, real-world scenarios to apply your learning. ServiceNow's Developer Program offers free access to a personal development instance.
- **Certification Pathway Planning**: Start with foundational certifications and gradually progress to specialized HRSD credentials for a structured learning path.
- **Join User Groups**: Connecting with regional or global ServiceNow user groups can provide networking opportunities and insights into best practices.

Appendix D: FAQs on Implementing ServiceNow for HR

This appendix addresses common questions related to implementing ServiceNow for HR, providing clear and concise answers to help HR professionals and organizations understand best practices, potential challenges, and key considerations during their implementation journey.

1. What is ServiceNow HR Service Delivery (HRSD), and how does it help HR departments?

ServiceNow HRSD is a comprehensive solution designed to streamline and automate HR processes. It helps HR departments by creating seamless workflows, centralizing employee services, improving case management, and providing self-service portals that enhance the employee experience.

2. How do we determine if our organization is ready to implement ServiceNow for HR?

Assessing organizational readiness involves evaluating current HR processes, technological infrastructure, and employee needs. Conducting a gap analysis and understanding how ServiceNow's capabilities align with business objectives is crucial for successful implementation.

3. What are the main steps involved in implementing ServiceNow for HR?

The main steps include:

- Assessing needs and defining objectives.
- Planning the project scope and allocating resources.
- Configuring ServiceNow modules and customizing workflows.
- Data migration and system integration.
- Training HR teams and conducting user acceptance testing.
- Launching the system and providing post-implementation support.

4. Can ServiceNow integrate with existing HR systems like payroll and talent management tools?

Yes, ServiceNow can be integrated with various third-party HR systems, including payroll, talent management, and benefits platforms. Using ServiceNow's IntegrationHub and APIs, organizations can create seamless data flow between ServiceNow and other HR tools to ensure cohesive operations.

5. What customization options does ServiceNow offer for HR workflows?

ServiceNow offers extensive customization options using tools like Flow Designer for building custom workflows and ServiceNow Studio for advanced scripting and app development. These tools allow HR teams to tailor workflows to meet specific business needs while ensuring compliance and efficiency.

6. How long does it typically take to implement ServiceNow for HR?

The timeline for implementation varies based on the complexity of the project and the organization's size. Small to medium-scale implementations may take 3 to 6 months, while more extensive projects with multiple integrations and customizations can extend to 9 to 12 months or more.

7. What are the biggest challenges faced during the implementation of ServiceNow HR?

Common challenges include:

- Resistance to change from employees.

- Insufficient training and user adoption.
- Data migration complexities.
- Integrating legacy systems with ServiceNow.
- Ensuring consistent communication and collaboration among stakeholders.

8. What measures can be taken to ensure data security when using ServiceNow for HR?

Implementing data security measures includes configuring user roles and permissions, enabling data encryption, conducting regular security audits, and ensuring compliance with regulations like GDPR. ServiceNow also offers built-in security protocols and the option for further custom security features.

9. How do we measure the success of our ServiceNow HR implementation?

Success can be measured through key performance indicators (KPIs) such as:

- Time saved in HR case resolutions.
- Reduction in manual HR tasks.
- User adoption rates and satisfaction surveys.
- Improvements in employee self-service portal usage.
- ROI analysis post-implementation.

10. What ongoing maintenance is required after implementing ServiceNow for HR?

Regular maintenance includes:

- System updates and patch management.
- Continuous monitoring of system performance.
- Periodic training for HR staff to adapt to new features.
- Gathering user feedback to make iterative improvements.
- Ensuring data backups and compliance with evolving data protection laws.

11. Can ServiceNow be used to support remote HR operations?

Yes, ServiceNow's cloud-based platform is designed to support remote and distributed workforces. It provides mobile access, self-service portals, and collaboration tools that facilitate HR operations from anywhere, ensuring flexibility and efficiency for remote teams.

12. What training resources are available for HR professionals to learn ServiceNow?

HR professionals can access various resources, including:

- ServiceNow's own training programs and certifications.
- Third-party online courses on platforms like LinkedIn Learning and Coursera.
- ServiceNow community forums and webinars.
- Customized training workshops tailored to an organization's needs.

13. Is it necessary to hire a consultant for implementing ServiceNow for HR?

While some organizations with robust in-house IT teams may implement ServiceNow on their own, hiring an experienced ServiceNow consultant can greatly reduce implementation time, address technical challenges, and ensure best practices are followed for a successful rollout.

14. What ongoing support does ServiceNow provide post-implementation?

ServiceNow offers ongoing support through its customer service portal, knowledge base, and technical support team. Additionally, premium support packages are available for more personalized and hands-on assistance.

15. How does ServiceNow support HR process automation?

ServiceNow supports HR process automation through configurable workflows, task assignment automation, and integration capabilities that reduce the need for manual data entry and streamline HR processes, leading to higher productivity and reduced human error.

This appendix aims to address the most common questions HR professionals and organizations may have when implementing ServiceNow for HR, providing clarity and aiding informed decision-making.

Appendix E: Further Reading and Industry Insights

To continue your journey of mastering ServiceNow and understanding the evolving landscape of HR technology, this appendix provides valuable resources for further reading and industry insights. These resources include influential books, authoritative articles, relevant industry reports, and respected thought leaders to follow for staying updated with trends and best practices.

1. Books and Publications

- **"IT Service Management with ServiceNow" by Ajaykumar Guggilla** – A practical guide that dives deep into various functionalities of ServiceNow, offering useful insights that extend to HR Service Delivery.
- **"The ServiceNow Development Handbook" by Tim Woodruff** – Offers a comprehensive overview of customization and development practices within the ServiceNow platform.
- **"Digital HR: A Critical Management Approach to the Digitalization of Organizations" by Bondarouk and Ruel** – Provides context on how HR technology integrates with broader business strategies and the future of digital HR management.

2. Industry Reports

- **Gartner Reports on Service Management Platforms** – Regular publications that evaluate the state of service management platforms, including ServiceNow, and their relevance to HR operations.
- **Deloitte's Human Capital Trends** – Annual reports that outline key trends impacting the HR industry, including the role of digital platforms like ServiceNow in workforce transformation.
- **Forrester's ServiceNow Wave Reports** – Analyze the capabilities of ServiceNow among other IT service management tools, providing valuable comparative data.

3. Online Articles and Case Studies

- **ServiceNow Blog** – The official blog offers product updates, use cases, success stories, and expert advice on implementing ServiceNow in HR environments.
- **HR Executive Articles** – Articles discussing how leading companies are leveraging ServiceNow to optimize their HR processes, including insights on case management and workflow automation.
- **Harvard Business Review** – Articles and case studies on digital transformation in HR and the importance of workflow efficiency in large organizations.

4. Websites and Portals

- **ServiceNow Community (community.servicenow.com)** – A hub for users to share knowledge, ask questions, and access support materials.
- **HR Technologist (www.hrtechnologist.com)** – Covers a wide range of HR technology topics, trends, and best practices.
- **CIO.com** – Offers insights into technology management, including articles related to IT service management and how it overlaps with HR functions.

5. Industry Conferences and Webinars

- **Knowledge by ServiceNow** – The annual ServiceNow conference where experts and users share experiences, present case studies, and discuss the latest in platform capabilities.
- **HR Tech Conference** – Focuses on how technology is transforming the HR landscape, with sessions that often include discussions on digital workflow solutions like ServiceNow.
- **Webinars Hosted by ServiceNow and Industry Leaders** – Provide up-to-date knowledge on recent platform developments and expert tips for implementation and optimization.

6. Influential Thought Leaders and Experts

- **Fred Luddy** – Founder of ServiceNow, known for his insights on digital workflow evolution.
- **Josh Bersin** – HR industry analyst who frequently discusses the role of technology in human resources and workforce management.
- **Stacey Harris** – An expert in HR technology trends who shares insights on best practices for implementing platforms like ServiceNow in HR.

7. Podcasts for Ongoing Learning

- **"Digital HR Leaders" by David Green** – Focuses on digital HR strategies and often features conversations that touch on workflow management solutions.
- **"The HR Happy Hour Show"** – A podcast that discusses HR technologies and practices, often highlighting the use of digital platforms.
- **ServiceNow Podcasts** – Explore episodes specifically aimed at showcasing customer stories and technical advice from ServiceNow practitioners.

8. Professional Journals and Whitepapers

- **Journal of Strategic HR** – Features scholarly articles on the integration of technology in HR and case studies of successful implementations.
- **ServiceNow Whitepapers** – Officially published whitepapers detailing technical and strategic insights on ServiceNow implementations.

9. Networking and Professional Groups

- **LinkedIn Groups** – Such as "ServiceNow Professionals" and "Digital HR Transformation," where HR and IT professionals exchange ideas and solutions.
- **HR Technology Forums** – Engage with communities like SHRM's HR Technology and Automation Group for discussions and shared experiences.

10. Courses and Learning Platforms

- **ServiceNow Learning Portal** – Offers courses and certifications to deepen knowledge about HR Service Delivery within ServiceNow.
- **Coursera and Udemy** – Provide courses tailored to understanding the practical use and customization of ServiceNow in professional settings.
- **LinkedIn Learning** – Features comprehensive training on ServiceNow fundamentals and HR process automation.

These resources are curated to equip you with a deeper understanding and continuous learning in leveraging ServiceNow for HR and staying ahead in the evolving field of HR technology.

Conclusion

The journey to implementing and optimizing ServiceNow for HR has been both insightful and transformative. Throughout this book, we have explored the critical aspects of how ServiceNow can reshape HR processes, from planning and preparation to advanced customization and future-proofing. This transformation is not just about adopting a new tool; it's about embedding a new mindset that embraces digital workflows and drives efficiency, compliance, and innovation within HR teams.

Embracing Change for Lasting Impact

Implementing ServiceNow for HR goes beyond the technical aspects—it requires fostering a culture of adaptability and openness to change. HR professionals must understand that the value of ServiceNow lies in its capacity to empower teams, improve service delivery, and enhance the employee experience. Organizations that successfully implement ServiceNow leverage its capabilities to streamline operations, reduce manual tasks, and provide a seamless HR service delivery model.

Lessons and Insights to Take Forward

As covered in the case studies and lessons learned from real-world implementations, successful integration of ServiceNow hinges on comprehensive planning, stakeholder engagement, and continuous training. It is crucial to focus on user adoption and maintain an iterative approach, gathering feedback and making adjustments to align with changing business needs.

Security, compliance, and data protection are equally vital to the successful deployment of ServiceNow in HR. By following best practices for data privacy and adhering to industry regulations, HR teams can build trust and confidence among employees and stakeholders.

The Future of HR with ServiceNow

The future of HR is digital, and ServiceNow is at the forefront of this evolution. As the platform continues to develop with new features and capabilities, organizations must remain proactive, exploring innovations and incorporating them into their HR strategies. From AI-driven insights to more seamless integrations with other enterprise systems, the potential for HR transformation continues to expand.

Continuous improvement should be at the heart of your strategy. By staying informed about new ServiceNow updates, training teams, and leveraging the data insights available within the platform, your HR department can remain competitive and responsive in a rapidly changing work environment.

A Final Word

Implementing ServiceNow for HR is not just about meeting today's needs—it's about preparing for tomorrow's challenges. This book has provided a roadmap, highlighting both the strategic and practical steps needed to harness the power of ServiceNow and transform HR processes. As you move forward, remember that success relies on a commitment to continuous improvement, learning, and adapting to the ever-evolving landscape of digital HR solutions.

With the insights and guidance provided here, you are well-equipped to embark on or refine your ServiceNow journey, driving impactful changes that benefit not only HR teams but the entire organization.

Thank you for choosing this guide as your companion in your digital HR transformation. Here's to your success in implementing ServiceNow and leading your HR team into a future defined by efficiency, innovation, and resilience.